THE WORLD ALMANAC® OF
PRESIDENTIAL
★ CAMPAIGNS ★

THE WORLD ALMANAC® OF
PRESIDENTIAL
★CAMPAIGNS★

Eileen Shields-West
Illustrated by Jeff MacNelly

92-977

WORLD ALMANAC
AN IMPRINT OF PHAROS BOOKS · A SCRIPPS HOWARD COMPANY
NEW YORK

First published in 1992.

Library of Congress Cataloging-in-Publication Data
Shields-West, Eileen.
The World almanac of presidential campaigns / Eileen Shields-West
illustrated by Jeff MacNelly.
p.   cm.
ISBN 0-88687-610-9 (hc). — ISBN 0-88687-609-5 (pb)
1. Presidents—United States—Election.
2. Electioneering—United
States—History. I. World almanac. II. Title.
JF285.S55 1992
324.973—dc20   91-28734   CIP

Pharos Books are available at special discounts on bulk purchases for sales promotions, premiums, fundraising or educational use. For details, contact the Special Sales Department, Pharos Books, 200 Park Avenue, New York, NY 10166.

Printed in the United States

World Almanac
An Imprint of Pharos Books
A Scripps Howard Company
200 Park Avenue
New York, New York 10166

10 9 8 7 6 5 4 3 2 1

DEDICATION

For Robin, Lily, and Kate, so loving and patient.
For my parents, so encouraging.
And for Jeff, so wonderfully talented.

★ ACKNOWLEDGMENTS ★

Thank you to researchers Eileen Scully and Eileen Shapiro; Clark Clifford on President Harry Truman, Dr. Marvin Krantz of the Library of Congress; Horace S. Merrill, biographer of Grover Cleveland; and Frances Turgeon, curator, of the *Kiplinger* Washington Collection.

★ ELECTION OF 1788–1789 ★

Major Candidate for President George Washington, 56, Virginia, Federalist

Major Candidate for Vice President John Adams, 53, Massachusetts, Federalist

Credentials Washington rose from major to colonel during the French and Indian War (1754–1763), served as a member of Virginia's House of Burgesses (1759–1774), was one of Virginia's delegates to the First and Second Continental Congresses (1774–1775) and commander in chief of the Continental Army (1775–1783). He was elected president of the Constitutional Convention (1787).

Adams helped edit and signed the Declaration of Independence, drafted the state constitution of Massachusetts (1779–1780), and served abroad in the Netherlands (1780–1782), securing recognition of American independence. In October 1782 he arrived in Paris to join others in negotiating the end of the war with Britain (the Treaty of Paris, 1783) and became the first minister to Great Britain (1785–1788).

Tickets There were no official nominations, no caucuses or conventions to select a first president and vice president, but it was always assumed at the Constitutional Convention and at state ratifying conventions that Washington would be president. In fact, without that assumption, the Constitution would not have been ratified.

While the electors were technically free agents, as the Constitution wanted them to be, they could not help but be swayed by leading Federalists, the press, and the public. Since Washington was from a Southern state, it was generally thought that the vice president needed to be from New England so that that area would feel it had a voice in the new government. John Adams became the obvious choice because he had a good record in government service and, more important, was "available."

Slogans Since Washington had no competition, slogans took the form of favorite-son toasts. In summer 1788, people raised their glasses to "Farmer Washington—may he like a second Cincinnatus, be called from the plow to rule a great people."

Songs In the months leading up to the election, songs touting Washington and the new union were sung not to promote him for the presidency but rather to confer the presidency on him. There was "God Save Great Washington" (to the tune of "God Save the King") and "A New Federal Song"

GEORGE WASHINGTON

in which "Great Washington shall rule the land, / While Franklin's council aids his hand."

Popular Labels   For Washington, Great White Father, A Second Moses, First of Heroes, the Great American Fabius, the American Romulus, and Father of His Country.

For Adams, Patriot of the Constitution, Architect of the Revolution, Apostle of Independence, and Honest Old John Adams.

Curious Facts   Three of the existing thirteen states did not participate in the first election. North Carolina and Rhode Island, too individualistic to submit at first, did not ratify the Constitution in time; Rhode Island (Rogues Island, as it was known) did not even try—no ratifying convention was called.

New York was another story. It ratified the new Constitution but there was so much squabbling between Federalists and Anti-Federalists that no electors were chosen by the January-first deadline.

The Press   There was little if any resistance to the thought of Washington as president and not much to Adams as vice president, as the *Pennsylvania Gazette* heralded: "With our American Romulus in the President's and a John Adams in the Vice President's chairs, the United States cannot fail of becoming respectable abroad, and of bearing down ignorance, selfishness and faction at home.''

Firsts Washington was the first and only unanimously drafted president.

The first presidential election in which electors were unanimous on their choice of a president.

Alexander Hamilton assumed the role of the country's first unofficial campaign manager.

Trend The inaugural-address tradition began.

Vote Only four states had some form of popular election of electors, and the vote was very light. In the six other participating states, legislatures chose the electors. There were supposed to be seventy-three electors, but only sixty-nine showed up to vote on February 4. (One absentee claimed gout, another icy rivers.)

Each elector cast two votes. George Washington with 69 votes was president. John Adams, the runner-up, received 34 votes. The rest of the electoral votes were scattered among ten others, mainly favorite sons.

Quote As Washington stood on the balcony of Federal Hall in New York's Wall Street after taking the oath of office on April 30, 1789, Richard Livingston (who had administered the oath), cried "Long live George Washington, President of the United States!" and a great shout went up with the booming of the cannon in the narrow streets.

AFTER years of revolutionary war and months of constitutional controversy, America was like a cat with its back arched. Only the election of George Washington, it was generally thought, would have a calming effect on the new republic. But would he accept?

Returning to Mount Vernon from the Constitutional Convention, Washington thought he had done enough. And Washington was tired of hearing the Constitution ridiculed as that "Gilded Trap," that "triple headed monster" with its three branches of government.

Starting in September 1787 states were asked to ratify the new Constitution. Surprisingly to many, three states ratified by the end of the year (even if in Pennsylvania, the second state to ratify, two Anti-Federalists had to be dragged from their homes, clothes torn, and held in their seats to complete a quorum). Then two more states in January, and three more by May. By July 1788 New Hampshire, Virginia, and New York had ratified.

Now all eyes turned to Washington. The expectation that he would be the first president had been the impetus for the establishment of a powerful, independent presidency and the argument used in many states for ratification. As Benjamin Franklin expressed it, "The first man put at the helm will be a good one." Washington did not think he could do the job and did not want it. He told friends that he felt "more diffidence and reluctance than I have ever experienced before" and that he just wanted to retire on his farm. Besides, he said, his hearing was going and at fifty-six he was too old for the job.

Letters like courtiers came to Washington at Mount Vernon. "We cannot, sir, do without you," emphasized former Governor Thomas Johnson of Maryland. Lafayette, who had fought alongside Washington during the war, wrote from Paris "You cannot refuse being elected President." Fellow patriot Thomas Jefferson tried to dissuade Washington from his "vast reluctance." But, more than anyone, it was Hamilton who held Washington's hand, telling him he was "indispensable" and could not refuse "the general call of your country." Washington never publicly put his hat into the ring. In one letter, he confided he would serve if elected, but only until his services could be "dispensed with."

John Adams, however, was looking for a high office (senator was not good enough). Some even supposed, knowing his "extravagant self-importance," that he had a penchant to be president. With reservations, because of Adams' vanity and wartime paranoia that Washington wanted to be king, Federalist leaders decided to support Adams for the vice presidency. Hamilton, though, could not bear the thought of Adams accruing a great many electoral votes. What if he got as many as Washington; what then? So Hamilton advised some electors to scatter their second votes.

In the final tally Washington received all sixty-nine electoral votes for the presidency while Adams landed the vice presidency with only thirty-four. Adams was insulted and said he would think twice about taking office. However, when the messenger came, officially calling him to serve, Adams was ready, his bags already packed.

Washington was wined and dined on his passage to New York, the capital at the time. Alternating between a carriage and a white mount, Washington was heralded with flowers and, in one case, mechanically crowned with a laurel wreath. Legend has it that Washington cast off the wreath but bent down to kiss the little girl who had lured him to the spot. "The President of Her [the country's] Affections," observed the *Boston Gazette*.

The election of 1789 did not represent a democratic contest for president, since the popular vote was practically nonexistent. But it certainly symbolized a heartfelt expression of the public will. As things turned out, the calm it brought would not last long.

★ ELECTION OF 1792 ★

Major Candidate for President   George Washington, 60, Virginia, Federalist

Major Candidate for Vice President   John Adams, 57, Massachusetts, Federalist

Credentials   See Election of 1788–1789.

Tickets   As in 1789, there were no congressional caucuses or nominating conventions for president and vice president. Washington's name was the only one bandied about for president. A move was made by many Republicans to undercut Federalist power by supporting Governor George Clinton of New York for the vice presidency.

In March 1792 Congress passed a new election law that moved up the timetable for the election of electors and the casting of their votes. Electors would now vote on the first Wednesday in December and the results would be announced on the first Wednesday in February.

Campaign Notes   So set against running again was Washington that in May 1792 he sent for his old friend James Madison to help him prepare words of farewell to the country. Madison took the opportunity to dissuade Washington from retiring. Others argued the same. Washington listened but remained silent. Gradually that silence was interpreted as acceptance of another term or, at least, part of a term.

Adams refused to lift a finger to help himself. In fact, he fled home to Quincy, formerly called Braintree, for the summer and fall. Resisting the urgings of his son, Alexander Hamilton, and other Federalists who felt he needed to be in Philadelphia, the new capital, Adams said he was sickly and not in the mood for any "electioneering."

Songs   Tunes honoring Washington continued to be popular. People danced to "The President's March" and adopted "God Save George Washington" as the first anthem.

Popular Labels   As president Washington was touted as "The First of Men." Adams called himself "Daddy Vice" and others picked up on it.

Name-calling   While Washington was spared for the most part, Adams was belittled as "His Rotundity" and "His Superfluous Excellency."

Curious Facts   Although Alexander Hamilton, a Federalist, and Thomas Jefferson, who was emerging as leader of the Republicans, were on different sides of so many issues that faced the first administration, they both ended

ALEXANDER HAMILTON

up urging Washington to run for a second term. In separate appeals they even used the same argument: Washington would probably be able to retire after a year or two.

Jefferson also supported Adams for the vice presidency on the strength of "his personal worth and services" even though he did not agree with Adams' "political creed."

The Press   Washington, still revered by most, was attacked mainly for his "royal manners" or the fact that he was "distant." In one instance *The National Gazette,* edited by Republican Philip Freneau, attacked the "absurdities of *levees* [Washington's official afternoon receptions] *and every species of royal pomp and parade.*"

Adams received the brunt of the criticism. A Republican in the *Massachusetts Centinel* referred to his "lawless lust of POW'R in embryo" and described him as "the first spawn of hell."

Firsts   Every state and every elector participated.

Anti-Federalists began calling themselves Republicans.

Trend   Washington set the precedent of a second term.

Vote   George Washington was elected president with 132 votes. John Adams became vice president with 77 votes. George Clinton received 50 votes, Thomas Jefferson 4 votes, and Aaron Burr of New York one vote.

Benchmarks   Washington was reelected unanimously.

Washington delivered the shortest inaugural address ever, just 135 words.

Quote   After the election Washington confessed he "would have experienced chagrin" had he not been reelected "by a pretty respectable vote."

G EORGE Washington's first term as president began with such equanimity in domestic politics that the Philadelphia *General Advertiser,* an opposition paper in waiting, complained there were "no party disputes to raise the printer's drooping spirits." Before long, the scene changed.

On the economic front, his first term was marked by true division, chiefly between Secretary of the Treasury Alexander Hamilton, the Federalists' whiz kid and Secretary of State Thomas Jefferson over many issues, including a central bank. Washington came to view his two feuding secretaries as spoiled children who argued even though they had so much to be thankful for. Always tactful, he gently urged them to find "some line . . . by which both of you can walk." But the only thing that Hamilton and Jefferson could agree on was the need for Washington to serve again as president.

That was not what Washington wanted to hear. He was tired of the squabbling, the responsibilities of the job, and the commute—it was about a week's coach ride from the new capital in Philadelphia to Mount Vernon. "Perhaps in no instance in my life," Washington wrote a friend, "have I been more sensible of the sacrifice than in the present." He did not see a way out.

Vice President Adams was the likely but not popular choice to be vice president again. In his role as president of the Senate, Adams got on colleagues' nerves and was voted down when he fought to have the president addressed as "His Majesty" (only heads of fire companies and cricket companies, he said, were "president") and tried to dictate how many times a messenger from the Senate must bow on entering the House with a bill. When Adams worried aloud "what I shall be" when the president came to the Senate "for I cannot be president then," many just laughed behind his back.

Even though Adams eventually gave up wearing his sword to the Senate and later left his white wig at home, which caused some to question who he was, Republicans continued their ridicule. Pennsylvania's Senator William Maclay compared him to "a monkey just put into breeches" with "such evident marks of self-conceit." The Republican press weighed in too, especially since Washington was almost untouchable. The *National Gazette* lambasted Adams' writings, particularly on the value of a hereditary president, as "poisoned doctrines."

Although there was no Republican opposition to Washington for president, many Republicans decided to back New York governor George Clinton, instead of Adams, for vice president. New York Republicans furiously wrote letters to sympathizers in other states, but since Clinton had won his last gubernatorial election under a cloud of stolen votes, his appeal was limited.

Washington had no intention of getting involved *in any way* in the forthcoming elections. When a candidate for the House rumored that he had Washington's backing, the president admonished in writing, "The exercise of an influence (if I really possessed any) . . . would be highly improper." Adams remained at home during the summer and fall, refusing to return to Philadelphia lest his motive be misinterpreted. "I am not of Caesar's mind," he once confided to a friend. "The second place in Rome is high enough for me."

The results were predictable. Celebration was marred by the fact that the French Revolution was at a fever pitch and Francophile Republicans criticized Federalists more than ever for any royal show. After consulting his advisers, Washington decided on the simplest of ceremonies. He rode alone in his coach to take the oath of office, made a brief address and returned home alone. The silence was soon broken by bitter partisan dispute.

★ CAMPAIGN OF 1796 ★

Major Candidates   John Adams, 61, Massachusetts, Federalist
Thomas Jefferson, 53, Virginia, Republican

Credentials   For Adams, see Election of 1788–1789.

Jefferson drafted and signed the Declaration of Independence, was a member of Virginia's House of Delegates (1776–1779), governor of Virginia (1779–1781), a member of the Continental Congress (1783–1784), and minister to France (1785–1789). He became the first secretary of state (1790–1793).

Tickets   Federalist party leaders met informally to decide on John Adams as their candidate for president and South Carolina diplomat Thomas Pinckney for vice president. Pinckney was brought on to garner crucial Southern votes and because he had managed to negotiate a popular treaty with Spain in 1795.

Republican congressional leaders picked as their candidates Thomas Jefferson for president and Aaron Burr of New York for vice president. (Burr had displaced George Clinton as leader of the Republican party in New York.)

Campaign Notes   Washington did not publicly state a preference for Adams or Jefferson to be his successor (although it is assumed that he preferred Adams), nor did he notify the vice president that he definitely planned to

JOHN ADAMS

retire. Like others, Adams read the President's Farewell Address to the country in the newspapers in September 1796.

Adams wanted to be president but did not want to fight for the honor. Saying he was "disinterested," Adams spent the summer and fall at home in Quincy, tending his farm and analyzing possible election results.

Jefferson did not want the presidency in 1796 and did nothing to attain it. He remained at Monticello, worried more about the state of affairs with Britain and France than his own future. When Jefferson discussed the presidency with Republican friends the year before he had said he had no such "ambition," and party leaders never confirmed to Jefferson that he was their candidate.

Symbols   White cockades were worn by Federalists in contrast to tricolor cockades for Jefferson and France.

Slogans   Adams was elegantly toasted: "To John Adams, inflexible to preserve, virtuous to pursue, and intelligent to discern the true interests of the country."

Jefferson was promoted in pamphlets, handbills, and the like as the "steadfast friend to the rights of the people." His supporters rallied to "Liberty, equality and no King!"

Popular Labels   Adams was affectionately called an "Old Fielder," referring to a hardy little horse, and "The First Planet from Our Political Sun."

Jefferson was known as the "Champion of the Revolution" and the "Moses of the Republicans."

Name-calling   Adams was called "Bonny Johnny" to ridicule his English pretensions.

As the French Revolution turned excessive, Federalists turned to calling Jefferson "Mad Tom" and the "Robespierre of the American mob."

Once the rivalry between Federalists and Republicans heated up, even Washington was not spared. "An Ape of Royalty" the most rabid administration critics sneered. "Stepfather of His Country" and an "American Caesar" were other partisan snubs.

Curious Facts   Party leaders never confirmed to Jefferson that he was their candidate, so fearful were they that he would refuse. Even James Madison, who founded the Republican party with Jefferson and lived just a half-day's ride away at Montpelier, did not visit Jefferson at Monticello in 1796 "to present him no opportunity of protesting."

The Press   The press played an important part in this election. The *Gazette of the United States* was the main voice for the Federalists, while the *National Gazette* and later the *General Advertiser* or *Aurora* were most vocal for the Republicans. Other papers followed their lead.

The *Gazette* proclaimed that Republicans were corrupting the young people with "the poison of atheism and disaffection." The *Columbian Centinel* characterized Jefferson as a disorganizer and anarchist "in short, as a thorn in the government."

Adams was labeled a "monarchist" who longed for a scepter, but Washington came away more scathed. First the custom of celebrating his birthday was called into question in the pages of the *Aurora* as having "too strong a tincture of monarchy." Then the man himself became a subject for criticism. The *New York Journal* printed that "reveling, horse racing and *horse whipping*" formed his basic education.

Firsts   The first real contest for president.

The first true test of the electoral college.

The first modern political party—the Federalist party—was formed in the Western world. A Republican movement solidified against it.

The first farewell address.

Trend   By retiring, Washington began the tradition of a two-term presidency.

Vote   Adams squeaked into the presidency with 71 electoral votes, one more than the necessary majority. Jefferson became vice president with 68 votes, while Pinckney received 59 and Burr 30.

Benchmark Because electors did not have separate ballots for president and vice president, the president-elect and the vice president-elect were of different parties.

Quote "The *Lion* and the *Lamb* are to lie down together" was Hamilton's characterization of the election.

FOREIGN rather than domestic concerns dominated this election. Friction between the Federalists in power and the Republicans in opposition grew more spirited as the French Revolution became more excessive. The sympathy some Federalists had felt for the French in their efforts to establish a republic turned to scorn with the Reign of Terror in 1793. But Jefferson and other Republicans, while shaken by the atrocities against aristocrats, felt that a country could not move from "despotism to liberty in a feather bed."

Two moves by the administration of George Washington and John Adams exacerbated the situation. Washington wanted the union, young as it was, to avoid a foreign war. When hostilities broke out between France and Britain, he declared American neutrality. This brought into the open clashes between "Gallomen" (supporters of France) and "Anglomen" who favored England.

Jay's treaty created an even greater divide. The English had been asserting themselves on sea and land. The Royal Navy seized about 300 American merchant vessels in the West Indies and impressed many of the sailors to work on British ships. On American soil, Britain had kept its Northern frontier posts in violation of the peace treaty of 1783 and, from them, supplied Indians with firepower against new settlers. In 1794 Washington sent Chief Justice John Jay to London to try to avoid a war Republicans were hungry for.

From the moment Jay, on presenting his credentials, kissed the Queen's hand, Jefferson's followers were on the attack. One American journal cried "Men of America, he betrayed you with a kiss!" Jay was also at a tremendous disadvantage because Federalist leader Alexander Hamilton, who wanted to avoid war with England at any cost, leaked America's bargaining position. As a result, Jay came away almost empty-handed but, if the Senate would sign, his efforts added up to peace with Britain.

"Damn John Jay!" echoed through the states. "Damn everyone who won't damn John Jay!" And then "Damn George Washington!" This was a turning point. The president who stood behind the treaty had become fair game. It took six months, but the Senate ratified the treaty in June 1795. With that, the Jay treaty became the symbol of irreconcilable differences between the Federalists and the Republicans.

By this time Federalists and Republicans had separate drinking taverns and strong words for each other. To one Federalist, Republicans were "fire-eating salamanders"; to Martha Washington they were "filthy democrats" who left dirty fingerprints on her wallpaper. Republicans retaliated in print by calling her husband an "eastern pashaw" who would be king. Both sides were ready for the next election.

In the spring of 1796 Washington dug out from his files the draft of a farewell address, prepared four years earlier on his first attempt to retire, and sent it off to Hamilton. Two months later, Hamilton sent it back—completely rewritten. Washington made some stylistic changes, then decided to release it to a Philadelphia newspaper "and suffer it to work its way afterwards." On September 19 the *American Daily Advertiser* ran Washington's text on page two with a one-column head. It was signed: "G. Washington, United States, September 7, 1796." The address was reprinted in papers across the country and ocean. People pored over his concern about the dangers of "the spirit of party" and entanglement "of our peace and prosperity" in European struggles.

For their own reasons, the two leading presidential candidates stayed silent. Adams, who thought the vice presidency "the most insignificant office" ever, coveted Washington's job but wanted the office to come to him. Jefferson, on the other hand, really did not want the presidency in this time of turmoil. His eyes were on 1800.

During the election Hamilton was up to his old tricks. Believing that Thomas Pinckney, Adams' running mate, would make a more pliable president, Hamilton devised a strategy to get more Federalist electors to vote for Pinckney than for Adams. The scheme backfired: not only was Adams elected president with seventy-one votes, but Jefferson, whom Hamilton hated as a Republican and as a man, became vice president with sixty-eight votes.

The inauguration went well. Adams described it in a letter to his wife Abigail as the "sublimest thing ever." Even the *Aurora* gave praise, simply pleased that Washington was out of office. But Adams was "President by Three Votes," as Republicans constantly reminded him. He himself had predicted before the election "a dangerous Crisis in publick affairs if the President and Vice President should be in opposite Boxes." Adams would not have it easy.

★ CAMPAIGN OF 1800 ★

Major Candidates   John Adams, 65, Massachusetts, Federalist
Thomas Jefferson, 57, Virginia, Democrat-Republican

Credentials   For Adams, see Election of 1788–1789; for Jefferson, see Campaign of 1796.

Tickets   In 1800 the congressional nominating caucus came into play. Federalist members of Congress supported John Adams and Charles Cotes-

AARON BURR

worth Pinckney equally for the positions of president and vice president. Adams was not specifically nominated for the presidential spot; in this way Hamilton, who was feuding with Adams, and other Federalists hoped that Pinckney would receive more electoral votes and become president. Pinckney, diplomat and brother of Thomas Pinckney, Adams' running mate in 1796, was from South Carolina and supposed to draw Southern votes to the ticket. He was famous for turning down the French demand for a bribe in the 1797 XYZ affair with the words "Not a sixpence!"

Republican members of Congress in May nominated Aaron Burr for vice president on a ticket with Jefferson. Burr was credited with swinging his home state of New York with its twelve key electors into the Republican camp earlier that month.

Campaign Notes Both Adams and Jefferson avoided the appearance of campaigning, since it was not proper, in those days, openly to seek the office of president. So, stumping was out and just as well; Adams, who had lost most of his teeth, refused to wear dentures and as a result talked with a lisp, while Jefferson had a weak voice and poor platform performance.

But neither candidate kept himself altogether aloof. Jefferson, much more than Adams, wrote numerous letters to his friends, asking them to politick in his place. He funded Republican newspapers and distributed political pamphlets.

Adams had an advantage as president: He could draw attention to himself in the course of his office. One trip, though, smacked of politicking—or so it seemed to opponents. Adams traveled from Philadelphia to Washington via Lancaster and York, Pennsylvania and Fredericktown, Maryland. Inquired the Philadelphia *Aurora*, a Republican newspaper, "How is it he has taken the route . . . *fifty* miles out of the strait course?"

Symbols Symbols were tied to issues in this campaign. After the XYZ affair, many Federalists, pro-British in sentiment, were eager for war with France. Supporters of Adams donned black cockades.

Jefferson's followers sometimes sported tricolor cockades to show their pro-French sentiments.

Slogans Again, the XYZ affair was the catalyst. "Millions for defense, but not one cent for tribute," Adams' Federalists shouted against France.

Jefferson's supporters rallied against "The Reign of Terror," as they termed the Alien and Sedition Laws, passed in 1787, which cracked down on aliens and critics of the administration. Their candidate was "Jefferson, the Friend of the People." They campaigned: "Is It Not High Time for a Change?"

Songs Pro-Adams songs included "The Green Mountain Farmer," "Adams and Liberty," and "American Spirit," which preached patriotism as well: "If Frenchmen come with naked bum, / We'll spank 'em hard and handy."

Republican songs to get out the vote included "Free and Fair Elections" and "Watching O'er Your Freedom": "At your next election, / Chuse for chief Columbia's son, / The immortal Jefferson."

Popular Labels Adams was called "The Father of the American Navy," while Jefferson was labeled "The Mammoth of Democracy."

Name-calling Adams was ridiculed as "President by Three Votes" and "a mere old woman and unfit for a President." Abigail Adams was not spared: "Mrs. President," chided critics who thought she had too much influence on her husband.

Jefferson was denounced as "atheist," "infidel," and "Jacobin."

The Press The Federalist *Gazette of the United States* headlined: THE GRAND QUESTION STATED. GOD—AND A RELIGIOUS PRESIDENT; JEFFERSON—AND NO GOD!!!

In 1799 Jefferson instructed his followers: "The Engine is the Press." Republican editors, even though restrained somewhat by the Sedition Act, harped on Adams' "monarchical party" and his "Toryism." The *Aurora* referred to that "old, querulous, bald, blind, crippled, toothless Adams."

Spending During the campaign, Jeffersonians denounced the spendthrift policies of the Adams administration, but it was the Republicans who spent much more in trying to win the election.

Firsts The first real test of strength between two parties in a presidential contest.

The first transfer of power in America from one political party to another in both executive and legislative branches of government.

The first use by both parties of congressional nominating caucuses.

The first of two times that the House of Representatives decided a presidential election.

The first known appearance of presidential campaign songs, particularly getting-out-the-vote ballads.

The first unofficial party platform, written by Jefferson for the Republicans.

Adams was the first President defeated for a second term.

The first inauguration in Washington, D.C.

Trends The rise of issue politics.

Formal party organizations appeared in many states.

The Fourth of July became a day of big celebrations tied to patriotism and parties.

The influence of a partisan press.

Vote See campaign narrative, below.

Benchmarks Adams was the last Federalist President, this election marking the beginning of the end of the Federalist party.

The political dominance of the Northeast was temporarily over.

One of the nastiest campaigns ever.

The deadlock in the House of Representatives led to passage of the Twelfth Amendment (1804), which brought separate balloting by presidential electors for president and vice president.

A strong Republican press was instrumental in Jefferson's victory.

Quote At his inauguration, Jefferson made a peace overture: "We are all Republicans, we are all Federalists."

THE aura that had somewhat protected the sacrosanct figure of George Washington had given way to savage partisanship. President John Adams, a Federalist, did not help matters. Adams had the unfortunate distinction of being ridiculed not only by Democrat-Republican rival Thomas Jefferson, who happened to be vice president, but also by members of his own party, led by first secretary of the treasury, Alexander Hamilton.

A brilliant but rather silly man who loved grand titles, Adams was secretly mocked by Federalist enemies as "His Rotundity." And, because in 1796 he received only seventy-one electoral votes to Jefferson's sixty-eight, Republican pamphleteers jeered "President by Three Votes" throughout his term.

As president, Adams had a brief flirtation with popularity in 1797 when French agents "X, Y and Z," as Adams called them, tried to bribe American officials. Many Americans clamored for war with France and paraded for patriotism and Adams.

But Adams pursued peace with France (a treaty was eventually signed in 1800) instead of war, which once again alienated Hamilton and his hawkish followers. Then, in 1798, Congress passed the Alien and Sedition Laws, placing undue restraints on aliens and the press. These only served to highlight the differences between Federalists, who advocated a strong central government and curbs on criticism, and the Republicans, who stood for states' rights and freedom of speech and press.

Although the Sedition Law stilled some Republican criticism of Adams (one critic was fined $100 for commenting that the cannon fired in honor of Adams would be better aimed at the president's pants), there was more than enough to make the campaign bitter and personal. The Republicans swiftly spread the rumor that President Adams planned to marry one of his sons to a daughter of George III in order to start an American dynasty with economic ties to England. Comic rumor even had it that George Washington himself got Adams to change his mind by donning his Revolutionary uniform and threatening to run him through with his patriot's sword. "See Johnny at the helm of State," Jeffersonians chorused, "Head itching for a crowny, / He longs to be like Georgy, great, / And pull Tom Jeffer downy."

Adams had a sharp tongue, but he often managed to stay cool under Republican onslaughts. When it was put about that he had sent General Thomas Pinckney (his running mate in 1796) to England in a U.S. frigate to procure four pretty girls as mistresses for them both, Adams replied genially: "I do declare upon my honor, if this be true General Pinckney has cheated me out of my two."

Other Federalists fought back, questioning Jefferson's courage during the Revolutionary War, mocking him as a dilettante inventor who dreamed up nothing but "Gim-Krackery," and claiming he copied the Declaration of Independence from a work of Britain's John Locke. That was the high road compared to one biographical précis of the sage of Monticello: "Tom Jefferson . . . a mean-spirited, low-lived fellow, the son of a half-breed Indian squaw, sired by a Virginia mulatto father." Were he elected, an editorial in the Federalist *Connecticut Courant* warned readers, "Murder, robbery, rape, adultery and incest will be openly taught and practiced."

In a land still largely agrarian, the Republicans had won the support of the country folk and were better organized. This was particularly evident when the effort of Aaron Burr brought New York State to the Republican side of the ledger in the spring of 1800. Hamilton did not help his party by writing that Adams had a "vanity without bounds" and openly trying to make Charles Pinckney, instead of Adams, the next Federalist president.

Even so, history records a neck-and-neck election result and intense finagling because of the peculiar ground rules regarding the presidency and the electoral vote. Jefferson and Burr both got seventy-three to Adams' sixty-five. "Lord! how the Federalists will stare / At Jefferson, in Adams' chair" Jeffersonians celebrated—a bit too early. The vote forced a runoff in the lame-duck Federalist House, which tried to avoid picking Jefferson. Finally, on the thirty-sixth ballot, with two states turning in blanks, Jefferson was chosen. Federalists promptly cried "President by No Votes!" because of the blanks. But the political power of the Northeast was broken, at least for the moment. Jefferson looked back on it as the "Revolution of 1800."

★ CAMPAIGN OF 1804 ★

Major Candidates   Thomas Jefferson, 61, Virginia, Democrat-Republican
Charles Cotesworth Pinckney, 58, South Carolina,
Federalist

Credentials   For Jefferson see Election of 1796.

Pinckney, a wealthy businessman and lawyer, was a delegate to the Constitutional Convention in 1787, became minister to France (1796) and famous during the 1797 XYZ affair for flatly turning down French officials' request for a bribe with the words: "Not a sixpence!" He was the Federalist candidate for vice president in 1800.

Ticket   Among Republicans from the House and Senate there was no discussion or doubt about the presidential nominee; Jefferson was renominated by acclamation. But no one wanted Vice President Burr on the ticket again. He had alienated too many party members, starting with his refusal to step aside in favor of Jefferson in the electoral tie in 1800. Burr received no votes. George Clinton received the most—67 votes. Clinton, 65, who was serving a seventh term as governor of New York, was nonthreatening and from a politically important state.

Federalist congressmen, in a departure from 1800, did not caucus. Leaders privately agreed on Charles Cotesworth Pinckney and Rufus King, but publicly many Federalist newspapers boasted that electors would not be "tied down to two candidates." King had been a U.S. senator and then minister to England, resigning in 1803.

Campaign Notes   Unlike 1800, Jefferson did not get involved in this campaign; he did not even want a say in the choice of his running mate and left it open to debate among Republicans.

The Republicans at this point were well organized. There was a Republican

THOMAS JEFFERSON

national committee and state and local committees in opposition states. In traditionally Federalist Massachusetts, Boston even boasted ward committees.

The Federalists were highly disorganized and splintered. There was neither an official slate of candidates nor a national effort to defeat Jefferson.

Slogans Republicans touted Jefferson as "Man of the People" and toasted the "Louisiana Purchase." Federalists, without a clear presidential choice, raised glasses to "Washington—he never deserted his post" and "The Friends of the People—Not Their Flatterers."

Songs "Jefferson's March" and several "Jefferson and Liberty" songs were popular. One went " 'Tis the wretches who wait / To unite Church and State / The name of our Jefferson ever to hate."

Since the Federalists were not candidate-centered, their songs were such old favorites as "Hail Columbia," "Yankee Doodle," and "Washington's Grand March."

Popular Labels Republicans began to call themselves Democrats, although Jefferson never adopted this more revolutionary term. Jefferson was referred to as "The Red Fox" and "Immortal Jefferson."

Name-calling "Anglomany" was coined by Jefferson for the Federalist obsession with Britain. "Midnight judges" was a derisive term applied by Republicans to judges appointed at the last minute by Jefferson's predecessor, John Adams.

Federalists called Republicans "demagogues" and their philosophy "mobocracy." "Black Sal" was the name for Jefferson's alleged mistress. Jefferson was "the anti-Christ."

The Press The Republican *Independent Chronicle* criticized the Federalist failure to announce a credible ticket in opposition to "Jefferson and Clinton": "Let the Federalists come forward . . . or the conclusion in the public mind must be that they have designs which they dare not present for public scrutiny."

The *Washington Federalist* belittled the president as another Napoleon: "To Thomas Jefferson, President of the United States, Emperor of Louisiana, Lord High Admiral of the Navy, MY LORD."

Firsts The president and vice president were chosen separately by electors, as a result of passage of the Twelfth Amendment.

The Republicans held the first truly public congressional caucus, making the caucus the formal nominating body for years to come.

The first nominating roll call at a caucus.

Trends The Republicans formed a campaign committee that became a forerunner of later national committees.

Vote Six states had legislatures choose electors; eleven had some form of popular election. Jefferson and Clinton came away with a landslide victory of 162 electoral votes to 14 for Pinckney and King.

Benchmarks Few presidential victories have been as overwhelming.

Formerly Federalist New England, except for Connecticut, went Republican.

Quote The pro-Jefferson *National Intelligencer* commented that, in contrast to 1800, the president had been reelected "without awakening either the rapturous exultation of his friends or the angry passions of his enemies."

As revolutions go, Jefferson's of 1800 was most significant for what did not happen. While power was transferred from Federalists to Republicans in both the executive and legislative branches of government—a historic first—there was no overthrow of the political system or bloodshed or rioting, as partisans predicted. Rather, the president and his followers tried to recast the system more to their liking. In doing so, they left much untampered with and even adopted a Federalist approach on some issues. Still, the Federalists detested and ridiculed Jefferson and did all they could to make his first term miserable.

But Jefferson was on a roll. His popularity increased with the informality he brought to the presidency. He did away with the stuffy social gatherings of his predecessors called levees; he dressed down during the day (some criticized his "yarn stockings and slippers down at the heel").

Federalist grumbles started with the removal of a slew of their party members from office and the cancellation of the Judiciary Act of 1801, under which President John Adams appointed sixteen new judges in the final days and hours of his presidency.

On the economic front, Jefferson left intact the Bank of the United States and federal tariff but convinced Congress to repeal the excise tax, which caused a million-dollar shortfall in revenues. Some economies were made by scaling back the army and pursuing a small-gunboat shipbuilding policy in the navy. Federalists had fun calling these small boats Jefferson's "mosquito fleet." They laughed harder when Gunboat Number One, sent to defend the coast, was found in a Savannah cornfield after a hurricane. At a political rally for Rufus King, the Federalist vice-presidential candidate in 1804, they toasted: "If our gunboats are no use upon the water, may they be at least the best upon earth."

The Federalists also took pleasure from the charges brought by James Thomson Callender against Jefferson. Callender, who previously had slandered Washington and Adams and received some financial support from Jefferson, turned on then-president Jefferson when refused a political post. Callender unveiled the "Sally story" in 1802, claiming, among other things, that Sally Hemmings, a slave, had "yellow Tom" and other children by Jefferson. The Federalist press reprinted Callender's articles and engaged in some biting doggerel to boot. The *Boston Gazette* ran: "What wife were half so handy? / To breed a flock of slaves for stock, / A blackamoor's the dandy." Neither Jefferson nor the Republican press replied.

They did not need to. The president, after the Louisiana Purchase, which acquired 828,000 square miles for about three cents an acre, was above criticism.

The purchase of Louisiana required a loose interpretation of the Constitution, which troubled Jefferson. He was finally persuaded that if he did not act quickly the deal would collapse. Ironically, many of the Federalists who loosely interpreted the Constitution to establish the Bank of the United States now cried "unconstitutional." They also called the purchase "a great waste," arguing "we already have too much" land. But agarian and commercial interests, eager to double the size of the union and gain control of the Mississippi, hailed "Immortal Jefferson."

By failing to nominate official candidates and select slates of electors in several states, Federalists were not the competitors they had been in 1800. (In mid-July, the Federalist party lost its best leader, Alexander Hamilton, in a duel with former Vice President Aaron Burr.) Nevertheless, they tried to thwart Jackson's reelection by opposing the Twelfth Amendment, knowing that once it passed they could no longer defeat Jefferson by switching votes to his running mate. When it was adopted in September, Jefferson looked forward to the "verdict from my country" that the election would provide. The size of his victory overwhelmed even Jefferson, who wrote a French friend: "The two parties which prevailed with so much violence when you were here, are almost wholly melted into one."

★ CAMPAIGN OF 1808 ★

Major Candidates   James Madison, 57, Virginia, Democrat-Republican
Charles Cotesworth Pinckney, 58, South Carolina, Federalist

Credentials   Madison was a member of Virginia's House of Delegates (1776–1777), defeated when he did not pass out free whiskey to voters; youngest member of the Continental Congress (1780–1783); member of the Virginia House of Delegates (1784–1786); delegate to the Constitutional Convention (1787), titled "Father of the Constitution" for doing much of the work; congressman from Virginia (1789–1797) and secretary of state (1801–1809).

For Pinckney, see Campaign of 1804.

Tickets   In the Republican caucus of senators and congressmen Madison was nominated on the first ballot with 83 votes and George Clinton, Jefferson's vice president, was renominated on the first ballot with 79 votes. But trouble surrounded the caucus. Some Republicans objected to the caucus system; some boycotted the meeting; and some refused to accept the decision of the caucus. Critics attacked the caucus as just a powerful clique. Those attending countered that they were acting as "private citizens." The Republicans again appointed a campaign committee, formally calling it "the committee of correspondence and arrangement."

Mirroring 1804, the Federalists did not hold a formal congressional caucus to decide on nominees. Instead, party leaders from Pennsylvania and the North once again chose Charles Pinckney, with former minister to England Rufus King as his running mate.

Campaign Notes   Ever since he lost a seat in the Virginia House of Delegates by not buttering up voters enough, Madison "despised" electioneering. Luckily, there was still no campaigning for the presidency: In these early days, the office was above that. So Madison remained aloof, had his writings distributed (his voice was too weak for speeches, anyway), and took no public notice of all the backbiting that was going on among Republicans.

JAMES MADISON

Federalists had their noses pressed against the window for the early part of the campaign, watching different Republican factions attack each other in print but failing to be real players themselves. Only when the embargo, the brainchild of President Thomas Jefferson and Madison (see below), produced such disastrous results did the Federalists finally have an issue, select candidates, and target New England for their campaign.

Slogans Republicans rallied "To the Principles of '76!"

Federalists coupled Pinckney's famous quote during the XYZ affair, "Millions for defense—not a cent for tribute," with one wrongly attributed to Madison by a Republican rival: "France wants money, and we must give it."

Songs Republicans sang "Madison, Union and Liberty" to their candidate: "So Jefferson to shade retires, / But Madison, like morn, appears."

Federalists in New England sang against the embargo: "Our ships all in motion once whitened the ocean; / Now doomed to decay they are fallen a prey / To Jefferson, worms and EMBARGO."

Popular Labels Madison was known as "Father of the Constitution" as well as "Little Jemmy." Clinton was "The Hero of the Revolution" and the "Old Fox."

"A Hero of Our Revolution" referred to Pinckney.

Name-calling Republicans labeled fellow Republican and vice president George Clinton "the stalking horse of Federalism" during his unorthodox run for the presidency.

Clinton's followers accused Madison Republicans of being "Bonaparte, Imperial Republicans." Northern Democrats joined Federalists in attacking the "Virginia Dynasty" in presidential succession and the "Virginia lordlings" in Washington.

Federalists belittled Madison as Jefferson's "crown prince" and "monkey on a leash." They also took aim at "Despot" Jefferson and the "Dambargo," as they called the Embargo Act of 1807.

Curious Facts George Clinton, in a cool political maneuver, made known his objections to his own "spurious nomination" as vice president but did not take himself out of the race. This left him as the vice-presidential nominee, while his followers continued to promote him as a challenger to Madison for the presidency.

The Press Much of this campaign was conducted through the press. In many cases, papers were published by the Republican press, giving Madison's record as secretary of state. When the correspondence of the *Chesapeake* affair (a British frigate's attack on the American *Chesapeake*) was published, partisan reviews came in.

The Republican *Richmond Inquirer* said: "A more valuable body of dissertation on the rights of neutrals and interests of the U.S. was never before condensed in the same place."

According to the New York *Evening Post*: "Never since the birth of Machiavelli has this game of politics been played so dexterously and knavishly."

Firsts The first major protests were heard against use of the congressional caucus to nominate presidents.

The first inaugural ball.

Trends By retiring after two terms, when health was not a factor as it was with Washington, Jefferson reinforced the two-term presidency.

Vote Once again, seventeen states participated. In seven states the legislatures chose electors; in ten the people voted by district or general ticket. Madison received 122 electoral votes to 47 for Pinckney and 6 for Clinton. In Virginia, Madison received 14,655 to 3,408 for fellow Republican and Virginian James Monroe.

Benchmarks Madison's election broke the pattern of vice presidents becoming president.

Madison brought more experience in the public sector to the office of president than had anyone before him.

No president-elect was ever closer to his predecessor than Madison was to Jefferson.

Quote "Never did a prisoner, released from his chains, feel such relief as I shall on shaking off the shackles of power," said Jefferson about leaving the presidency.

Ir isn't over until the fat lady sings," Federalists could have said to President Thomas Jefferson in the second term of his presidency. Jefferson had dreamed of a one-party system after his landslide victory in 1804, but the Federalists were not to be counted out yet—due to his own foreign policies.

When war broke out again between France and Britain in 1803, Americans were happily caught in the middle. Commercial vessels out of New England, neutrality flags unfurled, enjoyed several boom years, bringing wealth as well to Southern and Western producers of exportable goods. The bubble burst when the warring governments, Britain and later France, ordered a crackdown on ships entering each other's ports. The British had also resumed their policy of impressing American sailors to work on His Majesty's ships. Then, in 1807, the royal frigate *Leopard* fired on the U.S. *Chesapeake*. "All parties, ranks and professions were unanimous in their detestation of the dastardly deed," announced the Washington *Federalist*. "All cried aloud for vengeance."

Jefferson tried to avoid war by asking Britain to make amends. When that did not work, Jefferson, at the suggestion of Secretary of State James Madison, embargoed all American exports to the two feuding powers. Madison's belief was that Britain, at least, needed U.S. goods much more than America needed English "superfluities or poisons" and would be forced to come to peaceful terms. But the impact of the Embargo Act, passed in December 1807, was hardest on American merchants and farmers. Just as Campaign 1808 was beginning, the Federalist party had an issue to run on.

A Federalist circular in Massachusetts urged citizens to act against "this accursed thing, this *Embargo*." Critics roasted Jefferson: "May he receive from his fellow citizens the reward of his merit, a halter [hangman's noose]." By June Albert Gallatin, secretary of the treasury, was predicting "the Federalists will turn us out by 4th of March next." In August Gallatin calculated that only "the Western states, Virginia, South Carolina, and perhaps Georgia" were sure for Madison.

Ironically, not until September did a meeting of the Federalists select their candidates. The candidates and their backers attacked the embargo and "French influence" in the administration ("the chains of Bonaparte," as one newspaper put it), and hoped that divisions within the Republican party would give them a boost.

In its stride, the Federalist party had its Hamilton and Adams factions. Now, the party in power was engaged in intramural strife. Even the nominating caucus fell under attack. Several Republican members of Congress refused to attend the January meeting, denouncing the "midnight intrigues" that allowed "any set of men" so much power. Nevertheless, more than ninety congressmen did come to nominate Madison for president. He won easily but not unanimously. George Clinton and James Monroe each garnered three votes, and would have gotten more had some of their supporters not been part of the boycott. Clinton was also renominated for vice president.

After the caucus, the three-way contest continued because neither Clinton nor Monroe publicly removed himself from the presidential race. In fact, Clinton became adept at running for president and vice president at the same time.

One of Clinton's main arguments against Madison was the grip of Virginia, the most populous state at the time, on the presidency. Madison would become the third president out of four to come from Virginia. Clinton argued for "rotation." On the other hand, Monroe (a Virginian, too) and his followers viewed Madison as under the thumb of Jefferson. Madison would be ruled "from the top of Monticello," they argued.

Jefferson tried to observe "a sacred neutrality," but he obviously wanted Madison to win. In time, the Republican infighting lessened as it was shown that Madison's leadership position could not be assailed. By the fall, the race was truly between the Federalists, who got a surge of strength from the embargo, and the much more powerful Republicans.

The election was a sizable victory for "little Jim Madison," the slight man with a weak voice whose title "Father of the Constitution" almost seemed too massive for him. At the inaugural ball, Madison was clearly overshadowed by his buxom, exuberant wife, "Queen Dolley," in her white satin turban (from Paris) with two bird-of-paradise feathers. "I would rather be in bed," he whispered to a friend. Maybe Madison was thinking of all that he faced. "The present situation of the world is indeed without parallel," he said earlier that day, "and that of our own country full of difficulties."

★ CAMPAIGN OF 1812 ★

Major Candidates   James Madison, 61, Virginia, Democrat-Republican
DeWitt Clinton, 43, New York, Republican

Credentials   For Madison, see Campaign of 1808.
Clinton, nephew of Vice President George Clinton, was New York State

senator (1798–1802, 1806–1811), U.S. senator (1802–1803), mayor of New York City (1803–1807, 1810–1811), and lieutenant governor of New York (1811).

Tickets Only 60 percent of the Republican members of Congress were present in May to nominate a presidential and vice presidential candidate. All but one (a New York member for DeWitt Clinton who just observed) of the eighty-three members present voted for Madison for president, making it unanimous. Although many of the missing members were simply unavailable, other absences were an indication of sectional displeasure with Madison and growing concern over the caucus, centered in the Northeast.

The vice-presidential nomination was more complicated. George Clinton had died in April. First-choice former senator John Langdon, 70, declined the nomination because of his age. A second caucus met and selected, at Madison's suggestion, Elbridge Gerry, the former governor of Massachusetts.

New York Republicans had a different idea. They met about a week later to nominate DeWitt Clinton, now "boss" of the party in New York, for the presidency. Of course, Clinton needed a wider appeal—which is where the Federalists came in.

The Federalists held a "convention" in September to map their strategy in the upcoming election and maybe even nominate a presidential candidate. The most eloquent and moving speech was made in favor of Republican Clinton. While no specific nominee was chosen, most delegates except those backing former vice-presidential nominee Rufus King would work for Clinton's election. Jared Ingersoll, the Federalist attorney general of Pennsylvania, was the nominee for vice president.

Campaign Notes Like his predecessors, Madison did not actively campaign. But he did write two letters in defense of America's war in 1812 against the British that could be construed as campaign appeals. Madison thought his conduct of foreign affairs, specifically the war with Britain, was the main issue of the campaign.

Clinton's camp had to do some fancy footwork to make the most of the war issue (see below). For good measure, New York Clintonian strategists also attacked the "dangers" of the presidential nominating caucus, the Virginia succession in presidents, and the assumption of a second term in an "Address to the People of the United States." Published in August, this document became official campaign "propaganda."

By this election, both parties had well-established grass-roots organizations. In turn, state nominating conventions with popular election of delegates were supplanting state caucuses for the selection of slates of presidential electors.

Slogans "Free Trade and Sailors' Rights" and "On to Canada, On to Canada" were popular cries of war-hungry Republicans.

Those against the war were fond of calling it "Mr. Madison's War."

DEWITT CLINTON

Federalists toasted: "The Existing War—the Child of Prostitution. May no American Acknowledge it Legitimate."

Clintonians were for "Peace and Commerce" and against "Too much Virginia" and the "Virginia Dynasty." Their electoral choice: "Madison and War! or Clinton and Peace."

Songs Republicans had "Madison's March" and even "Mrs. Madison's Minuet," while the Federalists played tunes from earlier elections.

Popular Labels Vice-presidential nominee Gerry was known as the "Gentleman's Democrat."

Federalists started calling themselves "Federal Republicans" and their party the "Peace party."

The president's wife, Dolley, was hailed as "Lady Presidentress."

Name-calling Federalists scorned Madison as "the Little Man in the Palace" and his party as the "War party."

To Federalists, France's Napoleon Bonaparte was not only the enemy of England but also "the anti-Christ of the age."

"Madison's Nightcaps" was the name given to the barreled mastheads of ships idled by the 1812 embargo.

Curious Fact The Federalists, in an attempt to broaden their appeal, began to call themselves "Federal Republicans" or just "Republicans," which, of course, was the popular name of their opponents, although "Democrats" was also in use.

The Press The war issue forced the press to take sides. Niles' *Weekly Register* in Baltimore commented that the country was forced to choose between Britain and France as "our enemy" and chose Britain "on account of her more flagrant wrongs."

Boston's *Columbian Centinel* backed Clinton, arguing "The declaration of war is a signal deliberately made by our government, inviting and authorizing the capture and plunder of our vessels on the ocean."

Firsts The first wartime election and, for the first time, war was the primary issue of the campaign.

Clinton is considered the first "politician" to be a major candidate for president.

Federalists held the first convention to resemble modern national nominating conventions.

Trend By winning well in wartime, Madison set the stage for future wartime incumbents.

Vote In nine states citizens voted for presidential electors by district or general ticket; in the other nine, the legislatures chose. Madison received a total of 128 electoral votes to 89 for Clinton. Madison won most of the South, Clinton most of the Northeast.

Benchmarks This was the closest election since 1800.

The sectional pattern to the election was the most extreme before 1860.

The last serious Federalist battle for the presidency.

Quote War reversals tempered Madison's election victory. A month before his inauguration, one Federalist surmised "Such a ferment is raised that it is thought if the Presidential election was to take place now, Madison would not obtain a single vote in Virginia."

D OLLEY Madison was a star. Bedecked in plumed turbans (she removed the plumes when napping) and French frocks, Dolley probably enjoyed rumors that she painted and powdered some, for she flauntingly pinched snuff from lava-and-platina boxes. Her receptions or "Mrs. Madison's crush" on Wednesday nights were perfect moments for politicians to catch the normally stiff, solemn "Jemmy" at ease and for Dolley to parade in fantastic costumes of ermine and amethysts. (So dazzled was one young man that he tried to stuff a teacup in his pocket.)

Dolley graced the head of the table at White House dinners, wooed—and shared snuff with—young War Hawk Henry Clay, and invited to her parties Mrs. William Seaton, wife of the new editor of the influential *National Intelligencer.* Then war with Britain came and even the irrepressible Dolley felt its impact. "The world seems to be running mad," she wrote a friend, "what with one thing and another."

America's divisive and ill-fought War of 1812 became the central issue of the campaign. Madison felt forced into it; most of New England, with its commercial and pro-British interests, fought against it. As the first wartime president, Madison found himself in an untested electoral situation. And the opposition made the most of it. At first, the Federalists accused Madison of baiting Britain as an election-year ploy. When war was declared, they insisted on calling it "Mr. Madison's War" and the Republican party the "War party"; theirs was the "party of peace."

Madison had tried to avoid war by using trade as a carrot but the policy had not worked.

In late 1811, he appointed James Monroe secretary of state. Monroe came to the job intending to bring America back from the brink of war with Britain. But the new firebrands in Congress, "the boys" as they were derisively called, changed all that. Heady and headstrong, they were led by thirty-four-year-old Clay of Kentucky who, as if by magic, was elected Speaker of the House. "Free trade and Sailors' Rights" they bellowed, even though many, being Westerners, had never seen the sea. "On to Canada!" they cried, even though they had no idea how tough routing the British would be.

Against this backdrop, the Republican congressional caucus met in mid-May, with many members too busy or too angry to attend. Madison was worried about the "spirit of opposition" that was gaining in the Northeast, and rightly so. Later in May New York Republicans decided to back their lieutenant governor DeWitt Clinton instead of Madison.

During June Congress debated a declaration of war behind closed doors. On June 18, the Senate in a close vote went along with war, but not until two days later did the public find out. Federalist Samuel Taggert complained that Congress would not have been "mad enough" to vote for war if the issue had been debated "openly and fairly." New England, where war was generally not wanted, saw lowered flags and public fasts.

The Federalists held a national convention in September and came away agreeing that their only chance of success was to back a fusion candidate, the Republican Clinton. Clinton had once called Federalists fiends and once been pro-war himself, but now ran on a peace platform for Federalists, although he also spoke about "vigor in war" to appeal to dissident Republicans. His Janus-faced campaign worked pretty well. Clinton tapped antiwar sentiment in New England as well as dissatisfaction with the war's progress in the Middle Atlantic states.

Madison's people charged that Clinton was playing on sectional rivalries and that his slogan "peace and commerce" was what everyone wanted. At one point it was rumored that Ohio was going Federalist, but Madison won

Ohio and Pennsylvania too, which gave him the election. But he did not get New England, except for Vermont, which meant more trouble ahead. As if to underscore this, a newly elected congressman from New Hampshire, after his courtesy call on the president, remarked, "I did not like his looks any better than I like his Administration." The new legislator's name was Daniel Webster.

★ CAMPAIGN OF 1816 ★

Major Candidates   James Monroe, 58, Virginia, Democrat-Republican
Rufus King, 61, New York, Federalist

Credentials   Monroe was a member of the Continental Congress (1783–1786), voted against the Constitution at the Virginia Ratifying Convention (1788), arguing for more states' rights, and then became a supporter of the new government and a U.S. senator (1790–1794). He was minister to France (1794–1796), governor of Virginia (1799–1802), minister to Great Britain (1803–1807), ran against James Madison for president in 1808, and was secretary of state (1811–1817) as well as secretary of war (1814–1815).

King served in the Continental Congress (1784–1787) and helped draft the Northwest Ordinance of 1787, which banned slavery in that area. He was delegate to the Constitutional Convention (1787), U.S. senator (1789–1796), minister to Great Britain (1796–1803), ran unsuccessfully as the Federalist vice-presidential candidate in 1804 and 1808, and returned to the Senate in 1813.

Tickets   Republican congressmen caucused twice. Only fifty-eight members came to the first call. On the second try 119 of the 141 Republican members attended. Monroe was chosen by a slim margin, receiving sixty-five votes to fifty-four for Secretary of War William Crawford. New York governor Daniel Thompkins was picked as his running mate.

The Federalists did not nominate any candidates nor did they informally agree, as they had in 1804, to support particular candidates. Only the few Federalist electors who voted made a choice: King for president.

Campaign Notes   What contest there was took place among the Republicans. So out of favor were the Federalists that once the caucus was over, the campaign was over. Monroe's only public statement about the campaign is his letter accepting the nomination. "I can only say," he wrote, "should the suffrages of my people call me to that trust, I should feel a duty to enter it."

The Federalists did not campaign. Even King called it a "fruitless struggle."

RUFUS KING

Slogans   The "Virginia influence," the "Virginia Dynasty" and "Not Subservient to Virginia" were expressions of growing dissatisfaction among more and more Republicans and, of course, Federalists about Virginia's hold on the presidency.

"Moneyed Monster" Federalists called the Bank of the United States when Republicans wanted to revive it in 1816. In the days of Alexander Hamilton the Federalists had supported the Bank; now, as sectionalists, they viewed it as damaging to state banks.

"Not One Inch of Territory Ceded or Lost" Republicans jubilantly shouted at the end of the War of 1812, putting the opposing Federalists on the defensive.

Songs   Republicans praised Monroe in "Monroe Is the Man" as "Whose country's his Idol, her good all his care."

"The Star-Spangled Banner," a poem written by Francis Scott Key during the abortive British assault on Baltimore in 1814, sung to the tune of an old English drinking song, became a popular war song among Republicans and—more than a century later—the national anthem.

Popular Labels   Monroe was hailed as the "heir apparent" and "Old Sachem."

Thompkins' admirers called him the "Farmer's Boy of Westchester."

Name-calling Monroe was belittled as "James the Lesser."

Curious Facts New York's Daniel Thompkins was nominated for three different offices in 1816 and ended up winning two. On February 14 he was chosen by Republican members of the New York state legislature as a favorite-son candidate for president. A week later he was renominated for the governorship. A month later, Thompkins was chosen in the Republican caucus to be the nominee for vice president. He became governor of New York and vice president but subsequently resigned the governorship.

Rufus King was the Federalist candidate who ran against Republican Thompkins for governor of New York and lost. King was also the Federalist electors' choice for president who lost to James Monroe.

The Press The *Charleston Courier*, objecting to the Virginia dynasty, argued that "a few leading men in Virginia have outrageously violated Republican principles."

The *Boston Daily Advertiser*, published in one of the few states to choose Federalist electors, noted: "We do not know, nor is it material, for whom the Federal electors will vote."

Firsts The first time the same political party managed to elect three consecutive Presidents.

The inaugural speech took place outdoors.

Newspapers gave detailed accounts of the inauguration for the first time since Washington's.

More electors were chosen by popular vote than by legislatures.

Trend Increased annoyance with the caucus system to nominate presidential candidates.

Vote In ten states there was a popular vote—by general or district ticket—for electors, while legislatures chose electors in nine: Monroe received 183 electoral votes to 34 for King, which were all from the Northeast. Four electors did not bother to vote. Thompkins also had 183 votes, while General John Howard of Maryland received the most Federalist vice-presidential votes: 22.

Benchmarks The Federalists had a contender for the last time.

The death of the Federalist party as a national party.

Monroe was the last president of the Revolutionary War generation.

The most spectators at an inauguration so far.

Quote "It is quite worthy of remark," Federalist Rufus King commented just before the election, "that in no preceding election, has there been such a calm respecting it."

★ ★ ★

THE War of 1812 ended in 1815 with a whimper. Then with a bang. Of course, communications were such back then that Americans first heard about Old Hickory's stupendous victory over the British at the Battle of New Orleans. Then, ten days later, word came across the Atlantic that the Treaty of Ghent had been signed. In fact, the treaty was signed on Christmas Eve and the battle won on January 8. But few got that straight. As a Baltimore paper headlined: "Glorious News! Orleans saved and peace concluded."

For General Andrew Jackson, (Old Hickory, as his men fondly nicknamed him) the party began soon after British commander Sir Edward Packenham was buried under a pecan tree. Crowned with a laurel wreath and feted as he rode through the streets, Jackson ended up dancing the night away at the New Orleans Opera House. In Washington, the "White House" gleamed with a fresh coat of paint that covered smoke damage from its burning by the British in 1814. Men in new fashionable long trousers and women in sleeveless dresses toasted the news. Americans—who had not won Canada or anything else by the Treaty of Ghent—generally thought the Battle of New Orleans made them the victors.

By 1816 the Federalists were completely demoralized and unable to offer a candidate or wage any kind of campaign. Jackson's victory had stolen their thunder, and now James Madison had taken over their old tenets by proposing a national bank and a protective tariff in his last State of the Union message. When Federalist Rufus King lost the governorship of New York to Republican Daniel Thompkins in April 1816, King took it as a call to retreat, telling a friend, "Federalists of our age must be content with the past."

The rivalry that surfaced in this campaign was among the Republicans. As early as 1811, when Madison made Monroe his secretary of state, there were rumors that Monroe was being targeted for the presidency. He was a natural. He had Revolutionary credentials and a good public record. His main drawback was that he was Virginian. The Republican *New York Patriot* simply said: "We are adverse to the nomination of another citizen from Virginia." Former president John Adams, who wanted to see his son president some day, complained that would not happen " 'till all Virginians are extinct."

William Crawford of Georgia, forty-four, former senator and Madison's secretary of war, presented an alternative. Dashing, not dull like Monroe, representing the younger generation of Republicans, Crawford probably had the votes among his onetime colleagues in Congress to win the nomination. But he never publicly made himself available. As a result, when the Republican caucus met some of his backers stayed away, giving Monroe the vote by a narrow margin. The fact that Crawford almost won, even though Monroe had more backing at the state level, raised voices once more against the caucus system.

After his nomination, Monroe could take his election for granted. As inauguration day approached, the only hitch was the refusal of House members to let senators bring their favorite red-velvet armchairs into the House, where the ceremony was usually held. So Monroe took the oath of office outside on a platform built near the burned-out Capitol with as many as 8,000 people craning to see. The new president began his administration convinced, as he had told Andrew Jackson earlier, that the "existence of parties is not necessary to free government."

★ CAMPAIGN OF 1820 ★

Major Candidate for President   James Monroe, 62, Virginia, Democrat-Republican

Credentials   See Campaign of 1820.

Tickets   The Republican caucus called for April 8 was a disappointment—only forty congressmen came. Bad weather was part of the problem, apathy the other. There had been some talk of unseating Vice President Daniel Thompkins, but because of the poor showing nothing was done. At the meeting, members decided it was "not necessary" to make any nominations. The understanding was that Monroe and Thompkins would be the Republican ticket.

The Federalists did not have a nominee and, unlike 1816, Federalist electors did not rally behind a candidate. In this election, they all voted for Monroe.

Campaign Notes   Monroe did not do any campaigning in 1820, but his summer goodwill tour in 1817, which was so successful that the Federalist Boston *Columbian Centinel* proclaimed the "Era of Good Feelings," set the stage for this election.

Symbols   As a veteran of the Revolutionary War—the last to hold the presidency, Monroe often dressed up in the "buff and blue" of the war (buff knee breeches and a blue coat) and an old-fashioned cocked hat. This "uniform" became a symbol in itself of an era coming to a close with Monroe. In addition, Monroe was greeted along his goodwill tour with recovered flags and other memorabilia from the Revolution.

Also during his tour, school children wore red and white roses, sometimes intertwined, symbolizing partisan peace.

JAMES MONROE

Slogans "The President's Progress" referred to Monroe's 1817 tour. "The Era of Good Feelings" became the theme of Monroe's presidency.

Songs Besides "Monroe Is the Man," "Hail Columbia" and "Yankee Doodle" were popular.

Popular Labels Monroe was called "Last of the Fathers" and "Last of the Revolutionary Farmers."

Name-calling Forging the Missouri Compromise, which brought the issue of slavery into the political arena, caused increased tension between Southern extremists and Southern moderates with their Northern allies (called "doughfaces" by some extremists). The compromise itself was denounced as a "dirty bargain" by those unwilling to go along.

Curious Facts New Hampshire elector William Plumer, a Federalist turned Republican, spoiled Monroe's chances of matching George Washington's unanimous election to the presidency. Plumer's reasons have long been debated, but he said "Mr. Monroe during the last four years has, in my opinion, conducted, as president, very improperly."

Never satisfied with a single contest, Thompkins ran again for governor of

New York. This time he simplified matters by losing to incumbent Governor DeWitt Clinton before the Republican caucus.

Thompkins did not come to Washington for the second inaugural. He decided to stay in New York and ended up taking the oath of office twice. He originally took it on March 3, then found out that Monroe would not be inaugurated until March 5, and took it again then.

The Press   On October 17, 1820, the Republican *National Intelligencer* predicted: "The unanimous re-election of Mr. Monroe is morally certain, as certain as almost any contingent event can be."

Even before knowing all of the returns, the Federalist *New Hampshire Sentinel* said that Plumer's vote "is to be regretted because it will probably be the only one throughout the United States in opposition to the reelection of the present incumbent, and thus to prevent a unanimous election will be pronounced sheer folly."

First   Slavery surfaces as a political issue for the first time.

Trend   The caucus system loses more clout.

Vote   Of the twenty-four states, fifteen chose their electors by popular vote, either district or general ticket, and nine by legislatures. Although many more electors were selected by some form of popular vote than by legislatures (163 to 72), the popular vote was negligible.

Monroe received 231 electoral votes to 1 for fellow Republican John Quincy Adams. Thompkins took 218 electoral votes, with 14 divided among four other candidates.

Benchmarks   Monroe was the last resident of Virginia to be elected to the presidency.

The end of the first generation of party politics, Federalists versus Democratic-Republicans. In the spirit of partisan peace, Republicans invited Federalists to their party caucus.

Monroe shares with Washington the distinction of running unopposed.

One of the smallest popular votes on record.

Monroe was the only president to be reelected on the heels of a major financial panic.

Quote   "There is no mustering of troops, no thunder of artillery, no revelry, nor song, no bloodshed or destruction," noted the Massachusetts *Essex Register* on December 6, the day electors voted. "Even our public prints are silent, and not one person in one hundred knows of the election of the day."

CIRCUMSTANCES allowed James Monroe to become a "Teflon" president. In more normal times, a bank panic as severe as that of 1819 and an issue as burning as that of slavery would have damaged the president in power.

But the fact that there was no opposition party created an atmosphere in which Monroe was never targeted for blame. This allowed the Republican president to be remembered mostly for the Era of Good Feelings and the Monroe Doctrine, which is just as he wanted it to be.

From the start, Monroe designed to be head "of the nation" rather than "of a party." He knew that one of the first things he needed to do was to smooth feathers over the "Virginia influence" in government. So Monroe looked East and chose John Quincy Adams for State, kept Georgian William Crawford in Treasury, and turned West for War. When Henry Clay and others declined, Monroe asked John C. Calhoun of South Carolina to run that department. But he did not go as far as warrior Andrew Jackson suggested, which was to bring a Federalist into his cabinet.

Monroe had a better idea. He remembered George Washington's presidential tours to come closer to the people. Monroe planned to do the same for a more political end. His hope was to eradicate partisan differences by making Republicans of Federalists. Not knowing what to expect, the president set off in the summer of 1817 on a three-and-a-half-month "progress." What a sight he was, dressed in the old "buff and blue" of Revolutionary War days and a dated cocked hat! Monroe almost looked like Washington now—at least from a distance.

The president intended to travel as a private citizen, but that plan fell apart as early as Baltimore, when his carriage was met by several hastily assembled cavalry units. As he ventured farther into Federalist country, the pomp and circumstance increased. In Boston he was greeted by a mile-long procession of military and civilian might, while forty thousand people thronged the streets. When he rode onto Boston Common, thousands of schoolchildren lined the lawn, wearing roses of red and white to show that differences had ceased. Later, Federalists and Republicans ate together; it was years since that had last happened. On July 17, Boston's staunchly Federalist *Columbian Centinel* was moved enough to write about the "Era of Good Feelings" when "many persons have met . . . whom party politics had long severed."

Surprisingly, the good feelings toward Monroe and his era persisted in spite of the panic of 1819. The panic, which was sparked by events overseas as well as the speculative derring-do of the Bank of the United States and "wildcat" Western American banks, sent farm prices reeling, many merchants into bankruptcy, and thousands into unemployment and even into debtor's prison. But in the end the "moneyed monster," the Bank of the United States, rather than the administration bore much of the blame.

Another potential trapdoor for Monroe was Missouri, the first state to be formed from the Louisiana Territory. At the time Missouri sought admission to the union, there were twenty-two states—eleven slave and eleven free. In February 1819 a bill came before Congress that would allow Missouri to enter the union. An amendment curtailing slavery in the future state was tacked on and the issue of slavery exploded in the halls of Congress. Monroe stayed his distance and let leaders like Henry Clay in the House and James Barbour in the Senate construct a compromise.

Maine, a free state, was seeking admission about the same time. But anti-slavery Congressmen wanted something more than a straight exchange; they wanted to restrict slavery in the rest of the Louisiana Territory. Finally enough Southerners, who thought they had won their point by keeping Missouri a slave state, agreed to go along. The slavery issue was settled before the election, much to Monroe's relief. But almost everyone realized it would rear up again. As Jefferson put it, "We have the wolf by the ears and we can neither hold him nor safely let him go."

Word of the probable compromise gave Monroe some trouble in the Virginia caucus. States' rightists could not believe that Monroe would sign an agreement that excluded slavery from any territory. The president sent word that a compromise was needed to keep the union together and a slate of electors loyal to him was reluctantly selected.

Otherwise Monroe sailed into a second term, pulling Vice President Thompkins along with him. Before the Republican caucus there was talk that Clay would make a play for the vice presidency in the Republican caucus, but not enough members attended to make a fight feasible. Monroe won all the electoral votes but one (even former president John Adams, a Federalist, voted for him), a victory second only to that of George Washington. Without any rivalry, however, the election was so lackluster that few people bothered to vote. In fact, anticipation was already building for the next presidential contest. The writer "Virginius" in the Richmond *Enquirer* labeled it best: "The War of the Giants."

★ CAMPAIGN OF 1824 ★

Major Candidates   John Quincy Adams, 57, Massachusetts, Democrat-Republican
John C. Calhoun, 42, South Carolina, Democrat-Republican
Henry Clay, 47, Kentucky, Democrat-Republican
William Crawford, 52, Georgia, Democrat-Republican
Andrew Jackson, 57, Tennessee, Democrat-Republican

Credentials   Adams, son of President John Adams, was American minister to the Netherlands, Portugal, and Prussia (1794–1801), U.S. senator (1803–1808), minister to Russia (1809–1814), helped negotiate the 1814 Treaty of Ghent, and served as minister to Great Britain (1815–1817). He became secretary of state under President James Monroe (1817–1825).

Calhoun served two sessions in the South Carolina legislature and then was elected to the House of Representatives (1810), identifying with the young "War Hawks" led by Speaker of the House Henry Clay. Reelected

JOHN QUINCY ADAMS

in 1812 and 1814, he was an influential supporter of the War of 1812 and became secretary of war in 1817.

Clay served in his state house of representatives (1803–1806 and 1807–1810), becoming speaker, filled unexpired senate terms (1806–1807 and 1810–1811), served in the U.S. House of Representatives, and was elected Speaker (1811–1821 and 1823–1825). He helped negotiate the Treaty of Ghent (1814).

Crawford was elected to his state legislature (1803–1807), filled an unexpired senate term (1807–1810), won a U.S. Senate seat (1810–1813), becoming president pro tem. He became minister to France (1813–1815), secretary of war (1815–1816), and secretary of the treasury (1816–1825). He was James Monroe's main rival for the Republican nomination in 1816.

Jackson helped draft the Constitution of Tennessee (1796), was elected that state's first U.S. Representative (1796), became U.S. Senator (1787) but resigned in frustration after a year, defeated the British at New Orleans in 1815 (the biggest victory of the war of 1812), subdued the Seminole Indians in Florida in 1818, was elected again to the U.S. Senate (1823), and resigned again in 1825.

Tickets One of the biggest issues of this campaign was the congressional caucus with candidates, state legislatures, and newspapers coming down on both sides.

Calhoun got off to an early start by declaring his candidacy in December 1821. In July–August 1822 the Tennessee legislature followed with an endorsement of favorite son Jackson "at the approaching election for chief magistracy." In November Clay, who was angling for the backing of several Western legislatures, received Missouri's (the "Missouri Compromise" helped) and then Kentucky's and Ohio's. Finally it was New England's turn. Maine announced in January 1823 that Adams was preferred "for the important office of president." A week later Massachusetts expressed "unlimited confidence" in its favorite son.

All along Crawford presumed he was the heir apparent. In deference to Monroe, he said, he had not declared himself a candidate in 1816, resulting in Monroe winning the brass ring of the Republican nomination. By 1823 Crawford realized that Monroe was not going to back him and that his rivals were gaining on him. He looked to the congressional caucus for approval, but his nomination turned out to be an albatross. Less than one-third of the Republican members of Congress attended the meeting on the evening of February 14, 1824. Crawford easily won and former secretary of the treasury Albert Gallatin was chosen as his running mate.

Campaign Notes Jackson had the most active campaign organization. The candidate's views on issues ranging from the tariff to the national debt were made known by publishing his correspondence. Pro-Jackson newspapers conducted "voter-preference" polls, such as one by the *Pennsylvanian* that found Jackson received more Fourth of July toasts than any other candidate. And Jackson's campaign manager, John Eaton, prepared the *Life of Jackson*, a gloriously image-making campaign biography.

Clay and Adams adhered more to the norm of presidential candidates by not advertising their personal views. Clay did have a campaign manager and a biography of Adams did appear, but their campaigns were not as effective as Jackson's.

Slogans Early on in some states, support was expressed for an Adams–Jackson "People's Ticket" with the cry "John Quincy Adams / Who can write / And Andrew Jackson / Who can fight."

Jackson supporters likened their candidate to George Washington with the slogan "Under Washington our independence was achieved; under Jackson our independence has been preserved."

The Adams camp knew it had to win on the first ballot in the House of Representatives or some states would desert to Jackson. The pep talk was "Adams in One, or Nothing Won!"

Songs The only unmistakable campaign song was "The Hunters of Tennessee," which extolled the fighting men Jackson had led into the Battle of New Orleans: "For ev'ry man was half a horse, / and half an alligator." It became the theme song for Jackson's campaign.

Paraphernalia Items for Adams included a colorful sewing box with a portrait of the president-to-be inside the cover and a tag taken from a cookie tin with a sketch of Adams and the words *Peece. Liberty. Home. Industry.*

Jackson supporters wore black silk vests sporting a portrait of Adams' main rival and showed off Jackson medals inscribed *The Nation's Pride.*

Popular Labels Adams was called "New England Independent"; Calhoun won the name "The Young Hercules" for his efforts in Congress to supply the war effort of 1812; Clay's favorite must have been "Gallant Harry of the West"; Crawford was a "plain giant of a man"; and Jackson was idolized as "Old Hero" and "The Hero of New Orleans."

Name-calling Clay denigrated Jackson as a "military chieftain" who wanted to be president.

Crawford bore the stigma of "caucus candidate."

Jackson denounced Clay as "The Judas of the West," convinced there was a deal between Adams and Clay.

Curious Fact New York's vote was critical in the House of Representatives. The state's vote (each state gets one vote in the House) could give Adams thirteen states and therefore the election, but the New York delegates were pretty much deadlocked on a choice. General Stephen Van Rensselaer found himself in the middle. At one point he put his head in his hands, prayed for guidance, and opened his eyes to see a discarded Adams ballot on the floor. He scooped it up and placed it in the ballot box. With that Adams became president.

The Press Jacksonians were irate at the alleged "corrupt bargain." One supportive newspaper issued this death notice: "Expired at Washington on the 9th of February, of poison administered by the assassin hands of John Quincy Adams, the usurper, and Henry Clay, the virtue, liberty and independence of the United States."

Firsts Records on the popular vote were kept for the first time.

A president is elected without a majority of popular votes.

Trends New political parties arose from this contest.

Official campaign managers started to play a role.

Public opinion polls became a staple of campaigns.

The first election cartoon was published.

Vote In only six states were electors still chosen by legislatures. In the remaining twenty-two they were selected by popular vote, either general or district ticket. In a light turnout—about 27 percent of those eligible voted—Jackson received 99 electoral votes and 153,544 popular votes (43.1 percent), to 84 and 108,740 (30.5 percent) for Adams, 41 and 46,618 (13.1

percent) for Crawford, and 37 and 47,136 (13.2 percent) for Clay. Jackson was shy 32 electoral votes of the needed majority. Under the Twelfth Amendment, it was up to the House of Representatives to choose a winner among the top three candidates (see below). Calhoun easily won the vice presidency with 182 electoral votes.

Benchmarks The last campaign in which congressional caucuses were held to nominate a president and vice president.

For the second time in history (and so far the last) the election is forced into the House.

More major contenders than ever in history.

Quote When notified of his election by the House, Adams responded that he wished "the decision of this momentous question" could be referred to the people again for them "to express with a nearer approach to unanimity the object of their preference."

THE ballroom was beautiful on the evening of January 8, 1824. Garlands of laurel and colorful tissue swirled down pillars and stretched like shadows across the ceiling. American eagles and patriotic mottoes made even the floors festive. It was the ninth anniversary of the Battle of New Orleans and Louisa Adams, wife of the secretary of state, was giving a ball in honor of "hero" General Andrew Jackson.

Women in silk and taffeta, hair held high with combs, fans, or ribbons of stars, rustled through the rooms, arm in arm with the titans of their times. At one point, Daniel Webster posed with his hand inside his vest and talked with John C. Calhoun. Across the room General Jackson and his wife Rachel waited for Henry Clay and John Quincy Adams to turn toward them. Only President James Monroe declined, concerned about his presence in an election year.

The ball did wonders for Mrs. Adams' image. That she took Jackson's arm was considered the height of diplomacy and not at all hurtful to her husband's presidential campaign. After all, had not Adams once written that Jackson would be perfect as vice president? Jackson benefited too. Having just arrived in town as the new senator from Tennessee, people saw that "frontiersman" did not do him justice. He seemed such a gentleman.

Something else was happening at the same time. Jackson was being taken seriously as a presidential candidate. By January 1824 Jackson had cut into Western support for Speaker of the House Henry Clay and won an initial round in the contest with Secretary of War John C. Calhoun for Pennsylvania.

Still, the race was far from over. The field had narrowed from some sixteen in 1822 to five candidates—all impressive, all Democratic-Republicans, men of spirit (three duelists, in fact) and experience. Besides Clay, Calhoun, and Adams, Jackson had to beat Secretary of the Treasury Crawford, who considered himself Monroe's rightful successor. Monroe never expressed his preference but probably would have picked Crawford as closest to his philosophy, with Adams, the architect of the Monroe Doctrine, the runner-up.

Since the candidates held fairly similar views on many issues, the campaign focused more than ever on personalities and regional appeal. It became quite biting, even petty at times. Clay was called a drunkard and immoral and Jackson was a tyrant and a murderer. Crawford was accused of misuse of his office; although he was eventually cleared, Calhoun insisted the charges had been "made good." Adams was labeled aristocratic and questioned about his negotiating position at the Treaty of Ghent. He felt so persecuted he said he thought "every calumniator in the country was at work day and night" to destroy him.

The only divisive issue of the campaign was the use of the congressional caucus as a nominating body. Over the years, as more and more states expanded suffrage, the caucus was criticized as an elitist way of choosing candidates. Of all the major contenders, Crawford alone thought he needed the backing of the caucus to boost his candidacy (see National Tickets, above).

By March it was obvious that Jackson had captured a public mood. A convention of Democratic-Republicans in Pennsylvania overwhelmingly nominated Jackson for president and named Calhoun for vice president. In November Jackson won the popular vote by getting 43 percent of the votes cast but did not obtain the needed majority of electoral votes.

Jackson was convinced that he epitomized the "will of the people." However, the election was no longer up to them. Under the Twelfth Amendment, the House of Representatives would decide among the top three candidates: Jackson, Adams, and Crawford. Clay had come in fourth and was out of the running. But with his forty-seven electoral votes, Clay became the pivotal figure in the bartering and brokering of the second election. "The friends" of all three candidates showed him much "disinterested homage and kindness," Clay noted with irony. In one way or another, the Department of State was dangled as the reward for his support. The question remained whether these approaches were authorized by the candidates or not.

What is known is that a year and a day after Mrs. Adams' famous ball for General Jackson, Adams and Clay did spend the evening together, conversing, as Adams noted in his diary, "of the past and prospective of the future." It gave the appearance of intrigue and Jackson picked right up on this, writing "Intrigue, corruption and sale of public office is the rumor of the day." Clay claimed that he had not spoken with Adams about the cabinet. But on February 9 Adams won the House vote with the help of Clay and within three days Adams asked him to be secretary of state.

Jackson went on the warpath. "The people have been cheated," he declared and soon stormed back to Tennessee. Less than comfortable in victory, Adams came into the presidency predicting that his opponents were out to "bring in General Jackson as the next President. To this end, the administration must be rendered unpopular and odious."

★ CAMPAIGN OF 1828 ★

Major Candidates   John Quincy Adams, 61, Massachusetts, National
Republican
Andrew Jackson, 61, Tennessee, Democrat

Credentials   See Campaign of 1824.

Parties   Adams' followers, heirs to the old Federalists, as well as strong
nationalists and opponents of Jackson, called themselves Adams' Republicans, the Administration party, or National Republicans.

In 1825, the "Jackson party" was born. It included "old Republicans"
or "Radicals" who left Adams because of his desire for a strong central
government. Jackson's party was the link between Jeffersonian Republicans
and Democratic-Republicans, or simply the Democrats—as they would be
known by 1832.

Tickets   No nominating congressional caucus was held. Adams was renominated in a series of state conventions and partisan rallies. His running mate
on most slates was treasury secretary Richard Rush.

Jackson was nominated by his own state legislature in October 1825. His
nomination was then seconded in state conventions and mass meetings
around the country. His running mate was incumbent vice president John C.
Calhoun.

Campaign Notes   As was the custom, neither Adams nor Jackson campaigned publicly. They worked through surrogates and, in Jackson's case,
played an active role in campaign strategy.

The hallmark of this campaign was the effort by both parties to whip up
the electorate and create mass appeal. Jackson's campaign workers, known
as the "Hurra Boys," organized barbecues, rallies, hickory-pole plantings,
and parades. Republicans competed on a lesser scale.

In probably the coolest public relations move by any presidential candidate
until then, Jackson did travel by steamship to New Orleans for the celebration of his victory there on January 8. Greeting well-wishers along the way,
he arrived on the anniversary of the battle to thunderous applause. For
four days, he was feted but shied away from making any kind of campaign
statement. All his exploits were extensively covered in the newspapers.

In addition to handbills and broadsides, both sides spent heavily to establish and support newspapers favorable to their views. By 1828 some 600
"party" newspapers were being published in the country.

Symbols   Adams' supporters chose the oak as a symbol of their sturdy candidate.

ANDREW JACKSON

Jackson was given the name "Hickory" by his troops in 1813 because of his toughness. During the election, his followers used the hickory pole to symbolize his candidacy.

Slogans   "Tariff of Abominations" was a rallying cry of Adams' people after the Democrat-controlled Congress passed a tariff aimed at electing Jackson. They called the election of 1828 "The Great Contest" and responded to the planting of hickory poles with "Odd nuts and drumsticks!"

"Corrupt Bargain" and "Bargain and Corruption" shouted Jackson's side. Others chanted "Huzza for Jackson" and "Old Hickory, the Nation's Hero and the People's Friend."

Songs   Adams' side sang "Little Wat Ye Wha's A-Comin" about Jackson, who will "hang honest men," and Clay-for-Vice-President boosters belted out "Adams and Clay."

Jackson men had the "Jackson Toast" and "The Hickory Tree" in which "Jonny was lounging on crimson and down."

Paraphernalia   This was the first campaign to see decorative items advertising candidates: cotton bandannas with "His Excellency John Adams" and French thread boxes inscribed "Adams Forever."

There were cotton chintzes with a General Jackson motif; tortoiseshell combs with *New Orleans*.

Popular Labels   Adamites labeled themselves "The Friends of Adams" and the "Coalitionists."

Jackson was called "The People's Candidate," the "Hero of New Orleans," and "The Farmer of Tennessee."

Name-calling   To detractors, Adams was "The Puritan" and "John the Second." His cabinet was ridiculed as "the travelling Cabinet."

Jackson's opponents labeled him "murderer" and "adulterer."

Curious Fact   In early December, when Jackson's electoral victory was known, his wife Rachel remarked, "I assure you that I would rather be a doorkeeper in the house of my God than to dwell in that palace in Washington." On December 22, the day before a huge celebration in Nashville to celebrate Jackson's victory, she died of a heart attack, never becoming First Lady.

The Press   Both sides engaged in scandalous attacks on the other through their party newspapers. For Adams' benefit, Charles Hammond, editor of the Cincinnati *Gazette*, explored the circumstances of Jackson's marriage and asked his readers: "Ought a convicted adultress and her paramour husband to be placed in the highest office of this free and Christian land?"

Democratic editors harped on the "corrupt bargain" that they said gave Adams the presidency in 1824 and accused the Adams administration of ethnic and religious prejudice.

Spending   The National Republicans did not spend nearly as much as Jackson's party, which improved the art of raising and spending money. By some estimates, it cost hundreds of thousands to elect Jackson president.

Firsts   This was the first "modern" presidential campaign in the sense of trying to sway voters on a mass scale.

Jackson was the first president from the new West or beyond the Appalachians and not from one of the original thirteen states.

Jackson was the first "outsider" to win the presidency in that he had not been secretary of state or vice president.

This was the first million-vote presidential election.

The first political lithographs appeared.

Trends   The rise of "people power."

The beginnings of a vital two-party system.

Election as a form of popular entertainment.

Jackson's Washington-based committee was a step closer to later party national committees.

A New York–Virginia alliance again becomes crucial for Jacksonian and later Democratic strength until the Civil War.

Vote   Voter participation tripled that of 1824, from roughly 350,000 popular votes cast to 1,155,000. Two reasons were that the 1828 race generated more interest and that, since the last election four states, including New York, had changed from legislative to popular election of electors. Now only Delaware and South Carolina still chose their electors by the legislature. With 58 percent of adult white males voting, Jackson won 178 electoral and 647,286 popular votes (56 percent) to 83 and 508,064 (44 percent) for Adams.

In the separate vice-presidential race, Calhoun easily won over Rush with 171 electoral votes to 83.

Benchmarks   The second transfer of power to another party in the history of the country.

Jackson won with 56 percent of the popular vote, the best margin recorded in the nineteenth century.

This campaign is considered the dirtiest, most scandalous in history.

John Quincy Adams, like his father John Adams, was one of three presidents not to attend the inauguration of his successor.

Quote   One National Republican wrote of his party's defeat "It was the howl of raving Democracy."

ROBBED, he thought, of the presidency in 1824 by a pesky electoral college that chose John Quincy Adams over himself, Andrew Jackson had stormed out of the capital and home to Tennessee. There he prepared his second bid for the presidency.

What really stuck in Jackson's craw was, to him, the certain evidence that a deal had been struck between Adams and Henry Clay, who was speedily appointed the new secretary of state. Jacksonian anger at this "corrupt bargain" made, as he put it, "by the Judas of the West" (Clay was from over the mountains in Kentucky), fueled the campaign of 1828.

Adams' National Republicans stood for stronger central government, more federal expenditure, and a higher tariff than the Jacksonians. But the issues took a back seat to a personality struggle between Adams, seen as an effete representative of Eastern power and privilege, and Old Hickory, a brawling, rough-tongued, frontier-war hero, clearly a man of the people. The confrontation helped create a new populist party, the Jackson party, which swiftly became the new national Democratic party. It also fueled a campaign almost too silly, too scurrilous to be believed. One observer wrote: "God help the nation. I am afraid that it will run mad."

Adams, a brilliant and dedicated public servant who rose at five each morning and worked pretty much without ceasing until five in the afternoon, did not turn out to be a popular or successful president. Democrats poked fun at his "kingly pretensions" and said he acted like a ruling monarch.

That was the polite part. They also asserted that the President and his wife had premarital relations and freely labeled him "The Pimp" on the strength of their unfounded charge that, during his term as minister to Russia (1809–1817), Adams had procured an American girl for Czar Alexander I.

The Republicans, in turn, tried with all their might to scare the public out of its infatuation with "The Hero of New Orleans." Because Jackson had been obliged to remarry his beloved wife Rachel when it turned out that her divorce (a scandal in itself) was not legal, Republican editorialists turned him into a home-wrecker and seducer. His hot temper and execution of men during military campaigns led gleeful Adams supporters to sing "Oh, Andy! Oh, Andy, / How many men have you hanged in your life? / How many weddings make a wife?"

Republicans issued the "Coffin Handbill," meant to convince voters that Jackson was indeed a wild man and unfit for the presidency. It was edged in black with six coffins on the cover, one for each militiaman who had been tried for desertion, convicted, and shot on orders signed by Jackson. Under the heading *Some Account of the Bloody Deeds of Jackson*, it accused Jackson of their "murders." Besides such things, there were routine charges that his mother was a "COMMON PROSTITUTE, brought to this country by the British soldiers!"

But nothing deterred the rolling wave of Jackson people from street demonstrations, barbecues, and—above all—innumerable plantings of Jackson's symbol, the hickory pole, in parks and on streetcorners all over the country. On November 4, 1828, just before the election, Jackson's people tore up the sidewalk in front of Tammany Hall and the pro-Adams *New York Spectator* sneered: "The pole was erected amid loud yells . . . the beer-barrels were rolled out; and it required no vivid imagination to distinguish in the uproar the yell of the hyena, the cry of the panther and the whoop of the Winnebagoes."

The turnout was heavy, three times larger than in 1824. Old Hickory won by a wide margin. His inauguration party, with the common folk overrunning the White House, breaking furniture, spitting tobacco juice in corners, and leaving muddy footprints on the carpets, is regarded a classic symbol of democracy triumphant. This election has been called "The Revolution of 1828" and heralded as "the rise of the common man." Party spirit was anything but exterminated.

★ CAMPAIGN OF 1832 ★

Major Candidates   Andrew Jackson, 65, Tennessee, Democrat
Henry Clay, 55, Kentucky, National Republican

Credentials   For Jackson, see Campaign of 1824 and 1828. He was elected president in 1828.

For Clay, see Campaign of 1824. After the election Clay served as secretary of state to President John Quincy Adams (1825–1829) and then went back to the Senate in 1831.

Tickets   Although there were only two major presidential candidates, there were three parties in the race and the third set the tone and a precedent by holding a national nominating convention.

The upstart Anti-Masonic party, formed in 1826, opposed Freemasonry and other secret societies. By September 1831 this party had enough appeal to attract 116 delegates to a national convention in Baltimore. When the favorite, Supreme Court Justice John McLean, refused to be considered the convention was thrown open and the leaders looked around for another candidate. They had already sounded out several men before William Wirt, a former attorney general and former Mason, accepted and was nominated. Lawyer Amos Ellmaker of Pennsylvania was selected for vice president.

The National Republican convention, also held in Baltimore, was a much more predictable affair. As bad weather and worse roads delayed the arrival of many delegates those present heard the first keynote address and nominating speech of a convention; then the first roll call of states heard Clay named by all but one delegate. Pennsylvanian John Sergeant, a lawyer for the Bank of the United States, was selected as the vice-presidential nominee.

In May 1832 the Democrats held the last and dullest convention, also in Baltimore. This convention adopted a rule requiring a two-thirds majority for nominations and recommended a variation of the unit rule whereby state delegations would vote as a bloc. Turning to essential business and without any nominating speeches, which might cause controversy, delegates chose only a vice-presidential candidate, former secretary of state Martin Van Buren, handpicked by Jackson.

Campaign Notes   This campaign was primarily a campaign of issues although the personalities of the dominant players were powerful. Even so, a lot of the hoopla that had been spawned by the purely personal campaign of 1828 continued. The Democrats excelled in this form of entertainment, building sky-high bonfires, feeding hoardes at barbecues, and snaking through the streets in parades that were sometimes a mile long.

As a candidate for president for the third time, Jackson was quieter than ever, letting his presidential actions do the talking.

HENRY CLAY

As a senator, Clay could air his opinions in a public forum. Otherwise, he was reluctant to make personal campaign appearances.

Slogans Jacksonites cheered "Jackson Forever: Go the Whole Hog" and "Let the People Rule," while followers of Clay called for "Freedom and Clay."

"To the victor belongs the spoils" captured the sentiment behind Jackson's use of "rotation in office" or, as it came to be called, the spoils system.

Songs "The Hunters of Kentucky," which celebrated the Battle of New Orleans, was sung again for Jackson, while "Adams and Clay," which spoke of Jackson's "stern tyrant's command," was recycled for the candidacy of Clay.

Paraphernalia The bank issue came into play with a pro-Jackson medal bearing the inscription "The Bank Must Perish." Anti-Jackson forces produced their own, which declared: "The Constitution as I Understand It," a takeoff on Jackson's bank-veto message.

A life-size cast-iron bullfrog boasted "I Croak for The Jackson Wagon." A Jackson campaign poster framed Jackson's oval portrait with arrows, tomahawks, and the like and trumpeted "Jackson, Democracy, and Our Country."

Popular Labels Jackson was "Old Hero" and "Old Andy," and (of course) "Old Hickory."

Clay was "Prince Hal," "The Great Peacemaker," and "The Champion of Republicanism and the American System." Clay's men were called "Bankites."

Name-calling To Jackson and his followers, the Bank of the United States was a "Mammoth Monopoly" and a "hydra of corruption."

Democrats called Clay "gambler" and "immoral aristocrat."

Jackson was derided as "King Andrew the First" and "King Jackson" by Clay and other critics for acting more like a monarch than a president in his desire for dominance.

Curious Fact Clay did accept one speaking engagement, in Louisville and asked a boatman to take him there. The oarsman took a wrong tributary that was up Salt River and Clay never got to speak. "Up Salt River" became a expression for political defeat.

The Press The rich-versus-poor theme was used by both sides. On Jackson's team, the Washington *Globe* wrote that the enemy was "the Aristocracy."

For the opposition, the Boston *Daily Atlas* argued that the Bank veto "falsely and wickedly alleges that the rich and powerful . . . are waging a war of oppression against the poor and weak."

Firsts Political parties held conventions to nominate their candidates.

A significant third party was in the presidential race.

The keynote address, the nominating speech, appearance by a candidate, and semiofficial party platforms.

Trends Coalescence of the modern Democratic party.

Political cartoons develop as a campaign art form.

Vote Twenty-two states chose electors by popular vote on a general ticket. South Carolina and Maryland did not. Jackson won a big victory with 219 electoral and 687,502 popular votes (54.5 percent) to 49 and 530,189 (37.5 percent) for Clay. Wirt got Vermont's seven electoral votes and roughly 100,000 popular votes (8 percent).

Benchmarks Except for 1820, Jackson's electoral tally was the best in a two-party race since the presidency of Washington.

Jackson's slight percentage dip in the popular vote from 1828 is the only such decline for a second-term election.

Quote In September Jackson wrote Van Buren: "Mr. Clay will not get one Electoral vote west of the mountains or south of the Potomac, in my opinion."

As the curtain went up on Andrew Jackson's presidency, John C. Calhoun and his wife Floride had their eyes on the White House. They even dreamed it could happen in just four years, since Jackson advocated one term for a president. Besides, Jackson's health was not good and everyone could see it. Emaciated at 140 pounds, although over six feet tall, the president coughed fiercely and even looked deathlike. Calhoun was vice president—a second time for him—and expected to be the heir apparent, having switched his support from John Quincy Adams to Jackson in the last election. But the "Eaton Malaria" altered the ending of this scenario.

"If you love Margaret Timberlake, go and marry her at once and shut their mouths," president-elect Jackson admonished his friend Tennessee senator John Eaton. Jackson wanted Eaton in his cabinet and mistakenly thought that a marriage would silence the sounds of scandal about Eaton's relationship with a married woman. She was free to marry now because her husband had died at sea of disease, drink, or maybe even suicide, the rumor went. Eaton took Jackson's advice and soon became his secretary of war.

But at the inaugural ball, "this New Lady," adorned in pink accentuated by black plumes, was not spoken to or even approached by other Washington wives. At the first formal cabinet dinner Jackson, who defended "brave little Peggy," seated her next to him. All eyes would have turned to her anyway, dressed as she was boldly in a low-cut evening gown.

The cabinet was divided. Calhoun did not try to prevent Floride from avoiding Mrs. Eaton. In fact, he saw an advantage in her husband's fall, if it came to that. Eaton was allied with Secretary of State Martin Van Buren, the only other possible presidential heir. Van Buren, a bachelor, went out of his way to be nice to "Bellona," as some newspapers labeled her. He arranged parties for her and prompted his bachelor friends, the British and Russian ministers, to do the same.

The president had another reason for passing up Calhoun: nullification bravado from the vice president. As 1830 began, a famous debate in the Senate surfaced the philosophical differences between those who argued for the right of a state to nullify a federal law that violated its sovereignty and independence and those who felt nullification endangered the union. Jackson's views became known at a Jefferson Day dinner in April. He had rehearsed a toast and finally, after twenty-four others mostly favoring South Carolina, the president caught Calhoun's glance and raised his glass: "Our Federal Union—It Must Be Preserved." The vice president was next. His hand trembled, some wine spilled, yet he differed: "The Union, next to our liberty, the most dear."

A year later, with Jackson deciding to run again and Mrs. Eaton still in the news, Van Buren offered to resign—a way of getting Eaton to offer to resign, as a way of allowing the president to ask Calhoun's three cabinet loyalists to resign. The plan worked. Van Buren went off to London to become minister; an angry Calhoun cast the deciding vote to have Van

Buren's nomination rejected by the Senate. "It will kill him," the vice president remarked. Instead, Van Buren became Jackson's—and the 1832 Democratic convention's—choice for vice president.

As the National Republicans met in December 1831 to choose a standard-bearer, Henry Clay, who expected the nomination, was pessimistic. The "Nationals" had already railed against Jackson's "indiscriminate removal of public officers" (he replaced about 10 percent of appointees in his first eighteen months in office), but they had no big issue until Clay convinced Nicholas Biddle, president of the Second Bank of the United States, to ask Congress to recharter the bank four years early.

In June the Senate agreed to the recharter and the House followed on July 3. That evening Van Buren, just back from England, went to the White House. Jackson looked awful, lying down, propped with pillows. "The bank," he told Van Buren, "is trying to kill me, *but I will kill it!*" A week later he vetoed the recharter bill on the basis that it was unconstitutional and favored the rich. Both political camps were ecstatic, each thinking the veto message would help its cause. For his part, Jackson remained optimistic, predicting in August "The veto works well."

The usual bombast of a Jackson campaign was present. There were parades and barbecues, bonfires and hickory poles. The campaign became the craze. In one instance, the all-consuming political talk on a cruise ship bound for America caused British actress Fanny Kemble to cry out "Oh, hang General Jackson!" But there was no stopping the people. They reelected him by a margin of almost five to one in the electoral college.

★ CAMPAIGN OF 1836 ★

Major Candidates   Martin Van Buren, 54, New York, Democrat
William Henry Harrison, 63, Ohio, Whig

Credentials   Van Buren, a political animal, organized the first political machine, the "Albany Regency," in New York. He was New York state senator (1812–1820), U.S. senator (1821–1828) and then governor of New York (January–March 1829). He resigned to become Andrew Jackson's secretary of state (1829–1831). In 1832 he was elected vice president.

Harrison, son of a signer of the Declaration of Independence, became the first governor of the Indiana Territory (1800–1812), routing Indians led by Tecumseh at the Battle of Tippecanoe (1811). Promoted to major general during the War of 1812, he helped secure the Northwest from the British at the Battle of the Thames (1813), was elected to the House of Representatives (1816–1819), moved to the Ohio state senate (1819–1821) and then the U.S. Senate (1825–1828). He was appointed the first American minister to Colom-

MARTIN VAN BUREN

bia by President John Quincy Adams in 1829 but was recalled the following year by President Andrew Jackson.

Minor Candidates   Daniel Webster, 54, senator from Massachusetts, Whig.
Hugh Lawson White, 63, senator from Tennessee, Whig.

Tickets   A year earlier than usual, President Jackson suggested a convention of delegates "fresh from the people" to nominate candidates for president and vice president. Van Buren, Jackson's choice, was nominated unanimously on the first ballot. Controversial Congressman Richard Johnson of Kentucky, who got credit for killing (it could never be proved) Indian leader and British ally Tecumseh during the War of 1812, with the backing of Jackson and Van Buren won the nomination for vice president on the first ballot.

The Whigs lacked an obvious candidate and were not organizationally prepared to hold a convention. As a result their strategy was to nominate the strongest candidate in each section of the country and draw enough popular and electoral votes away from Van Buren to send the election to the House of Representatives, where they would unite on one candidate. The Whig candidate of the West was William Henry Harrison of Ohio; Daniel Webster of Massachusetts for the Northeast; and for the South, Hugh Lawson White, once a very good friend of Jackson's and a Jacksonian Democrat. For vice president the Whigs ran former New York gubernatorial candidate Francis Granger, an anti-Mason, and Virginia senator John Tyler, once a Democrat.

Campaign Notes   None of the candidates did any real campaigning, but each made distinct overtures for votes. Van Buren, for example, knowing that the nomination of Johnson for vice president antagonized Virginians, who had put up their former Senator William Rives, took his own carriage and drove at night over bumpy roads to explain to Rives in person the need for a Westerner on the ticket and to argue for Democratic unity.

Webster traveled around New England to seek support from anti-Mason party leaders, while Harrison made a precedent-setting tour of some Eastern states, and was hailed by thousands as a hero, pledging to maintain "the honor, glory and dignity of my native land."

In addition, Van Buren, Harrison, and White all used the technique of public letters to air their views. Van Buren was by far the most prolific.

Slogans   In the hope of holding on to Southern support, Van Buren was hailed as a "Firm Friend of the South." The Democrats chanted that Whigs wanted to "Divide and Conquer" by fielding several candidates against Van Buren. Van Buren was publicized as the man "Who Can Justly Appreciate Liberty and Equality."

Songs   Johnson was the focus of most of the singing—for good and bad. In a bid to advertise their vice-presidential nominee and overshadow the reputation of Whig presidential candidate Harrison, who had once defeated but not killed Tecumseh, Democrats sang (and tried to rhyme) "Rumpsey dumpsey, rumpsey dumpsey, / Colonel Johnson killed Tecumseh."

Cynical Whigs retorted "Rumpsey dumpsey / Who killed Tecumseh?"

Paraphernalia   That this was not a rousing campaign is indicated by campaign items, which were rare and lacked popular appeal. For Van Buren, an ornate star-studded horseshoe encircled a filigree star and a small painting of the candidate. A Harrison medal was modeled after one he received from Congress to celebrate his victory at the Battle of Thames.

Popular Labels   Jackson liked to call Van Buren "Matty," whereas the party promoted him as "Young Hickory" and Johnson as "Warrior Sage" or "The Hero of the Thames." Not to confuse things, Whigs hailed Harrison, who happened to have been Johnson's commander at the Battle of Thames, the "Hero of the Battle of Tippecanoe."

Name-calling   To Democrats, the make-up of the Whig party was nothing more than "organized incompatibility."

To enemies, Van Buren was "King Martin the First" and a "first-class second-rate man."

Curious Fact   In anger, Tennessee sent no delegates to the Democratic convention in Baltimore. But someone spied Tennessean Edmund Rucker, a bit politician, in a local tavern and convinced him to represent his state. Rucker's vote gave Johnson the vice-presidential slot on the first ballot and made *to ruckerize* part of American political slang.

The Press   To make up for Van Buren's lack of Jacksonian appeal, Democratic newspapers put more emphasis on the party than on the party's candidate. "What republican will fail to rally around him?" the Washington *Globe* asked defiantly. The same paper threw barbs at Van Buren's main opponent, calling Harrison "a red petticoat general" and "the hero of forty defeats."

Opposition papers attacked both Van Buren and Johnson on a personal basis. The *New York American* painted Van Buren as "illiterate" and "politically corrupt."

Firsts   The first national election for Whigs.

Van Buren is considered the first politician to become president.

The first and only time the vice-presidential election was decided by the Senate.

Trends   The donkey became the symbol of the Democratic party.

Verse put to song became a popular campaign tool.

Harrison's tour as a candidate set a standard.

Vote   Twenty-six states (all except South Carolina, which used the legislature) selected electors by popular vote and the general ticket, and the turnout was slightly higher than in 1832. Van Buren received 170 electoral votes and 765,483 popular votes (50.9 percent) to 113 and 739,795 (49.1 percent) for his three Whig opponents. Harrison was the strongest challenger, with 73 and 584,000 (39 percent).

In the vice-presidential race, Democratic candidate Johnson did not win a majority of electoral votes and the election was sent to the Senate, under the terms of the Twelfth Amendment. There he won over Granger, the next highest electoral vote-getter, on a strict party vote of 33 to 16.

Benchmarks   A second two-party system was launched.

Sectional voting patterns were no longer predictable.

Quote   In his inaugural address Van Buren praised Jackson's presidency, adding: "I may hope that somewhat of the same cheering approbation will be found to attend upon my path."

V AN Buren was a little "big" man. At five feet six inches he made himself appear grander by standing very straight and grooming himself to the nines. He had a penchant for yellow gloves, velvet collars, and lace-trimmed cravats, but as the election approached he dressed more conservatively, more "presidentially." His preference for fine things extended to wine and food and thus also to his waistline, although this too made him look more respectable. After all, Van Buren had a reputation to live down.

He was a master politician—the "wizard of Albany"—and his "Albany Regency" a powerful political machine. In 1828 the "Red Fox of Kinderhook," as Van Buren was called by those who found the man born in Kinderhook, New York, too cunning for their tastes, caught two brass rings. He was elected governor in New York and helped elect Andrew Jackson president. Two and a half months after Jackson's election Van Buren resigned the governorship to become secretary of state. Four years later he became vice president. Some opponents said he manipulated Jackson or worse. "A crawling reptile whose only claim was that he had inveigled the confidence of a credulous, blind, dotard, old man," scorned young Whig leader William Seward. Others, however, had to admit that Van Buren could be charming, and, of course, the vice president did not have any better friend than the president.

Van Buren was in the difficult position of being less popular than the man he wanted to succeed and having to defend unpopular Jacksonian policies. Senator John C. Calhoun, Jackson's first vice president and now a Whig, teamed up with colleagues to make trouble for Van Buren, who presided over the Senate. They winked at disturbances in the galleries, manipulated tie votes that Van Buren would have to break, and hurled insults. In one floor debate, Calhoun compared Jackson to "the lion or the tiger" and Van Buren "to the lower order, the fox."

Two election-year publications by Whig sympathizers added more colorful attacks. In the *Life of Martin Van Buren*, advertised as a biography by frontiersman Davy Crockett, the author said the vice president "struts and swaggers" to the Senate chamber "laced up in corsets." In the novel *The Partisan Leader* Van Buren was pictured as "tastily and even daintily dressed" down to his "delicate" slippers. In addition, Van Buren was called the illegitimate son of Aaron Burr and "a first-class second-rate man."

But Jackson was firm in his support of Van Buren for president. Stunned when the legislature of his own state of Tennessee decided to nominate favorite son Senator Hugh Lawson White in January 1835, he called for a Democratic convention before more states were lost. Van Buren easily won on the first ballot. But Jackson's choice of Kentucky congressman Richard Mentor—a Westerner who would balance the ticket—for vice president was hard to swallow. Only by inventing some votes did Johnson's name go over the top. The Virginia delegation, which hated the railroading, hissed and walked out.

Johnson's selection was boosted by a recent book glorifying his exploits during the War of 1812. Still, many Democrats were not persuaded that "a lucky random shot, even if it did hit Tecumseh, qualifies a man for Vice President." The Whigs went further, pointing out his "connection with a jet-black, thick-lipped, odoriferous negro wench, by whom he has reared a family." They also rumored that Johnson himself was black.

The Whigs were a new party, united more in their antipathy to Jackson and his policies than in a uniform program. As a result, they decided not to hold a convention and instead to support three strong regional candidates: William Harrison in the West, Hugh Lawson White in the South, and Daniel Webster in the East.

The Whigs tried to lure Democrats too, especially Southern Democrats, by stating that they believed in the democratic principles of Jefferson and Jackson *in 1829*. They objected to "the Jackson dynasty" or Martin Van Buren and his Northern views.

The Democrats tried less to defend their candidate than to stress loyalty to the "party" and its past leaders. Cartoonists picked up the theme and showed Van Buren hanging onto Jackson's coattails, but he won the close race. Jackson's handpicked successor now had to deal with Jackson's legacy of overspeculation through wildcat banks and his "Specie Circular" credit crunch. Within one month of his inauguration the new president woke up to headlines about the panic in New York. It was the Panic of 1837.

★ CAMPAIGN OF 1840 ★

Major Candidates   William Henry Harrison, 67, Ohio, Whig
Martin Van Buren, 58, New York, Democrat

Credentials   See Campaign of 1836. (In 1832, Van Buren was elected vice president and four years later president.)

Tickets   The Whigs held their first party convention in December 1839 in William Henry Harrisburg, Pennsylvania. In initial canvassing Henry Clay, leader of the Whigs in Congress, garnered the most votes but not the needed majority. By the third day, behind-the-scenes maneuvering gave Harrison the nomination in the only "official" ballot of the convention. To bring the party together, John Tyler, a pro-Clay delegate and speaker of the Virginia House of Delegates, was nominated for vice president.

Van Buren was renominated unanimously at the Democratic National Convention. But there was so much dissension over the renomination of Vice President Richard M. Johnson because of his personal life (he had several black mistresses and even took a leave of absence from the vice presidency in 1839 to manage his own hotel in White Sulphur Springs, Virginia) that no vice-presidential nominee was chosen. In effect, though, Johnson was Van Buren's running mate.

At their convention the Democrats came up with a new campaign tool—a national platform.

WILLIAM HENRY HARRISON

Campaign Notes   Some said that Harrison was the first president "sung into the Presidency." There were indeed more than a hundred Whig songs, plus poems and chants, poking fun at Van Buren or inflating the legend of Harrison. The most famous of these dealt with Harrison's exploits at Tippecanoe and were published in the *Log Cabin Song Book*.

No campaign before or since has exceeded the hype, hoopla, and paraphernalia of 1840. The Whigs portrayed Harrison as a folk hero and man of the people and chose the theme "Log Cabin and Hard Cider Democracy." As a result, log cabins or facsimiles turned up everywhere. There were log cabin floats decorated with coonskins, log cabin facades on campaign headquarters, and "log cabin cider" freely flowed at campaign rallies. One of the most sought-after items was a miniature log cabin filled with "Old Cabin Whiskey" bottled by the E. C. Booz Distillery. By the end of the campaign the word *booze* had entered the language.

Stump speaking was more popular and speeches lasted longer than ever.

Symbols   Besides the omnipresent log cabins and hard cider, Harrison's followers rolled giant slogan balls, made of buckskin, paper, twine, or tin through the streets from town to town to symbolize the snowballing majority for Harrison.

Van Buren's side, in an effort to compete, borrowed directly from 1828 by organizing "Hickory Clubs" and erecting hickory poles.

Slogans "Tippecanoe and Tyler, Too" is the most memorable campaign slogan ever. "Keep the Ball A-Rollin' " and "We Need Tipp to Guide the Ship" are examples of many more. Harrison's supporters also promised "Two Dollars a Day and Roast Beef" against "Matty's Policy, Fifty Cents a Day and French Soup." They also shouted "Down with Martin Van Ruin!"

The Democrats were weak on catchy slogans in their favor, although they did have a quick reply when asked if Harrison would win: "Read his name backwards—Nosirrah!"

Songs Naturally, log cabins and hard cider were favored in such Harrison songs as "The Log Cabin Waltz" and "The Hard Cider Quick Step." Van Buren was the target in "Little Vanny" ("too tender a dandy to shoulder a musket") and in "Van Buren."

Van Buren's side had fewer songs, in general, and practically none extolling the virtues of its candidate.

Paraphernalia Harrison souvenir items surpassed any campaign before and probably since. In addition to the more traditional thread boxes, snuff boxes, and silk bandannas, there was everyday china, depicting Harrison at his plow in front of a log cabin, at an affordable seven cents a plate; there was "Tippecanoe Shaving Soap," "Tippecanoe Tobacco," "Harrison Letter Paper," "Log Cabin Breast Pins," "Hard Cider Canes," "Tippecanoe Extract" for handkerchiefs, gloves, and the hair.

The Democrats decried such "factitious symbols" and stayed with the usual clothing buttons, pitchers, and ribbon badges.

Popular Labels The Whigs likened their candidate to Democrat Andrew Jackson, calling him "Old Buckeye" and "The Hero of Tippecanoe."

The Democrats also invoked Jackson; they nicknamed Van Buren "Young Hickory." Other nicknames were "Old Kinderhook," from Van Buren's birthplace in New York, and "The Magician from Kinderhook" because of his political prowess.

Name-calling Van Burenites criticized Harrison as "General Mum," saying he was silent on the major issues, and "Granny Harrison, the Petticoat General," claiming Harrison was not the hero the Whigs made him out to be.

Van Buren was belittled as "King Matty" and "Martin Van Ruin."

The Press Ironically, it was a Democratic paper that gave the Whigs their successful campaign theme. "Give Harrison "a barrel of hard cider and a pension of two thousand a year," said the *Baltimore Republican*, "and . . . he will sit the remainder of his days in a log cabin."

The Whig press claimed the election was "a contest between cabin and palace, between hard cider and champagne."

Spending   Both sides spent freely and raised more money than ever before. The Whigs, who were backed by the wealthy DuPont family of Delaware, bested the Democrats, spending more by tens of thousands to elect Harrison.

Firsts   1840 represented the first full-fledged modern campaign.
The Whigs held their first national convention.
The Harrison campaign was the first "image" campaign.
"Tippecanoe and Tyler, Too" was the first official campaign slogan.
The first national platform was designed at the Democratic convention.
Harrison was the first presidential candidate to make a campaign tour.
The birth of national campaign newspapers, such as the *Log Cabin* (Whig) and *Extra Globe* (Democrat).
The DuPont family was the first group of wealthy individuals to support candidates with cash gifts.

Trends   It became the norm for both parties to nominate candidates for president and vice president by general party conventions.
Voter participation remained high—70 percent or above—through 1900.
Image advertising.
The entrenchment of the two-party system.
Humble origins as a popular myth for presidential candidates.
The political parade with all its trappings, including professional campaign banners, floats, bands.

Vote   Roughly 80 percent of eligible voters participated—up from 59 percent four years earlier—more than ever before. Harrison won 234 electoral and 1,274,624 popular votes (53.1 percent) to 60 and 1,127,781 (46.9 percent) for Van Buren.

Benchmarks   Eighty-percent voter participation was not to be excelled except in 1860 and 1876.
The most evenly competitive contest between two parties up until then.
Campaigns became mass entertainments.
Political paraphernalia became widely available and affordable.
Several popular expressions became permanent features of the American language. *O.K.*, for example, stood for Van Buren's nickname "Old Kinderhook."
Harrison delivered the longest inaugural address ever (and died a month to the day after taking office).

Quote   "We have been sung down, lied down and drunk down," commented the Democratic *Wheeling Times* after the election.

★   ★   ★

THE Democrats, the party of Andrew Jackson, had mostly themselves to blame for "the great commotion" that made Whig candidate William Henry Harrison a folk hero and swept him into the presidency. It was as if only the Whigs had learned lessons from Jackson's successful "common man" campaign for the presidency in 1828 and that the Democrats, in office for over a decade, felt they did not have to stoop to win.

Martin Van Buren, an astute politician in his own circles, was having difficulty as Jackson's successor. He lacked Old Hickory's charisma, and even some Democrats were wont to call him the "bastard politician" for being handpicked by Jackson for the presidency. He inherited a banking mess that led to the Panic of 1837 and made things worse by trying to set up an independent treasury. Van Buren did not help himself any by appearing courtly and vain and dressing flamboyantly.

Still, the Democrats were optimistic when the Whig convention met in December 1839 and nominated William Henry Harrison, an aging military hero who had run against Van Buren in 1836 and lost. They also thought it a good sign that the Whig party, an amalgam of National Republicans, States' righters, Abolitionists, protectionists, and free-traders, united merely in its opposition to Jackson, would not or could not come up with a national platform on which to run.

It was then that the Democratic *Baltimore Republican* decided to have a little joke at Harrison's expense. The paper printed a remark made by a friend of Whig leader Henry Clay that General Harrison, given a pension of two thousand dollars and a barrel of hard cider, would be perfectly happy spending the rest of his days in his log cabin thinking big thoughts. The joke turned out to be on the Democrats.

Whig imagemakers picked up on the symbols and created their "log-cabin–hard-cider candidate." Practically overnight, Harrison was transformed from a Virginia aristocrat (he owned a Georgian mansion and sipped gentlemen's whiskey) into a popular, log-cabin-dwelling, hard-cider-swigging hillbilly.

The tunefully reinforced image caught on and the Democrats could never discredit it or expunge another song-inspired inference that their own hapless candidate was a pantywaist who wore corsets and bathed more often than a good man should. Democratic protests were drowned out by rousing choruses of "Old Tip he wears a homespun coat / He has no ruffled shirt-wirt-wirt / But Mat has the golden plate / And he's a squirt-wirt-wirt." The *wirt-wirts* were embellished by spitting (usually tobacco juice) through the singer's teeth.

It was that kind of campaign year. Whig lawyer Abe Lincoln, running for state legislature, reached over and tore open his Democratic opponent's tightly buttoned cloth coat to reveal the ruffled silk shirt and velvet vest hidden beneath. Stumping for Harrison, Daniel Webster shook off his satin-lined coat, donned one of linsey-woolsey, and apologized for not being born in a log cabin. Harrison even took to the road, stung by attacks that he was a "superannuated and pitiable dotard," and turned out to be quite an entertainer. He whooped Indian war cries and paused midspeech to swig hard cider.

Van Buren watched from the White House while Jackson and other party dignitaries campaigned for him. Vice President Richard Johnson provided some needed color when he stumped in the red jacket he said he tore from Indian chief Tecumseh after killing him. For added effect, Johnson displayed his seventeen battle scars.

The election turned especially nasty when congressman Charles Ogle, a Harrison supporter, delivered a three-day discourse on "The Regal Splendor of the Presidential Palace," claiming that the president strutted by the hour before huge golden-framed mirrors and wanted a crown, scepter, and jewels. The Democrats retaliated by saying that Harrison's "log cabin" was really a mansion, that he had an annual income of $6,000, "as rich as any man in this country," and that he was not the hero he was made out to be.

By then the public was busy making merry, for the Whig uproar was contagious. City-to-city celebrations lasted several days; men, women, children marched five abreast in lines two, sometimes three, miles long, towing log cabin floats, slogan balls, and singing "What has caused the great commotion, motion, motion / Our country through? / It is the ball a-rolling on / For Tippecanoe and Tyler too."

"Log cabin hard cider and coon humbugery," scoffed Jackson, the Whig's unwitting tutor. But the appeal to the common man worked wonders. It wasn't the public's fault that Harrison was sixty-eight years old, delivered an interminable (8,578-word) inaugural speech without a hat or coat, then died of pneumonia a month later. With the election of 1840, political campaigning had become a staple of American entertainment.

★ CAMPAIGN OF 1844 ★

Major Candidates   Henry Clay, 67, Kentucky, Whig
James K. Polk, 49, Tennessee, Democrat

Credentials   For Clay, see Campaign of 1824. Clay served as secretary of state to President John Adams (1825–1829) and then went back to the Senate (1831–1842).

Polk served in his state's house of representatives (1823–1825) and in the U.S. House of Representatives (1825–1839), becoming speaker for the last four years. He became governor of Tennessee (1839–1841) and tried for reelection in 1841 and 1843 but was defeated.

Tickets   The Whigs met for just one day in Baltimore. With the death of William Henry Harrison and the enormous dislike of President John Tyler, Clay had no equal. He was the unanimous choice of the 275 delegates. Former New Jersey senator Theodore Freylinghuysen was nominated for vice president. The Whigs produced their first platform, which was less than a hundred words.

JAMES K. POLK

The Democrats chose Baltimore as well. Going into the convention, it was a good bet—but not certain—that former president Martin Van Buren would win the presidential nomination. A few weeks before, Van Buren had hurt his standing with Southern Democrats by coming out against the immediate annexation of Texas. What did him in, though, was the 1832 rule that two-thirds of the vote was necessary for nomination. In a field of seven Van Buren won a majority of votes on the first ballot, but not two-thirds. By the seventh ballot he was no longer in the lead. The convention recessed and the next day, a new name—a "dark horse"—surfaced when the roll call of states began. James K. Polk was proposed by New Hampshire. Several states followed the lead to give Polk a total of 44 votes. On the ninth nominating roll call, the Polk candidacy could not be stopped as states stampeded each other to give him all their votes. The convention chose George Dallas of Pennsylvania, a former minister to Russia, as the vice-presidential nominee.

For the second time in its history, the abolitionist Liberty party held a national convention. In a repeat of 1840, the party nominated James G. Birney of Michigan, a former slaveholder, for president. Thomas Morris of Ohio was the vice presidential candidate. The party platform dealt with only one issue: slavery.

Campaign Notes   Once nominated, Clay said he would no longer make public appearances out of a "sense of delicacy and propriety" and immediately refused an invitation to make an acceptance speech before the Whig convention. But he could not resist writing down his opinion on all sorts of subjects.

Polk played the silent type, not making any tours and writing only one letter for publication.

Symbols The extrovert Whigs went from mere coonskins in 1840 to the whole raccoon to make the wealthy, urbane Clay more appealing to the common man. Live "coons" were carried in boxes and paraded on floats.

The raccoon was up against the rooster. The Democrats took their emblem from the fighting gamecock that crowed defiance at British warships from the deck of the victorious American flagship *Saratoga* during the War of 1812.

Slogans The Whigs shouted "Huzza for Clay" and "Hooray for Clay." In their view the choice was "Polk, Slavery and Texas or Clay, Union and Liberty." And they made a joke about "dark horse" Polk's relative obscurity. "Who is James K. Polk?" became a constant refrain.

Democratic expansionist sentiments were expressed in the slogan "The Reoccupation of Oregon and Reannexation of Texas." Or, stronger: "All of Oregon or None." Their catch-all slogan was "Polk, Dallas, Texas, Oregon and the Tariff of '42."

Songs The Whigs picked on the Democratic candidate: "Ha, ha, ha, ha such a nominee, / As Jimmy Polk of Tennessee!" And, since they could not sing for Tippecanoe, they sang Tippecanoe songs for Clay, such as "Clear the Way for Harry Clay" (formerly "Tip and Ty"). New tunes included "Harry of the West" and "That Same Old Coon."

The Democrats borrowed "Tip and Ty" as well, renaming it "That Same Old Tune." They reminded voters of Clay's past ("your bargain with Adams we've not forgot"), ridiculed Whig rule in "Hard Times," and sang of the future in "Polk, Dallas and Texas."

Paraphernalia The Whigs went all-out once again, but items were not as folksy as in the log-cabin-and-hard-cider days. Long-stemmed pipes and snuff boxes, cigar cases and cane handles had Clay's likeness. Clothing buttons, medals, and lapel badges variously pitched Clay as a farmer, the workingman's friend, and an ally of business.

Less demonstrative, the Democrats had less of everything. But the Texas issue was more prominent with a silk ribbon badge that pictured Polk and Dallas beneath the Texas star and motto "Alone but Not Deserted."

Mass-produced portraits of the candidates sold for ten or fifteen cents and gave many Americans their first look at presidential candidates.

Popular Labels Clay's followers called him "Glorious Harry Clay," "Gallant Harry Clay," "The Farmer of Ashland," "the Old Coon," and just plain "Harry."

To perk up Polk's image, Democrats christened him "Young Hickory" as they once had Van Buren, and "Little Hickory." He was also known as "Tennessee Polk" and "Dark Horse" Polk.

Name-calling The Democrats used the slang term *coons* for Whigs. Clay was "the corrupt bargainer"of 1824 and the "Same Old Coon."

To Whigs, "Gallant Harry" was running against "Polk the Plodder" or the "mum candidate."

The Press Democratic papers liked to make a class comparison with Polk "emphatically the candidate of the *People*, the other [Clay] that of the *Aristocracy*."

The pro-Whig press criticized Polk's credentials. Said the *New York Herald*: "A more ridiculous, contemptible and forlorn candidate was never put forth by any party."

Firsts The first "dark horse" candidate nominated by a major party.

The first convention "stampede" to nominate a candidate.

Trend A third party influences the election outcome.

Vote All states but South Carolina had the popular election of their electors with a high (79 percent) turnout. In a close race, Polk won 170 electoral votes and 1,338,464 popular votes (49.6 percent) to 105 and 1,300,097 (48.1 percent) for Clay. The Liberty party received no electoral but 62,300 popular votes (2.3 percent).

Benchmarks Polk was the youngest president-elect yet.

One of the most closely fought elections.

The second time a president is elected without a majority of popular votes.

Quote "who is j.k. polk will be no more asked by the coons. A.J."—Andrew Jackson's postelection note to Polk.

L IKE a reluctant actor, slavery took its sweet time setting foot on stage, but might have waited in the wings longer if President John Tyler had not been such a troublemaker. The Whigs could hardly believe their bad luck at the sudden death of President William Harrison when Tyler, who succeeded him, started acting more like a Democrat than the Whig he was supposed to be. Tyler, a proud, obstinate Virginian had started out as a states'-rights Democrat but broke away to the Whigs over differences with Jackson. In 1840, he had been put on the ticket with Harrison to muster Southern support, although some surmised it was really because "Tippecanoe" sounded so good with "Tyler Too."

Before long most Whigs wished they had never heard of the alliteration. They started calling him "His Accidency" and "Traitor Tyler" and even named a virulent influenza the "Tyler grippe." Annoyance began with Tyler's veto of a bill to reestablish a national bank and surged to outrage when a second bank bill was given the presidential boot. The entire Harrison cabinet resigned, except for Secretary of State Daniel Webster, and a caucus of congressional Whigs ruled that the party could no longer be "held responsible" for Tyler's actions.

Tyler chose a cast of conservative Democrats to be in his new cabinet and then proceeded to make his legacy the annexation of Texas, a state with a slave economy. The circle was complete when John C. Calhoun became secretary of state in March 1844. Tyler submitted the annexation treaty to the Senate on April 22, 1844, together with a defense of slavery written by Calhoun. It was the "Texas bombshell." Suddenly, slavery was onstage.

The "cheerful" Whigs, as they called themselves, convened first and only had eyes and songs for Clay: "Laughing girls with raven curls / Give all their smiles to Harry." The balconies of Baltimore overflowed with local belles, while below marched parades of people with Clay badges, coons in boxes and banners, banners everywhere. Texas was barely mentioned in the hall and not at all in the platform (which did call for a revenue tariff and a single-term presidency), and Clay won the nomination hands down.

At the Democratic convention, about all anyone could talk about was Texas and how Van Buren had "ruined his prospects gratis." Did he not realize the pull of slavery on Southern Democrats? It took eight tries before Van Buren was eliminated and "dark horse" James K. Polk, who favored statehood for Texas "at the earliest practicable period" and also the "reoccupation of Oregon," was nominated. The crowd went wild.

"Who is James K. Polk?" the Whigs taunted. This nomination, the *National Intelligencer* added, "may be considered the dying gasp" of the Democratic party. Clay reportedly had a different reaction: "Beaten again, by God." But his followers were too giddy to think of anything but victory: "He'll sweep the whole / Like summer chaff away." While the Democrats in their platform decried such "displays and appeals" as the Whigs used, they were noisier than four years earlier, singing back: "Run Clay koons, we come. We come." They also published "Twenty-one Reasons Why Clay Should Not Be Elected" and said a pistol, a pack of cards, and a brandy bottle ought to be the "standard of Henry Clay."

Clay was caught in a vise between the Liberty party, which challenged his right to be called "The Abolitionist Candidate of the North," and his own penchant to compromise. When he heard the complaints of Southern Whigs, Clay altered his antiannexation stand to accept the addition of Texas if achieved "without dishonor, without war." Then Northern Whigs nudged him back to opposition.

In the end, five thousand votes made the difference. Clay lost New York by that number—the Liberty party probably siphoned off most—and, with that, the election. Polk cared less about the closeness of the race than his desire to acquire more land. Since Congress agreed to the annexation of Texas before the inauguration (President Tyler saw to that), Polk set his sights on all of California and most of Oregon in what came to be romanticized as the country's "manifest destiny."

★ CAMPAIGN OF 1848 ★

Major Candidates   Lewis Cass, 66, Michigan, Democrat
Zachary Taylor, 64, Louisiana, Whig

Credentials   Cass was the youngest member of the Ohio legislature (1806), became a brigadier general in 1813 and fought under Gen. William Henry Harrison (during the War of 1812), served as governor of the Michigan Territory (1813–1831), secretary of war (1831–1836), and was appointed minister to France (1836), resigning in 1842 over a treaty with Britain. He was elected to the Senate in 1844.

Taylor was made a first lieutenant (1808), promoted to captain (1810), fought in the War of 1812 and was breveted major, rose to lieutenant colonel (1819) and colonel (1832). He served in the Black Hawk War (1832) and the Second Seminole War (1837–1840), was breveted brigadier general during the war. He fought in the Mexican War (1846–1848); won victories at Resaca de la Palma, Monterrey, and Buena Vista; and became a major general.

Tickets   When the Democrats met in Baltimore they needed a new candidate because President James K. Polk declined to run for a second term. On the third day, nominations began with Cass in the lead. He won on the fourth ballot with 179 votes. The convention quickly made it unanimous. Two more ballots and General William O. Butler of Kentucky became the vice-presidential nominee. The Democrats appointed a national committee and a national chairman, both firsts, to oversee the campaign and handle party matters between conventions.

The Whigs met in Philadelphia, and on the third day, on the fourth ballot, Taylor was nominated, trailed by another war hero (Winfield Scott), Henry Clay, and Daniel Webster. New York state comptroller Millard Fillmore was nominated for vice-president on the second ballot.

There were several other conventions, but the one that mattered was the Free Soil convention in Buffalo, a gathering of about 400 delegates, many dissatisfied with the nominees of both parties, in the only facility that could hold them, a large tent pitched in the city park. They chose former president Martin Van Buren their presidential nominee and Charles Francis Adams, son of former president John Quincy Adams, for the vice-presidential spot.

Zachary Taylor

The Free Soil platform pledged "no more slave states and no more slave territory."

Campaign Notes   Cass did not speak or write on his own behalf.

Taylor behaved like everyone's pen pal until worried advisers told him to stop.

Van Buren did not campaign but his son John did, and scores of Free Soilers stumped in the North.

Symbols   A military motif appeared on many campaign items in an attempt to identify both major candidates as war heroes.

Slogans   Democrats sloganized a statement of defiance, supposedly made by Cass during the War of 1812: "While I Am Able to Move I will Do My Duty."

Whigs picked up Taylor's war words and put them into slogans too: "General Taylor Never Surrenders" and "A Little More Grape [shot], Captain Bragg" were Taylorisms that rallied the troops during the Battle of Buena Vista.

The Free Soilers started off with an official party slogan: "Free Soil, Free Speech, Free Labor, and Free Men." They made up more along the way, concocting catchy appeals such as "Vote the Land Free" and, it is believed, "Vote Early and Often."

Songs The Democrats sang for "Cass and Butler" and "The Brave Old Volunteer."

"Old Zack Taylor is the man . . . to fill the chair of Washington," Whigs warbled. In "Rough and Ready" and "The Bold Soger Boy" they praised "gallant" "darling" Taylor.

The Free Soilers sang even more freely in "Martin Van of Kinderhook": "He who'd vote for Zacky Taylor / Needs a keeper or a jailer. / And he who still for Cass can be, / He is a Cass without the C."

Paraphernalia The Democrats had almost as many themes as trinkets. A ribbon stressed "Freedom of the Seas," a medalet the "Tariff of Forty Six," while other items, lapel pins to prints, promoted "The Union" and "True Democracy."

The Whigs focused on the military front. A working cast-iron parlor stove showed off a military bust of General Taylor; colorful silk bandannas portrayed his military exploits; lacquered cigar boxes pictured him in full military regalia; and ribbons, buttons, and banners had other military poses.

Popular Labels About the best the Democrats could do for their candidate was "General Cass," while the Whigs had more affectionate terms for Taylor such as "Old Rough and Ready" and "Old Zach."

Name-calling Whigs had much fun with Cass' name and physique, calling him "General Gass" and a "pot-bellied, mutton-headed cucumber."

To Democrats, Taylor was a "military autocrat," likened to Napoleon, and "economical, comical Old Zach" for a trait of penny-pinching.

The Press Democratic editors criticized Taylor's letter-writing, saying what he wrote was banal, inconsistent, and "fatal."

The Whig press revived old charges against Cass, even some that had been disproved.

Firsts A military man with no officeholding experience or real political party membership became president.

The first president from the Deep South and a state west of the Mississippi River.

The first broad-based antislavery party.

Trends The issue of slavery starts to break up established parties.

The Free Soilers sow the seeds of a new Republican party.

Stump speaking—literally on a stump—comes into its own.

Vote   Thirty states voted, half slave and half free. The vote was close, with Taylor receiving 163 electoral votes and 1,360,967 popular votes (47.4 percent) to 127 and 1,222,342 (42.5 percent) and the Free Soilers attracted no electoral but 291,263 popular votes (10.1 percent).

Benchmark   Taylor became the third president, to win by less than a majority of popular votes.

The most votes polled yet by a third party.

Quote   The voters, said abolitionist William Lloyd Garrison, decided "a Whig General should be made president because he had done effective work in carrying on a Democratic war."

A MERICA was growing up. The steam locomotive, which once had embarrassed itself in a well-publicized 1830 race with the horse-drawn carriage, was connecting the country bit by bit. On the seas, stately Yankee clipper ships, newly crafted by New England shipwrights, made cargoes fly and took the breath away. A game called baseball had become so popular that it needed its own set of rules, and a showman known as "the Prince of Humbug" was making a living off bearded ladies and elephant men.

On the frontier, old-timers sang to newcomers: "Come filthy, come lousy, come just as you are." But in Northeastern cities the mounting thousands of Irish and German immigrants who crowded into open spaces were told angrily that enough was enough. And antislavery activists were arguing that the principles of democracy did not bend to the bondage of slavery. The issue of slavery was about to explode. The explosion came closer with "Jimmy Polk's war."

The Whigs claimed that Democrat president James Polk had started it all by placing troops, led by Gen. Zachary Taylor, so near the disputed Rio Grande boundary as to dare the Mexicans to attack. When they did, in April 1846, Polk found it easy enough to get Congress to declare war to atone for the spilling of "American blood on American soil." It was not as easy to quiet one Whig congressman, Abraham Lincoln of Illinois, who demanded to know what particular spot of American soil was red with American blood or the uproar caused by the "Wilmot Proviso," which proposed to ban slavery in all territories to be won from Mexico.

And win Polk did. With victories by generals Taylor and Winfield Scott, the president secured a treaty in February 1848 that included the Rio Grande boundary for Texas, New Mexico, and California, with gold just waiting to be discovered, for fifteen million dollars plus another three million for war claims. But the Whigs, who had protested the war from start to finish, were also winners. They had another Tippecanoe. Only this time Zachary Taylor was an undisputed war hero and a legend in his own right.

The Whigs needed somebody new. Their old favorite, Henry Clay, had run and lost too many times and, more important, his various positions on slavery had angered both factions of the party. Taylor was attractive because he had not expressed any political opinions, had never voted, and had no publicized party affiliation—that is, until so pestered that he finally said "I am a Whig but not an ultra Whig."

When the Whigs nominated "Old Rough and Ready," as Taylor was affectionately called for doing battle in baggy pants and a battered straw hat, they promised nothing. Initially some Whigs were appalled, especially followers of Clay. But generally, Northern Whigs liked his military record and Southern Whigs felt secure in the fact that he owned hundreds of slaves.

The Democrats also nominated a military hero, Gen. Lewis Cass, who served with honor during the War of 1812, at one point breaking his sword rather than surrendering it. But the Democrats' focus was not heroism but compromise on the issue of slavery because the party was already divided in New York between the status-quo Hunkers and the antislavery Barnburners. So they chose a "northern man with southern principles" who was against the Wilmot Proviso but favored "squatter sovereignty," having settlers in new territories decide on slavery.

The Barnburners walked out anyway, eventually joining with disgruntled Whigs, Liberty party types, and Free Soilers to nominate former president Martin Van Buren and to push for the Wilmot Proviso. Messianic Free Soilers stumped the Northern states, providing the only real color of the campaign.

The two major parties, which had glossed over the slavery issue, were left to engage in petty attacks. The Whigs called Cass a "doughface" who would be swayed by Southerners and ridiculed him as "General Gass." The Democrats retorted that Taylor was a "candidate of many parties" and joked that he was as knowledgeable about national issues as his horse "Old Whitey." But the Whigs rallied around their candidate. Lincoln gave a rousing speech in Congress, defending Taylor's right to reserve his opinions until elected.

The large Free Soil vote in pivotal Northern states really decided the election. Attracting five times as much support as in 1844, the antislavery cause took crucial votes away from Cass and gave the presidency to "Old Rough and Ready." As with "Tippecanoe" in 1840, the country had a President it knew only by image. Poet James Russell Lowell posed the problem in Yankee dialect: "He hezn't told ye wut he is, an' so there ain't no knowin'."

FRANKLIN PIERCE

★ CAMPAIGN OF 1852 ★

Major Candidates   Franklin Pierce, 48, New Hampshire, Democrat
Winfield Scott, 66, New Jersey, Whig

Credentials   Pierce was elected to the New Hampshire house of representatives (1829–1833), becoming speaker (1831–1832). He became a U.S. representative (1833–1837) and then a senator (1837–1842), resigning in February to practice law, appointed federal district attorney for his state (1845), volunteered for the Mexican War (1846–1848), and served as a brigadier general under General Scott.

Scott entered the military in 1808, fought in the War of 1812, was promoted to brigadier general and then brevet major general, led troops in the Black Hawk War (1832), the Second Seminole War (1835–1837) and the Aroostook War (1839). He became general in chief of the U.S. Army in 1841, commanding the forces during the Mexican War (1846–1848) and winning victories at Vera Cruz and Mexico City, which ended the war.

Tickets   When the Democrats met in Baltimore they had more than enough candidates and more than enough delegates. Three contenders were of the older generation: 1848 nominee Lewis Cass, James Buchanan of Pennsylvania, and William Marcy of New York. The fourth was the young senator from Illinois, Stephen Douglas. On June 5, as no candidate had been able to win, on the thirty-fifth ballot, Virginia gave its fifteen votes to "dark horse" Pierce and over the next thirteen ballots his strength increased until on the last there was a stampede to him. To balance the ticket, Senator William King of Alabama was chosen as the vice-presidential nominee.

The Whigs also convened in Baltimore and cast even more ballots before giving Scott the presidential nomination. The delegates had three serious choices before them: President Millard Fillmore, Scott, and Daniel Webster. The Whigs fought long and hard on everything. From the start, Fillmore and Scott were neck-and-neck and Webster a distant third. For two days and forty-six ballots, this horse race continued until Fillmore's managers agreed to back Webster if the Massachusetts senator could get 41 votes in the North. He failed even to get the votes of his own state. When voting resumed, Scott pulled ahead to win on the fifty-third ballot. Secretary of the Navy William Graham of North Carolina was unanimously named for the second spot.

The Free Soilers were now calling themselves the Free Democrats, but the party that convened in Pittsburgh was but a shadow of its former self. It nominated Senator John Hale of New Hampshire for president and Indiana's George Julian for vice president.

Campaign Notes   Pierce remained at home and stayed silent. Scott, stumped in Pennsylvania, Ohio, and other states on a military-related jaunt, all the while protesting "I do not intend to speak to you on political topics."

Symbols   To promote Pierce as from New Hampshire the Democrats formed "Granite Clubs," and, to boost him as following in the tradition of President Jackson, raised hickory poles. Scott's symbol was the soup bowl because he had made famous the expression "a hasty bowl of soup."

Slogans   Pleased with their first dark-horse victory, the Democrats chanted "We Polked 'em in '44; we'll Pierce 'em in '52." They reduced to slogans two of Scott's more ridiculous remarks: "Fire upon the Rear" and "Hasty Plate of Soup."

The Whigs promoted "General Winfield Scott—First in War, First in Peace" and pleased that they had the well-known candidate, they chided: "Who is Frank Pierce?"

The Free Democrats used the Free Soil slogan: "Free Soil, Free Speech, Free Labor and Free Men."

Songs   The Democrats published verses in campaign newspapers that were sometimes sung to popular tunes, such as: "Feathers and Soup and Fuss / They cannot frighten us."

The Whigs sang of "Scott, Who Oft to Victory Led," and in "Scott and

Graham'' they sang of Pierce in the Mexican War: ''He took a sudden fainting fit / And tumbled off his horse.''

Paraphernalia   As in 1848, the Whigs were running the more important military man. Still, the Democrats did their best to promote the military side of Pierce's past. On ribbons and medals he was often called ''The Statesman & Soldier'' or ''Citizen and Soldier.'' His portrait, many times with Pierce in uniform, appeared on handkerchiefs and medallions.

The Whigs made the most of their upper hand by using ribbons, bandannas, ceramics, and prints to advertise their candidate as ''The Hero of Many Battles,'' ''First in War, First in Peace,'' and ''Triumphant in War.''

Popular Labels   Pierce was dubbed ''Young Hickory of the Granite Hills.'' He was also called ''Handsome Frank.''

Scott was variously ''The Hero of Bridgewater,'' ''The Hero of Lundy's Lane,'' and the ''Hero of Vera Cruz.'' Best of all, his troops liked to call him ''Old Fuss and Feathers'' because of his meticulous military dress and love of pomp. Not surprisingly, the Democrats got more mileage out of his nickname than did the Whigs.

Name-calling   To Whigs, Pierce was ''The Fainting General.''

To Democrats, Scott was a ''military chieftain'' whose appeal was nothing more than ''Gunpowder Glory.''

The Press   There was so little interest in the campaign and so much silliness that the *New York Herald* called it the most ''ludicrous, ridiculous, and uninteresting Presidential campaign since the country had been emancipated from British rule.''

First   Pierce was the first Democratic candidate from the Northeast.

Trends   The political balance was tipping in favor of the free states.

Both Democrats and Whigs started the practice of adopting platforms before nominating candidates.

Vote   Thirty-one states voted. All but four voted for Pierce, giving him 254 electoral votes to 42 for Scott. Pierce's win was less spectacular (1,601,117 to Scott's 1,385,453) in the popular vote, but better than recent presidents had done. Hale garnered 155,825 votes.

Benchmarks   Pierce was the second dark-horse candidate and second to be nominated by stampede by a major political party.

The Whigs suffered their worst electoral setback and never nominated another candidate.

There was no inaugural ball.

The dullest campaign since 1820.

Quote The Whig party, it was said at the time, "died of an attempt to swallow the Fugitive Slave Law."

THEY were truly giants, towering in political thought and its expression, and together "the immortal trio." Henry Clay, John C. Calhoun, and Daniel Webster all had begun their political careers in the House during the War of 1812, had been secretaries of state and more, and had served (and fought) with each other in the Senate for over a decade. As 1850 broke, they were fighting still, only this time with dying voices on an issue that would not die, the issue of slavery.

Then the greatest debate of all began. It came as the territories acquired in the Mexican War were trying to turn themselves into states, either slave or free but probably free, as pressure mounted to abolish slavery in the nation's capital and as Southerners said their runaway slaves, about a thousand a year, were finding safe places in the North. Clay proposed a package of compromises. To please the North, Texas would be a free state and the District of Columbia's slave trade would end. For the South, the territories of New Mexico and Utah would decide on their own about slavery and the Fugitive Slave Law would be tightened. On February 5 and 6, the "Great Pacificator," now seventy-three and so feeble that he needed to be helped up the Capitol steps, rose to defend his proposals, speaking for four hours, his strength only in words: "All now is uproar, confusion and menace to the existence of the Union."

On March 4 Calhoun, bundled in blankets, suffering from tuberculosis and too weak to give his own defiant speech, spoke through a protégé. The equilibrium between slave and free states had been destroyed, he said. Let the North compensate the South or "let the States we both represent agree to separate and part in peace." Three days later, Webster, like Calhoun sixty-eight and not well at all, gave the speech of his life. "I speak to-day for the preservation of the Union," he declared, as spectators sat hushed, wondering which way he would turn on the Fugitive Slave Law, the litmus test in Northern eyes. "The South, in my judgment, is right, and the North is wrong."

Webster's Seventh of March speech lost him the Whig nomination two years later, but it helped win passage of the Compromise of 1850. In pieces it passed, after opponents Calhoun and President Zachary Taylor had died, shepherded through in the hands of thirty-seven-year-old Stephen Douglas, the "Little Giant." Celebrations erupted across the country as word passed that the slavery issue had been settled, once and for all.

It certainly seemed that way when the two major parties convened in June 1852 to decide on their nominees and prepare platforms. In both cases, the platforms were easier to handle and so they tackled them first, stating in effect that the Compromise of 1850 was to be the last word. But it took the Democrats forty-nine ballots and bitter debate before they finally chose Franklin Pierce, a much darker horse than James Polk had been in 1844 and, like Lewis Cass in 1848, a "Northern man with Southern principles." The Whigs had even more difficulty, taking fifty-three ballots to nominate "Old Fuss and Feathers," Gen. Winfield Scott. In choosing Scott, the Whigs passed over Webster as well as President Fillmore. Webster was devastated and died in October, several months after Clay.

From the start, the Democrats were out in front. Pierce was personable with matinee-idol looks and no known strong opinions. The Democrats easily came together around him, joined by many Free Soilers who wanted to give the Compromise of 1850 a chance. The Whigs, on the other hand, were divided. Southerners, who questioned Scott's commitment to slavery, held back their support, while Northerners, who could not stomach the Fugitive Slave Law, said openly "We accept the candidate but spit on the platform."

With slavery sidelined by similar party platforms, the nitty-gritty of the campaign became an issue of personalities. Mudslinging flourished in this atmosphere. Both candidates were vulnerable. Pierce was called a drunkard and a coward, even though his "fainting fit," as the Whigs called it, occurred when his horse stumbled and caused him a painful groin injury. The Democrats never let "Old Fuss and Feathers" forget his army nickname, which the Whigs were less fond of, or two ludicrous statements he once made about "a hasty plate of soup" and "a fire upon the rear."

The Whigs were frightened and so they sent Scott on an extended tour of several states, ostensibly to select sites for military hospitals but really to engender some enthusiasm for their candidate. It did not matter. The people, especially those in the South, felt safer with Pierce and elected him by an overwhelming electoral majority. They were only buying time. Harriet Beecher Stowe's novel *Uncle Tom's Cabin* was turning the publishing world inside out and the uncommitted against slavery.

★ CAMPAIGN OF 1856 ★

Major Candidates   James Buchanan, 65, Pennsylvania, Democrat
John C. Frémont, 43, California, Republican

Credentials Buchanan served in his state house of representatives (1815–1816), was elected to the U.S. House of Representatives (1821–1831), became minister to Russia (1832–1833), U.S. senator (1834–1845), secretary of state (1845–1849), and minister to Great Britain (1853–1856).

Frémont surveyed the region between the Mississippi and Missouri rivers (1838–1839), explored the Oregon Trail (1842) and across the Sierra Nevadas into the Sacramento Valley (1843–1844). He became a captain in the army, came back to California and helped overthrow Mexican rule (1846), and served as one of California's first two U.S. senators (1850–1851).

Tickets   The Democrats met in Cincinnati. From the start, Buchanan had a small lead. His two main opponents—President Franklin Pierce and Stephen Douglas—were tainted by the uproar over the Kansas–Nebraska Act, which had turned the slavery issue into bloodshed. At first, Buchanan was ahead of Pierce, then Douglas, until Douglas withdrew and Buchanan was unanimously nominated on the seventeenth ballot. Former representative John Breckinridge of Kentucky was chosen for vice president.

The new Republican party held its exuberant national convention in Philadelphia. The meeting was clearly sectional—only Northern states and four border slave states sent delegates. After scores of earnest, messianic speakers addressed the revivalist-type meeting, an informal ballot put Frémont far in front; his nomination was then made unanimous. William Drayton, former senator from New Jersey, was chosen as his running mate. His runner-up was Abraham Lincoln.

The Americans or Know-Nothings, who were antagonistic toward new immigrants as well as Catholics, convened, and after many delegates left over a split on the slavery issue, chose to run former president Millard Fillmore and Tennessee's Andrew Donelson, Andrew Jackson's nephew and editor of the *Washington Union*. The Whigs—what were left of them, since many had joined the Republicans—supported the Know-Nothing ticket.

Campaign Notes   Buchanan, Republicans joked, was dead of lockjaw because he was so quiet during the campaign. He stayed at his estate, Wheatland, not commenting on events.

Also true to form, Frémont did not campaign for himself. Frémont was lucky to have some very effective substitutes. Jessie, his wife and daughter of the famous Democratic senator Thomas Hart Benton, campaigned for him, spawning popular "Oh Jessie!" buttons. Abraham Lincoln, Whig-turned-Republican, took to the stump and made over fifty speeches.

Symbols   Democrats used the rooster, while Republicans paraded with bear flags and formed "Bear Clubs" in honor of Frémont's role in founding the state of California.

Slogans   The Democrats rallied for "Buck and Breck," promised to "Take the Buck by the horns," and appealed for "James Buchanan—No Sectionalism." When Republicans shouted "Free Soil, Free Men, Free Speech and Fre-mont," Democrats snickered "And Free Love" to remind voters that Frémont had been born out of wedlock.

Republicans, of course, proselytized other aspects of Frémont's past. They hailed him as "Pathfinder of the West," even "The Pathfinder of Empire." Buchanan's shortcomings were sloganized as "Opposition to Old Bachelors" and "Buchanan's Workshop: Ten Cents a Day." (Buchanan was reported to have said that ten cents a day was enough for mechanics.)

JAMES BUCHANAN

Songs Like 1840, this campaign was hard-fought and hard-sung, with Republicans the feisty underdogs. The Democrats, in "Buchanan and Breckinridge," sang of Buchanan as the only one to hold the Union together.

For Republicans, "We'll Give 'Em Jessie" was a popular song and battle cry, standing for "We'll give 'em hell!"

Paraphernalia The Democrats were not above using fear to sway voters. One ribbon, featuring a runaway slave with a knapsack, was titled *Black Republican*. Another showed a skull and crossbones and underneath "Frémont and Dayton."

Republicans inevitably stressed the issue of the day over personality. Pictures of Frémont were more often than not coupled with some variation of the "Free Soil" message.

The Know-Nothings peddled "Know-Nothing candy," "Know-Nothing tea," and "Know-Nothing toothpicks."

Popular Labels Followers called Buchanan "Old Buck" and themselves "Buchaneers" or "Buchaniers." He was also hailed as "The Sage of Wheatland" and "Old Public Functionary."

To Republicans, Frémont was "The Pathfinder" and "The Mountaineer."

Name-calling To Republicans, the Democratic candidates were "Old Fogies" and Buchanan himself was "Ten Cent Jimmy."

"Woolly Horse" was a characterization of Frémont used by both Democrats and Know-Nothings, based on a fictitious animal circusmaster P.T. Barnum promoted as once found by Frémont's exploring party.

Firsts The Republican party had its first national candidates and platform.

Estimated to be the first million-dollar election, including national and local expenditures by both parties.

The first electoral votes won by a third party.

Trends The rise of sectional politics.

The rise to power of a party not prone to compromise on the slavery issue.

Vote Thirty-one states participated. Buchanan won 174 electoral votes and 1,832,955 popular votes (45.3 percent) to 114 and 1,339,932 for Frémont and 8 and 871,731 for Fillmore.

Benchmarks Buchanan was the last Democratic president until Cleveland.

The fourth time a president is elected without a majority of popular votes.

The Democratic party was the only really national party in this race.

Quote Poet and antislavery crusader John Greenleaf Whittier wondered about the Republicans' future: "If months have well-nigh won the field, / What may four years do?"

★ ★ ★

UNTIL now, preservation of the Union was more important than any other issue, even slavery. But the self-serving actions of Illinois senator Stephen A. Douglas changed all that. A pit bull of a man, short and stocky and wired for combat, the "Little Giant" did not intentionally destroy the delicate balance between North and South crafted by the Compromise of 1850, which he himself had helped nudge through Congress. But he was set on becoming president and becoming rich. To realize these ambitions he needed Southern states to support him politically as well to back the idea of a Pacific railroad that would terminate in Chicago, the city of his investments. Douglas proceeded to woo them.

He went too far. Working under the assumption that the principle of "popular sovereignty" was now widely accepted, in January 1854 Douglas proposed a bill to divide the Territory of Nebraska into Nebraska and Kansas, with their settlers deciding on slavery. The bill amounted to nullification of the "sacred" Missouri Compromise. Northerners attacked the bill as a "monstrous plot" to profit the Southern slavocracy and denounced Douglas as a "Benedict Arnold" and a "Judas." But the Democratic senator was the better pugilist. Sparring with arguments about how the Missouri Compromise had stigmatized slavery and felling his opponents with bruising words, Douglas and his Southern colleagues pushed the bill through Congress.

Fed up with "Neb-rascals" and their "Nebraska swindle," antislavery advocates met in Ripon, Wisconsin, on February 28. Drawing their ranks from Conscience Whigs, Northern Democrats, and Free Soilers, they made history. A greater number of them gathered on July 6 in Jackson, Michigan, called themselves Republicans, and organized to fight "the great moral, social and political evil of the day."

The Know-Nothings, a new party antagonistic to immigrants and Catholics, along with the Republicans, did relatively well in the midterm elections and many wondered which group would challenge the Democrats for the presidency in 1856. Slavery decided. It split the Know-Nothings in two and made the Republicans even stronger. Kansas was torn asunder by feuds between "settlers" from free Northern states toting "Beecher's Bibles" that were really new breech-loading rifles, and "border ruffians," five thousand strong, who crossed over from slaveholding Missouri and voted in a proslavery legislature. The free-state settlers then set up their own seat of government, which President Franklin Pierce condemned as revolutionary. Now Kansas was bleeding with John Brown's massacre and more.

Against this backdrop the Democrats and Republicans convened. (The Know-Nothings had met earlier, disagreed, and the antislavery segment had wired Republicans: "The North Americans are with you." Those remaining nominated former president Millard Fillmore.) The Democrats needed somebody who was not scarred by Kansas. That eliminated Douglas and Pierce and singled out Buchanan, who had been minister to Great Britain during most of the uproar. The Republicans ran the romantic "Pathfinder" John Frémont, whose reputation as an explorer was probably a bit overblown but who made up for it in dash and daring and his lovely wife Jessie, so that "Frémont and Jessie" sounded right in song and slogan.

This time the parties distinctly differed on the issue of slavery. Democrats supported the Kansas–Nebraska Act and said that Congress could not interfere with slavery in the territories, while Republicans opposed the repeal of the Missouri Compromise and said Congress had the duty to prohibit "those twin relics of barbarism, polygamy and slavery," in the territories. "Black Republicans," "Nigger Worshippers" shouted the Democrats, and Buchanan warned that the opposition "must be boldly assailed as disunionists, and this charge must be reiterated again and again." It was, by Whigs who remained Whigs and did not join the Republicans (as Abraham Lincoln and William Seward had done) and by Fillmore, who was saying that the country was "treading on the brink of a volcano."

The campaign was set in the North because the Republicans did not run tickets in most of the South. The Democrats with deeper pockets spent liberally in states like Indiana and Buchanan's own Pennsylvania. The Republicans compensated with enthusiasm and fervor. They excelled in torchlight parades and "staccato" cheers; they had the Wide Awakes and the Pioneers, California Bear Clubs and Rocky Mountain Clubs, and more songs, longer slogans ("Free Labor, Free Speech, Free Men, Free Kansas and Frémont) and stinging ditties about bachelor Buchanan: "Who ever heard in all his life, Of a candidate without a wife?"

But Frémont was not well known and was hurt by Know-Nothing pamphlets, "The Romish Intrigue" and "Papist or Protestant, Which?", falsely charging that he was a Catholic. Coupled with no Southern support, this led to Buchanan's win. But it was an uneasy victory for the Democrat who had only 45 percent of the popular vote, almost 10 percent below Pierce's popular support four years earlier. Also, voting patterns showed a clear-cut sectionalism, with Frémont favored by most of the states in the North and Buchanan by all of the South. President-elect Buchanan was warned "You are not to lie in a bed of roses for the next four years."

★ CAMPAIGN OF 1860 ★

Major Candidates   Stephen Douglas, 47, Illinois, Democrat
Abraham Lincoln, 51, Illinois, Republican

Credentials   Douglas held local office, was appointed judge of the state supreme court (1841), elected to the House of Representatives (1843–1847), and then the U.S. Senate (1847–1861). He wrote the Kansas–Nebraska Act of 1854.

Lincoln was appointed a local postmaster by President Andrew Jackson (1833–1836), was elected to the Illinois general assembly (1834) with bipartisan support and was then reelected as a Whig (1836–1842), became a U.S. representative (1847–1849) and switched to the Republican party (1856). He was nominated to run for the U.S. Senate (1858) but lost to Douglas.

Tickets   The Democrats were divided over slavery when they met in Charleston, South Carolina, in late April. After fifty-seven tries to pick a candidate, the delegates gave up, deciding to reconvene later.

In June they met in Baltimore, where there was another walkout by many Southern and anti-Douglas delegates. Douglas was chosen on the second ballot. The vice-presidential nominee was former Georgia governor Herschel Johnson.

Between the Democrats' two deliberations the Republicans convened in Chicago, where the convention delegates decided to abandon the unit ru!e and to elect with a majority of the voting delegates. New York senator William Seward was the acknowledged front-runner, but the mood of the convention was more moderate toward slavery than his stance had been. Anti-Seward forces backed Abraham Lincoln and on the third ballot, Lincoln was just a vote and a half short of a majority, with $231\frac{1}{2}$ to 180 for Seward. When Ohio switched four of its votes to Lincoln, a stampede followed; his nomination was secured and made unanimous. Maine's senator Hannibal Hamlin, a Democrat-turned-Republican, became Lincoln's running mate.

Two other conventions were held, both by disaffected parties. Splinter

STEPHEN DOUGLAS

Democrats who wanted slavery protected in the territories, nominated Vice President John Breckinridge, President Buchanan's protégé, for the top spot and, to run with him, Senator Joseph Lane of Oregon. The Constitutional Union Party, made up of onetime Whigs and Know-Nothings, after some squabbling nominated former senator John Bell of Tennessee for president and the well-known orator Edward Everett as his running-mate.

Campaign Notes Douglas made a clean break with tradition by taking to the stump and selling himself.

   Lincoln declined to campaign. Instead, he received visitors at Springfield, shook hundreds of hands, and wrote lots of letters to party leaders. His wife, Mary Todd Lincoln, assumed an important and new role for a candidate's wife, welcoming journalists to their home, helping choose campaign portraits, and accompanying her husband on preconvention speaking engagements.

   Neither Breckinridge nor Bell campaigned.

Symbols The split rail was favored for Lincoln, although the bull was also used for the Republican effort.

Slogans The regular or Douglas Democrats rallied for "Douglas and Johnson: The Union Now and Forever." They claimed "Cuba Must Be Ours" and "We Want a Statesman Not a Railsplitter as President."

Republicans cheered for "The Man Who Can Split Rails and Maul Democrats" and promised "The Man That Can Split Rails Can Guide the Ship of State."

Songs To the tune of "The Star-Spangled Banner," Douglas Democrats sang " 'gainst the treason of Lincoln and Breckinridge too." And they laughed at Lincoln for his looks, singing that Republicans could make up any lie about their candidate or mixture (of lies), "But, oh don't, we beg and pray you— / Don't for land's sake, show his picture!"

Lincoln's side had more campaign songs, most of them legend-building. There was "Old Abe, The Rail Splitter," "Honest Abe, the Flatboatman," and "The Gallant Son of the West."

Paraphernalia Douglas items did not emphasize the candidate so much as the Union and the principle of popular sovereignty, with ribbons, flags, medals, and lithographs.

Lincoln items were abundant, with advertising weighed more to the candidate and his legendary characteristics than the issues of the day. Much ado, for example, was made about Lincoln's rail-splitting skill. There was *The Rail Splitter* campaign weekly, local rail-splitter clubs, rail-splitter badges and envelopes, featuring "The Fence That Uncle Abe Built," a bust of Lincoln and the words: "What though it be a homely face . . . God speed our brave splitter of rails."

This campaign saw the first photographic ferrotypes of all four candidates; these were usually worn in ornate lapel-size brass frames.

Popular Labels Douglas' followers called him the "Little Giant" and themselves "Little Giants" and "Little Dougs."

Lincoln's nicknames were "Old Honest Abe," "Honest Abe," or just "Old Abe." Lincoln had earned the title "Little Giant Killer" for debating Douglas so well in the Illinois senate race of 1858. He was also the "Rail Splitter" and "Hannibal of the West."

Name-calling To opponents, Douglas was the "Squatter King," Lincoln a "Big Baboon" and "The Slave Hound of Illinois."

The Press The Illinois *Gazette* lambasted Douglas for campaigning: "Douglas is going about peddling his opinions as a tin man peddles his wares."

The South, said Georgia's *Southern Confederacy*, would never submit to "such humiliation and degradation as the inauguration of Abraham Lincoln."

Firsts Lincoln was the first Republican President.

Douglas was the first to stump for the presidency.

First prearranged all-out demonstration at a party convention for a candidate (for Lincoln at the Republican convention).

Vote Thirty-three states took part. Lincoln won 180 electoral and 1,865,593 popular votes (39.8 percent) to 72 and 848,356 (18.1 percent) for Breckinridge, 12 and 1,382,713 (29.5 percent) and 39 and 592,906 (12.6 percent) for Bell.

Benchmarks Lincoln became the fifth minority President, winning by the smallest percentage of popular votes, except for John Quincy Adams in 1824. Voter participation was the second highest ever.

Quote President-elect Lincoln told reporters: "Well boys, your troubles are over now, mine have just begun."

"M R. Lincoln is elected," a saddened Stephen Douglas murmured to himself and his secretary in October. Statewide elections in Pennsylvania and Indiana had favored the Republicans and predicted his fate. Three months earlier, this same Democratic powerhouse, the major challenger to Republican presidential candidate Abraham Lincoln, had exuberantly told a supporter that "the chances in our favor are immense in the East." But Douglas never really had any chance. He was toying with smoke and mirrors.

This election was decided, before a single hat made it into the ring, by events that fatefully divided the Democrats and brought into national focus a gangling small-town lawyer and single-term Republican congressman who still said *git, thar*, and *to home*. The Supreme Court's Dred Scott decision was the beginning. Southerners cheered while Northerners raged over the Court's slip into "the filth of pro-slavery politics."

And the Democratic party began to break apart. President James Buchanan set the last straw in place by backing Southern "fire-eaters" who wanted to push through Congress the minority Lecompton Constitution, which would have brought Kansas into the union as a slave state. Senator Douglas, the "Squatter King" to his enemies, openly split with the president on this, arguing that a majority of the territory's residents wanted Kansas to be free. Catfights and fistfights marked the debate in Congress, with the document finally sent back to Kansas for another vote. (Kansas entered as a free state in 1861.)

Without a Southern flank, Douglas had little hope of winning the presidency—his ultimate goal. Still, there seemed to be no other Democrat (Buchanan wanted to retire) or any Republican, for that matter, standing in his way. But when the senator returned to Illinois in 1858 to run for reelection, he met his match. "Abe" Lincoln had just about dropped out of politics at one point, only to be roused "as he had never been before" by the Kansas–Nebraska Act, which Douglas authored and Lincoln detested. Douglas knew he was up against "the best stump speaker in the West" and uneasily agreed to a series of seven debates across the state.

They were an extraordinary pair: Douglas "handsome" in some eyes, Lincoln "grotesque"; Lincoln towering six foot four in stocking feet, Douglas stretched at five; and Douglas famous for sartorial splendor, Lincoln for carrying a crumpled stovepipe hat and, over his left arm, a gray woolen shawl in case of a chill. They were equal, though, in eloquence, except that when Lincoln spoke he united his party behind him whereas Douglas divided his. Thousands came to hear Lincoln declare that the Union could not last "half slave and half free" and Douglas debate the Dred Scott decision and uphold popular sovereignty. Douglas kept his seat, but Lincoln the head-lines—LINCOLN FOR PRESIDENT, 1860—and eventually admitted "The taste *is* in my mouth a little."

The Democrats met in April for their national convention, ready to do "battle." When their version of the platform calling for protection of slavery in the territories was rejected, many Southerners walked out, leaving Doug-las forces in charge but their man unelectable. Finally a second convention in June did choose Douglas, while the renegade Democratic Southerners picked Vice President John Breckinridge, who was Buchanan's choice. The new Constitutional Union party, also Southern-based, nominated Tennes-sean John Bell.

The convention that really mattered took place in a wigwam-shaped build-ing in Chicago. Designed for ten thousand, it was immediately inadequate, overflowing with delegates, journalists, and spectators. At first glance, Wil-liam Seward, New York's adamant antislavery senator, had the convention in his pocket, with so many young, radical followers singing "Oh, isn't he a darling?" But behind the scenes, Lincolnites were saying "Success rather than Seward," and, in any case, they were bargaining cabinet posts for votes and minting counterfeit tickets. When the balloting began, Lincoln "shouters" were sitting in the places of Seward "boys" and squealing so loudly it sounded like "all the hogs slaughtered in Cincinnati." Lincoln won on the third ballot.

In effect, there were two contests. One in the North, where the majority of electoral votes were, between Lincoln and Douglas; the other in the South, between Breckinridge and Bell. Lincoln sat in Springfield resolved to stay silent. Others did the work for him. Pretty girls were sent by wagonloads to spruce up rallies, stump speakers spoke against slavery but also for home-steading and higher tariffs, and the Wide Awakes, in their oilcloth capes, did a special zigzag march to mimic a split-rail fence. Douglas had the Little Giants and the Chloroformers ("to put the Wide Awakes to sleep"), but mostly he relied on himself, speaking for two months, sometimes twenty times a day, in every major city, except unruly Charleston. Even in October when Douglas knew Lincoln would win, he did not quit. "We must try to save the Union," he said. "I will go South."

The campaign was mean. Lincoln was called "sooty and scoundrelly" and his running mate Hannibal Hamlin a mulatto. Douglas was accused of drink-ing and berated for speaking out in "utter disregard for the proprieties of his position." Most of all, the campaign was predictable. Douglas could not win with a divided party, and Lincoln's election would divide the Union. "We will never submit to the inauguration of a Black Republican President," cried Southerners.

"We are elected!" Lincoln shouted to his wife on hearing the news. His victory was short-lived. On December 20, South Carolina took itself out of the Union, and then six more states rapidly followed to form the Confederate States of America. Lincoln tried to reason in his inaugural address: "We are not enemies, but friends. We must not be enemies."

The guns of Fort Sumter sounded April 12.

★ CAMPAIGN OF 1864 ★

Major Candidates   Abraham Lincoln, 55, Illinois, National Union
George McClellan, 38, New Jersey, Democrat

Credentials   For Lincoln, see Campaign of 1860. He was elected president in 1860.

McClellan served in the Mexican War and was breveted captain (1846–1848), worked as an army engineer, resigned his commission (1857), and became a railroad executive. He joined the Union army as a major general (1861). In July he headed the Army of the Potomac and in November became commander of the army. Lincoln relieved him of his duties in March 1862 for falling short of expectations. He returned to head up the Army of the Potomac, only to be removed again in November 1862.

Tickets   As usual, the Republicans welcomed to their convention in Baltimore all who wanted to come under their banner, including many Democrats who supported Lincoln's war aims. Lincoln easily won on the first ballot, with 494 votes to Missouri's twenty-two for General Ulysses S. Grant. Missouri then made it unanimous. Lincoln favored Andrew Johnson, the military governor of Tennessee, for the second spot over the current vice president, Hannibal Hamlin, and got his way.

The Democrats, deserted by those who favored Lincoln and the Southern Confederate wing, held off their convention until August, better to judge the military situation. On the first ballot, as predicted, General George McClellan won with 174, then raised to 202½ of 226 votes cast. The nomination was made unanimous. As McClellan's running mate the convention unanimously chose Ohio representative George Pendleton on the second ballot.

Campaign Notes   Lincoln did not actively campaign. McClellan remained in retirement and did not solicit votes.

Symbols   Personalities were played down and the Union played up, as both sides featured flags, drums, cannon, and eagles.

ABRAHAM LINCOLN

Slogans   Lincoln once said and his followers now shouted: "Don't Swap Horses in the Middle of the Stream." Lincolnites also hailed "Uncle Abe and Andy" and argued "Vote as You Shot" and "Lincoln and Liberty—Good for Another Heat."

Democrats wanted "The Constitution as It Is, The Union as It Was, and the Negroes Where They Are." They bragged "Old Abe Removed McClellan, We'll Now Remove Old Abe."

Songs   The Civil War was Lincoln's war and so "Battle Hymn of the Republic" and "Marching Along" were almost like campaign songs for him. In addition, there was "We Are Coming Father Abraham, 600,000 More" and "Rally Round the Cause, Boys."

The Democrats sang back "Little Mac Shall Be Restored" and "Little Mac! Little Mac! You're the Very Man." Many lyrics lambasted Lincoln for his liberation efforts, as in "Fight for the Nigger."

Paraphernalia   The 1860 folksy images of Lincoln as "The Railsplitter" and "Honest Old Abe" were not sufficient this time. Items more often stressed the Union, freedom, and the war effort. Ribbons heralded "Lincoln and Johnson, Union and Liberty" and "Union Forever."

McClellan's side also emphasized the Union, as well as their candidate's past efforts to preserve it. Tokens showed him in his military uniform with such inscriptions as "One Flag and One Union Now and Forever."

Popular Labels   Lincoln was known as the "Great Emancipator," "Uncle Abe," and "Old Abe."

McClellan liked to be called "Little Napoleon." He was also "Little Mac."

Name-calling   To opponents, Lincoln was "Lincoln the Last," the "Illinois Ape," "The Tyrant," and "Prince of Jesters."

McClellan was belittled as "Tardy George," and "Mac the Unready."

The Press   The Democratic New York *World* denounced the Lincoln-Johnson ticket as "a rail-splitting buffoon and a boorish tailor, both from the backwoods, both growing up in uncouth ignorance."

The Richmond *Dispatch*, headquartered in the Confederate capital, weighed in with its opinion about the Democrats: "They are as bitterly opposed to separation as Lincoln himself, or any of the thieves and murderers who lead his armies."

Cartoons   The appearance of *Harper's Weekly* in 1857 and *Vanity Fair* in 1859 provided an outlet for a new generation of cartoonists who used a freer style and more caricature than their predecessors. During this period Thomas Nast began in *Harper's* two decades of graphic humor on behalf of the Republicans.

First   The first general election for any nation during a major civil war.

Trends   No subject was too sensitive for the political arena.

"Don't Swap Horses" became a well-worn campaign sentiment.

Vote   Of the thirty-six states, nine seceded Southern states chose not to appoint any electors. Results were counted in twenty-five Northern and border states (elections in Louisiana and Tennessee had been denied validity).

Lincoln won 212 electoral votes and 2,206,938 popular votes (55 percent) to 21 and 1,803,787 (45 percent) for McClellan.

Benchmarks   Lincoln's percentage of the popular vote was the highest since Jackson's in 1828.

The Union (formerly Republican) party proved itself as strong as any political party had been.

Eleven Southern states did not participate in the election.

Quote   General Ulysses S. Grant telegraphed Lincoln after the election: "The election having passed off quietly, no bloodshed or riot throughout the land, is worth more to the country than a battle won."

★ ★ ★

As a warrior president, Abraham Lincoln was about to take the nation where it had not been before: into a general election during a period of civil war. At times Lincoln doubted not only his own chances but also the country's ability to pursue democracy without peace.

The bloody Battle of Bull Run woke the North to the enormous task ahead, but it would still be years before the war played favorites. Youthful and slow George "Mac the Unready" McClellan, general in chief of the Union army, was beaten back from Richmond, the Confederate capital, in the spring of 1862 by his counterpart, masterful Robert E. Lee with "Stonewall" Jackson at his side. Blood was spilling. A few months later at a second Bull Run, Union forces were defeated once again. On September 17 at Antietam, Maryland, McClellan, demoted to commander of the Army of the Potomac, scored in one of the bloodiest battles of the war. He was able to push Lee back across the Potomac but was removed from command for not pursuing him.

Antietam was a sufficient victory to give Lincoln a platform from which to issue the Emancipation Proclamation. While it made slaves "forever free" only in rebellious states, Lincoln believed such a step toward abolition would help "to save this Union" by adding a moral tone to the war and maybe the military might of freed blacks to the North's cause. But delighted Democrats thought it would eventually strengthen their hand against the president.

The battles and blood continued while a Northern general who did not know the meaning of *quit* made Lincoln look westward. In April 1862 at Shiloh Church in Tennessee, "Unconditional Surrender" Grant had fought until his side won. Grant went on to take Vicksburg on the Mississippi River in July 1863, effectively severing one part of the South from the other.

About the time Grant was storming Vicksburg his ultimate enemy Lee was commanding a Confederate charge on Gettysburg, Pennsylvania. Lee's decision to send 15,000 infantry at the heart of the Union forces was a mistake. On November 19 the president traveled to Gettysburg to deliver a simple ten-sentence address, saying that "these dead shall not have died in vain."

Amid mixed public emotions Republicans, who were now calling themselves the National Union party to include outsiders, convened in June 1864 and readily renominated Lincoln for a second term. The president wanted and got Andrew Johnson, a pro-war Democrat, as his running mate. It became the "Abe and Andy" ticket, supported by marching bands, torchlight parades, and freedom songs. But Lincoln knew that people were becoming tired of a war that was not won and even his advisers were talking defeat at the polls.

The Democrats held their convention in Chicago in August and, led by the so-called Copperhead faction, decided to run an antiwar platform. General George McClellan, who had proved popular with the men in the field although not with Lincoln, agreed to be their standard-bearer—at a price. In his acceptance letter, McClellan repudiated his party's platform, writing "The Union must be preserved." Ironically, this boosted his stock.

In spite of the war, the campaign went on and became as bitter as any. McClellan was accused of being a "traitor" and a "coward." The Democratic platform, argued Republicans, "gives a silent approval of the Rebellion itself." Lincoln was called a "tyrant" and a "dictator" for suspending the writ of habeas corpus during the war. Democrats cried that lives were being sacrificed not for the Union but for "degraded negro slaves" and warned that Lincoln's reelection would extend the war four years or more. They circulated stories about how "Abe, the vulgar joker" had asked to be sung a "lively" song as he toured a battlefield where "the dead were piled highest." And they used an anonymous, scholarly-sounding pamphlet against the Republicans. Titled "Miscegenation: The Theory of the Blending of the Races," it stated that grafting black stock onto white would make "the finest race on earth."

The party in power had the advantage. Government clerks were often used to send out campaign literature and all federal employees, postmasters to cabinet officers, were expected to contribute to the president's campaign chest. War contractors were also tapped for funds and came in with some big contributions.

But the campaign really had to be won on the battlefield. Gettysburg was a beginning but by no means the end. In the following months, the Union blues, including new black recruits, pursued the Confederate grays without clear-cut victories. Grant hunted Lee in the Wilderness area of Virginia during May and June of 1864, pushing until as many as half of his hundred thousand men were killed; Lee lost about half of his, some twenty-five thousand. Blood kept on spilling on June 3, when Grant ordered an impossible attack on Cold Harbor and seven thousand died in just a few minutes. Finally, on September 3, Lincoln held in his hand the word he had waited for—a short dispatch from General William Tecumseh Sherman that read: "Atlanta is ours and fairly won." The South had lost.

In October Lincoln was at the War Telegraph Office, a favorite haunt of his during the war and, having in his head the number of electoral votes of each state, grabbed a piece of telegraph paper and a pencil and started calculating. Listing each state and its votes, he came up with a total of 117 for himself and 114 for McClellan. A friend came over and added three to his column for the Nevada that he forgot. The President knew that he would win, but the size of his vote would surprise him. In his second inaugural address, Lincoln asked to bind up the nation's wounds "with malice toward none, with charity to all." For some strange reason, Mary Todd Lincoln had felt uneasy and ordered a thousand dollars' worth of mourning clothes.

ULYSSES S. GRANT

★ CAMPAIGN OF 1868 ★

Major Candidates　Ulysses S. Grant, Illinois, 46, Republican
　　　　　　　　　Horatio Seymour, New York, 58, Democrat

Credentials　Grant, a career military officer, served in the Mexican War (1846–1848) and the Civil War (1861–1865), becoming lieutenant general and commander of all Union armies in 1864 and then general of the army in 1866, the first general to hold that rank since George Washington. He filled in as secretary of war (1867–1868).

Seymour was a New York state assemblyman (1842 and 1844–1845) and then governor of New York (1853–1854 and 1863–1864).

Tickets　The Republicans convened in Chicago three months after Radical Republicans in the House had voted to impeach President Andrew Johnson for "high crimes and misdemeanors" and a week after his acquittal in the Senate. With the president completely out of the picture, a few names were in the air, but only General Ulysses S. Grant's name was placed in nomination and he won unanimously on the first ballot. House Speaker Schuyler Colfax was selected for the vice-presidential slot.

The Democrats met, unified after the Civil War, in New York. There were forty-eight potential candidates, including charismatic George Pendleton of Ohio, the vice-presidential candidate four years earlier; President Johnson; Francis Blair of Missouri, a former Republican; and Pennsylvania's General Winfield S. Hancock. After considerable jockeying a compromise candidate, convention chairman Horatio Seymour, was cajoled into accepting the nomination. After a further bit of back-room maneuvering, the vice-presidential slot went to Blair.

Campaign Notes The "party of Lincoln" waged a cautious campaign, not wanting to make any mistakes and lose the great advantages it possessed at the outset. For the most part, Grant refused to campaign or say anything about issues.

In 1868 the Democrats started out way behind, and knew it. By October the party's prospects were so dim that many urged switching horses in midstream. But party chiefs decided to stop trying to re-do the convention, and Seymour undertook a tour through major cities in Pennsylvania, Ohio, Indiana, New York, and Illinois.

Symbols Grant's people used Union military themes and songs. His "segar" (cigar) was an instantly recognizable symbol. Republicans even played up Grant's tannery experience with little mock tanneries and figurines of "The Tanner of Galena," showing Grant in a black leather-tanner's apron.

Democrats relied on the "Democratic Rooster" to crow the praises of their candidates.

Slogans Republicans dared their rivals to "Match Him." The most widely used slogan was borrowed from Grant's plea in his nomination acceptance speech: "Let us have Peace."

Democrats pleaded "One Currency for the Bondholder and the Plowholder," "Reduce Taxation before Taxation Reduces Us," and, more controversial, "White Men to Govern the Restoration of Constitutional Liberty."

Songs Republicans sang "The Sword of Ulysses," "Brave U.S.G.," "Grant, the Daring, the Lion-hearted," "The Man Who Saved the Nation," and "For Grant and the Union," among several others.

Democrats crooned "Union and Justice," "The Irish Volunteers," and "The White Man's Banner."

Paraphernalia In 1868 the Republicans literally showered the voters with medals, badges, pins, buttons, ribbons, flags, banners, and trinkets. Cigar cases with the candidate's name and bust were an effective reminder of Grant's trademark "segar." Military-theme ribbons listed major battles and such paeans to Grant as "First in the Hearts of His Soldiers." A much-sought-after item was an army knapsack pin that opened to a military bust portrait.

Democrats' paraphernalia was low-key: with some medalets, ribbons, and prints.

Popular Labels   Grant was hailed as "Unconditional Surrender," the "Man from Appomattox," "The Tanner of Galena."
Seymour was the "Man of Peace."

Name-calling   Grant was "the Drunkard," "the Butcher," "the Speculator," and "the Dummy Candidate."
Seymour was "The Great Decliner" because he had repeatedly turned down the nomination.

Curious Fact   Seymour might have been the most reluctant nominee ever. He wept in frustration again and again at being nominated against his wishes, but was persuaded by friends to accept what fate, and (rumor said) New York Democratic party leader Samuel Tilden handed to him.

Spending   The Republicans reported spending upwards of $150,000, almost twice the expenditures of Seymour's Democrats.

First   The first election in which freed Southern blacks voted.

Trends   Republican domination of postwar politics.
New black voters were overwhelmingly Republican.

Vote   Of the thirty-seven states, three Southern states were still "unreconstructed"—not yet readmitted to representation in Congress. Grant won 214 electoral votes and 3,013,421 popular votes (52.7 percent) to 80 and 2,706,829 (47.3 percent) for Seymour.

Benchmark   Suffragette Susan B. Anthony asked the Democratic convention to support women's right to vote, but was laughed into silence.

Quote   After the election, one headline screamed THE SECOND REBELLION CLOSED.

G RANT'S acceptance plea "Let Us Have Peace" reflected a genuine sentiment within the "party of victory," but, on the other hand, party managers were not above waving the bloody shirt and, in other ways, keeping the specter of sectionalism and treason alive, if that was what winning the presidency required. Voters were urged to "Vote as you shot." The *New York Tribune* claimed: "Scratch a Democrat and You'll Find a Rebel under his Skin." The Democrats, too, were determined to use the campaign to limit the political costs of having lost the Civil War.

As the 1860 and 1864 campaigns had been about war—whether it was to come and then when it was to end—that of 1868 was about the peace: whether it was to come and how painful it was to be for the losers. While some talked of tariffs and greenback activists, who wanted an expansion of the money supply, spoke in terms of rich versus poor, the main issue was Republican Reconstruction of the South, particularly the extension of the vote to freed blacks. Moderates had prevailed against Radicals in the Republican convention, winning the adoption of a compromise platform plank that supported black suffrage in the South only, leaving the North on its own.

Even so, the Democrats played on widespread racism in both parties by waving "The White Man's Banner," predicting that "we will raise and conquer with it, too!" They portrayed Reconstruction as an unconstitutional invasion of the South by a locust plague of carpetbaggers, who posed as friends of the freed blacks simply to get their votes in order to consolidate control of the federal government. Racial tensions led to race riots in Eastern cities and lynching rampages of the Ku Klux Klan throughout the South.

There was plenty of personal pillorying of the candidates as well. Grant was widely lampooned as a boozer, a speculator, an anti-Semite, and a "butcher." He was accused of wartime atrocities at Andersonville, of excessive ambition in uniform, and of intemperate public drunkenness. An order he issued in 1862 expelling Jews from his command in Mississippi, an order conforming with a Washington policy of retaliating against individuals who were found to be "trading with the enemy," was resurrected and used to flog him in the press. Republican vice-presidential candidate Colfax was accused of harboring Know-Nothing anti-Catholic views.

Life was no gentler for Democratic candidates. In 1863, as mayor of New York, Seymour had addressed draft rioters as "my friends" and Republicans alleged that this "proved" his lurking treasonous Copperhead sympathies. His father's suicide was used to "prove" a history of family suicide. Seymour's running mate Blair was labeled "a spoon stealer," a "revolutionist," and a drunkard.

Perhaps to demonstrate his own sobriety, Grant did meet with various delegations at his home in Galena, Illinois, where he waited out the campaign. Though making no speeches, he took several short trips to Kentucky, Colorado, Missouri, and Ohio. In general, though, Grant let others work their magic. Party-sponsored "tanner" clubs emphasized Grant's humble origins, military daring and brilliance, and deep American roots. Much was made of the fact that Grant's great-grandfather had died in action during the French and Indian War and that his grandfather had fought at Bunker Hill. "Boys in Blue" marched in torchlight parades in support of their hero. Party songs promised that Grant would "make the nation brighten up/Just like his own segar." The Democrats responded by warning voters about "a man on horseback."

No doubt figuring that nothing was to be lost by trying to fool all of the people all of the time, some Democrats courted newly enfranchised Southern blacks. An article in a Southern paper entitled "The Colored Voter: A Sober Appeal to His Interest and His Sober Reason" said, in part: "If your State and her sister Southern States had not seceded from the Union you would not today have been free . . . which of the two parties has the greater claim on you for your support? The Democratic Party!''

By early September the Democrats were in trouble. The New York *World* led the ground swell for a new candidate, insisting that honor demanded Seymour and Blair step down for two men who had any chance of winning. Seymour held his ground but did feel compelled to take to the hustings in October, if only to show voters that he was a sane, sober fellow. He campaigned from New York to Chicago, covering Buffalo, Cleveland, Columbus, Pittsburgh, and the state of Indiana, following a route mapped out by Andrew Johnson's 1866 ''swing around the circle'' to sell his Reconstruction strategy. Reports of vicious and unprovoked killings of Southern blacks by vigilante groups undermined Seymour's efforts to reassure Northern voters that his party was sufficiently chastened by the recent war and ready to accept political as well as military defeat. Though Seymour was a well-regarded orator, the hastily arranged speaking tour left him with only one or two boilerplate speeches, which he continuously recycled.

The Republicans won decisively in the electoral column but by only a margin of 300,000 popular votes. It became clear that newly enfranchised black votes had been crucial and that to make further inroads in the South, they would need more. Right after the election, Republicans set their sights on getting the Fifteenth Amendment, giving black males the right to vote, passed. As preparations for the inauguration began, Grant informed the planners that he would not ride with President Johnson to the Capitol or even speak to him. Johnson chose to stay at the White House working while Grant, seated alone, rode off in his carriage to take the oath of office. He told those assembled: ''The responsibilities of the position I feel, but accept them without fear.''

★ CAMPAIGN OF 1872 ★

Major Candidates   Ulysses S. Grant, Illinois, 50, Republican
Horace Greeley, New York, 61, Liberal Republican/
Democrat

Credentials   For Grant, see Campaign of 1868. He was elected president in 1868.

Greeley, founder of the *New York Tribune* in 1841, helped start the Republican party in 1854.

Convention Tickets   The Republicans met in Philadelphia and unanimously renominated President Ulysses S. Grant on the first ballot with all 752 votes.

Grant's incumbent vice-president, Schuyler Colfax, was dropped because of his involvement in the just-breaking Crédit Mobilier scandal, something that might have been forgiven had he not revealed to Grant his own presidential aspirations. Massachusetts Senator and co-founder of the Free Soil party Henry Wilson was selected on the second ballot.

Unhappy with "Uncle Sam" Grant, Liberal Republicans walked out of the party and into their own convention in Cincinnati. More than four thousand delegates met to see a runoff between Charles Francis Adams of Massachusetts, son of former President John Quincy Adams, and New York editor Horace Greeley. Greeley won on the sixth ballot. The vice-presidential slot went to Missouri governor B. Gratz Brown.

The Democrats convened in Baltimore without a candidate. After only six hours of discussion, the Liberal Republican platform was adopted intact and Greeley was nominated. But Greeley did not satisfy all the Democrats and some bolted.

Campaign Notes Grant's campaign managers wanted to keep the support of newly enfranchised blacks, who had helped them win in 1868, and so appointed former slave and leading abolitionist Frederick Douglass to a federal post and sent black campaign speakers to key areas.

After losing in September state elections, the Liberal Republican/Democratic coalition sent Greeley out to campaign, although it was still not quite the acceptable thing to do. He gave more than two hundred speeches, talking up the Grant scandals and talking down the Civil War, as he preached bridging "the bloody chasm."

Victoria Woodhull, who ran for president on Equal Rights Party ticket with Frederick Douglass as her running mate also took to the stump, preaching woman suffrage and reform, but was often ridiculed as an advocate of "free love."

Symbol Grant's cigar held its own; Greeley's white parson's hat became the emblem of his supporters.

Slogans Republicans yelled "Grant Us Another Term" and "Grant, Wilson & Prosperity." Opponents wanted to "Turn the Rascals Out."

Greeley supporters called for "Universal Amnesty, Impartial Suffrage," and "Liberty, Equality and Fraternity."

Songs Republicans sang "We'll Fight on the Line," "The Fighting Tanner," and "Ulysses Tried and True." They taunted Greeley for his belief in Fourierism, a brand of utopian socialism, in "Hurrah! Hurrah for Grant and Wilson!" and also chorused "Goosey Greeley" and "Greedy or Greeley."

Greeley supporters crooned about "Farmer Greeley" and hailed "The Wise Man of the East," "The Old White Hat and Coat," and sang of his difference with Grant: "Horace had no relations / To fill the public stations."

HORACE GREELEY

Paraphernalia The "Boys in Blue" marched for Grant carrying paper Chinese lanterns. Less peripatetic supporters expressed themselves through prints, banners, ribbons, small trinkets, and lapel pins, most of which emphasized Grant's military prowess.

Democrats and Liberal Republicans boasted their choice on buttons and tokens acclaiming "The Sage of Chappaqua" (the New York City suburb where Greeley had a house and farm). His trademark parson's hat was adorned with ribbons, in one case also showing two clasped hands representing sectional reconciliation. Supporters also wore badges shaped like quill pens inscribed with "The Pen Is Mightier than the Sword."

Popular Labels Grant was—fondly—"Uncle Sam," "The Soldier's Friend," and "Ulysses the Invincible."

Greeley was "Old Honest Horace," "Our Uncle Horace," "Old White Coat," "The Chappaqua Farmer," "The Sage of Chappaqua," and "The Old Tree Chopper."

Name-calling Detractors attacked "Useless Grant" as "Caesar," "Dictator," "Loafer," "Swindler," "Ignoramus," "Utterly depraved horse jockey," and militaristic "man on horseback."

Greeley was attacked as a Copperhead "doughface" and "the stalking horse of the secessionists." His penchant for fringe causes gave him the name "the Quack" or, more respectfully, "Dr. Quack."

The Press   The *New York Sun* called the race "a shower of mud."

Spending   Republicans reported spending $250,000 to $50,000 for the Democrats.

Firsts   Victoria Woodhull became the first woman in U.S. history to seek the presidency.
    Susan B. Anthony cast the first woman's vote in a national election. New York City police arrested her, and she was fined $100.
    A presidential candidate died before the electoral votes were cast.

Trends   Continued role of dissident wings of the parties.
    Liberal Republican reform proposals on the civil service and the tariff have an impact.

Vote   With thirty-seven states voting (but the votes of Louisiana and Arkansas were not counted in because of irregularities) Grant received 286 electoral votes and 3,596,745 (55.6 percent) to 66 (although Greeley, who died between the popular vote and the meeting of the electoral college, was never awarded them) and 2,843,446 (43.9 percent).

Benchmark   Grant won the highest number of electoral votes in U.S. history up to that point and was not surpassed until McKinley with 292 in 1900, when there were forty-five states.

Quotes   Greeley called himself "the worst beaten man who ever ran for high office."

IN 1868, the popular military hero Ulysses S. Grant had been wooed by both Democrats and Republicans to head their party. But, following a term of incompetence and scandals, Grant's own party was bitterly divided on renomination, so much so that liberal foes made common cause with Democrats, backing an ill-suited, eccentric candidate, Horace Greeley, the muckraking editor of the *New York Tribune*. The result was odd indeed. Greeley in his paper had tarred Democrats as horse thieves, traitors, and "all saloon keepers." Now, too, Northeastern liberals were turning up "in bed with" Southern "race-baiting" Democrats, partners in "Anything to Beat Grant."

    "A great soldier might be a baby politician," rued historian Henry Adams, the descendant of two presidents, when he saw that Grant was filling his cabinet with his best cronies instead of the best men. Grant appeared to be personally scandal-free, although he was certainly guilty of nepotism, patronage, and inattention to the dishonesty that thrived under him. "The Gilded Age," as Mark Twain and Charles Dudley Warner called post-Civil War society, was an age of miscreants, "robber barons," and "Boss" Tweed with all that glitters as their goal. There was the gold scam, dreamed up by millionaires "Jubilee Jim" Fisk and Jay Gould, in which the price of the metal was bid up with the aid of Grant's brother-in-law until the Treasury belatedly released its hoards. There was the Whiskey Ring, in which government officials made themselves tipsy with illegal profits. And there was Crédit Mobilier, the largest of the scandals, in which two congressman and the vice president were found with unpaid-for stock certificates in their back pockets.

Liberal Republicans and Democrats attacked Grant's sordid and disastrous first term, singing "His nephews and his cousins all came up to win the race / And every man who gave a dog / Was sure to get a place." They vilified him as a power-hungry Caesar and tried to forge a coalition of veterans, workers, immigrants, and reform advocates. But Liberals splintered in the course of the campaign, hated themselves for nominating Greeley, and tried to get him to withdraw in favor of a winner. The Democrats continued to bicker over their decision to fuse with Republicans and the Straight Outs, the Democrats who did not, attacked Grant and Greeley as forcing a choice between "hemlock and strychnine."

The Republicans' strongest argument for "Grant us another term" was the quixotic figure of Greeley. His ever-present steel-rimmed spectacles, old white coat, tall white parson's hat, and green umbrella made him an easy target, as did the sometimes eccentric causes he embraced like vegetarianism, atheism, free love, and communalism. Foes ridiculed him as a "white-hatted, lost-cause fanatic" and a "make-believe farmer." More serious charges of treason were bandied about because Greeley had been one of the signers of a bail bond to release Confederate president Jefferson Davis from jail, prompting Republicans to rant: "Grant beat Davis—Greeley bailed him."

Greeley's tendency to embrace eccentric schemes convinced campaign managers of the wisdom of keeping him off the hustings. Thinking that the tide was turning in his favor that summer, Greeley agreed. Early returns in August and September caused him to change his mind. Greeley followed his own famous advice ("Go West, young man") and took the stump to deliver his message. Ironically, it was the same one Grant had run on four years earlier: "Let us have peace." However, the "incendiary" style of his campaign, as *The New York Times* put it, made the handshake of peace seem anything but. He stereotyped blacks as "ignorant, deceived and misguided" for not backing him and said that while he had once been an antislavery crusader, "That might have been a mistake!" He toured Kentucky, Indiana, Ohio, New Jersey, and Pennsylvania, making a record number of speeches each day, but, unfortunately, did not target his audiences well and ended up urging sectional reconciliation to Northern veterans. His vice-presidential running mate knew his audiences better but often arrived too intoxicated to talk straight.

Grant in the main kept a low profile, avoiding political appearances almost entirely. His habit of thinking out loud and a life-long tendency to mumble convinced Grant that "I am no speaker, and don't want to be beaten" by those more skilled in the arts of oratory. Superior organization and better fund-raising gave the Republicans the edge. Critical states like Ohio, Indiana, and Pennsylvania were inundated with speakers, campaign literature, and lots of "spending money." Liberal Republicans could not compete, and it seemed at times they were more interested in letting "Useless Grant" know how angry they were than in doing what was needed to win.

The face of politicking changed in this campaign through the sharp pencil of cartoonist Thomas Nast. Known for helping to bring down the Tweed Ring ("them damn pictures," Tweed had screamed), Nast took after Greeley in 1872. Drawing him as disheveled with thick eyeglasses and carrying around such pamphlets as "What I Know About Liars" and "What I Know About Eating My Own Words," he aided the image of Greeley as vacillating, unprincipled, and a pawn of Southern racists. Rival cartoonist Matt Morgan of *Frank Leslie's Illustrated Weekly* produced vicious caricatures of a boozing incompetent president, unable to make his way out of his own cigar smoke except to lay claim to "gifts" from "admirers."

After all the "nastiness" Grant won an epic victory, holding on to support from freedmen, veterans, ethnic and labor groups, and—predictably—business interests. Greeley had the support only of white Southerners and middle-class reform groups. Many agreed with *Nation* editor Edwin Godkin that the voters cast their "contempt for Greeley" rather than love for Grant.

★ CAMPAIGN OF 1876 ★

Major Candidates   Rutherford B. Hayes, 54, Ohio, Republican
Samuel J. Tilden, 62, New York, Democrat

Credentials   Hayes served in the army during the Civil War (1861–1865), rising to major general, became a member of the House of Representatives (1865–1867) and governor of Ohio (1868–1872, 1876–1877).

Tilden, as chairman of the New York Democratic committee (1866–1876), became known for heading the prosecution and bringing the infamous Tweed Ring to justice. He became governor of New York (1874–1876).

Convention Tickets   The Republicans met in Cincinnati with most of the errant Liberal Republicans back in the fold. The front runners represented the three factions of the party: Radical leader New York Senator Roscoe Conkling; House Speaker James G. Blaine of Maine, leader of the "Half-Breeds"; and Reform champion Kentucky's Benjamin Bristow, former sec-

RUTHERFORD B. HAYES

retary of the treasury, best known for going after the Whiskey Ring. Blaine broke away from the rest on the first ballot but dark horse Rutherford Hayes from electorally important Ohio finally bested Blaine on the seventh ballot. New York representative William A. Wheeler was named by acclamation as the vice-presidential candidate.

The Democrats convened in St. Louis, and it was immediately a two-way contest between New York governor Samuel Tilden and Indiana governor Thomas A. Hendricks. Tilden began well ahead on the first ballot and by the second nabbed the nomination. Hendricks, the Independent Democratic nominee in 1872 and a Greenback (paper-money advocate), had to settle for the second spot on the ticket.

The Greenback party ran a candidate of its own, businessman and philanthropist Peter Cooper of New York.

Campaign Notes The Grant administration, worried about the vote in Tilden's New York, where Tammany Hall made a practice of stretching it for its needs, spent $80,000 in an effort to track votes. There were detailed street maps, four thousand registration books, and alphabetical indexes, all to keep tabs on voters.

To sway voters, Republicans put together an elaborate "campaign textbook" that included party positions, a biography of the candidate, his acceptance letter, and much praise for the current administration.

Democrats turned professional too, their "campaign textbook" telling all one had to know about corruption in high places, plus Democratic party and candidate information.

Symbols   *Harper's Weekly* cartoonist Thomas Nast first used the elephant to represent the Republican vote. At this time, Nast portrayed the Democrats as a donkey as well as a tiger. Neither was intended to laud the parties, but over time were appropriated by them and transformed into instantly recognizable, endearing symbols.

Slogans   Hayes supporters hailed "Our Centennial President." In the best "bloody shirt" tradition of identifying the Democrats as the party of treason and rebellion, they shouted "Avoid Rebel Rule," "Vote As You Shot," and "The Boys in Blue Will See It Through."

Tilden's men answered back "Honest T. Is the Best Policy," "Turn the Rascals Out," "Let Us Have a Clean Sweep," and "Hayes, Hard Money and Hard Times."

Songs: The "bloody shirt" was bloody popular in Republican songs too, as the Republicans belted out "Our Watchword," "We'll Fight Traitors to the Death," "Hurrah! for the Army Blue," "Empty Sleeve," and "The Boys In Blue."

The Democrats sang of scandal and depression, the Republican brand, in "Tilden and Reform," "The Times Are Sadly Out of Joint," and "Hold the Fort for Tilden."

Paraphernalia: Both parties had lapel badges, ribbons, tokens, and the like, but a lot less than usual because of the 1873–1874 nationwide depression.

The Republicans sported "Boys in Blue" ribbons and held high "Boys in Blue" banners. They also had "Honest Money/Honest Government" tokens.

Democrats sang their own praises in song and joke books, and reinforced their reform slogans with medals shaped like long-handled brooms that could be worn as a pin with *Reform* inscribed on the handle.

Popular Labels   Hayes was "Brave Rutherford."

Tilden was "Uncle Sam," "The Sage of Greystone" (his home estate), and "The Aggressive Leader of Reform."

Name-calling   Hayes was "The Great Unknown."

Tilden's corporate law career made him "The Great Forecloser" and "Slippery Sam."

Spending   The Republicans reported spending $950,000 to $900,000 for the Democrats.

First   The first time major parties nominated incumbent governors for president.

Trend   The merchandising of candidates.

Vote   Thirty-eight states voted, but the election was in doubt between November 8 and March 2 (see the campaign narrative, below). "The Compromise of 1877" finally made Hayes the winner with 185 electoral votes and 4,036,572 (48 percent) to 184 and 4,284,020 (51 percent) for Tilden. Greenback's Cooper received no electoral and 81,737 popular votes.

Benchmarks   The most disputed election in history, with the highest voter turnout ever.

Hayes was truly a minority president, without even a plurality of popular votes.

Black leader Frederick Douglass spoke at the Republican convention on racial equality.

Quotes   Of the election result, Tilden noted: "I shall receive from posterity the credit of having been elected to the highest position in the gift of the people, without any of the cares and responsibilities of the office."

IT was America's hundreth birthday and James Russell Lowell was not alone in thinking there was little to show for it. On the occasion of Philadelphia's Centennial Exposition in May, where others also exhibited their gifts to mankind, Lowell's lyrics were biting: "Columbia, puzzled what she should display / Of true home make on her Centennial day, / Was urged to exhibit scandals, graft and rings, / And challenge Europe to produce such things." But once the Centennial doors opened, proof was there of American ingenuity, unstifled by "Grantism" and all that that implied. An odd-looking "typewriter" was on display and a contraption called the telephone. America, for better and worse, was also moving west, pushing the proud Sioux and other Indian tribes out of the way and making railroads the steel bridges from coast to coast. And America's first class of multimillionaires, from Andrew Carnegie to John D. Rockefeller, was dreaming of ways to make more money and dreaming up the business trust.

In this climate the race of 1876 began, with the major parties pieced together again after splintering in 1872 and both selling "reform" candidates. Rutherford B. Hayes won the Republican nomination over the dashing but suspect speaker of the house James G. Blaine because he was from the right state and had the right credentials. Hayes' Ohio was a swing state, ranking third in electoral votes. He was Blaine's opposite in personality as well as the perception of virtue. While Blaine was either loved or hated, Hayes, wrote contemporary Henry Adams, was "a third-rate nonentity, whose only recommendation is that he is obnoxious to no one." Hayes also had fought and been wounded several times, once seriously, in the Civil War, whereas Blaine could only talk about other brave "Boys in Blue" and was ridiculed as "invisible in war, invincible in peace."

Once theirs, Republican leaders decided to keep Hayes at home and mostly quiet during the campaign. They played up his military scars in the battle for Antietam and the like, hoping to hold on to the soldier vote and keep the "rebel rule" issue alive. Hayes felt that the party's strategy should be to wave the bloody shirt once again. And so "Boys in Blue" clubs sang louder than ever about "the blood of half a million Noble Union men" and the rank and file labeled their Democratic opponents "rebel traitors" and "Confederate thieves."

Above all, Hayes said, he wanted to deflect attention from "our deadliest foe," the issue of hard times. Coupled with the scandals of the Grant years was the depression of 1873–1874. It was precipitated by the collapse of financier Jay Cooke's banking empire and rippled to about fifteen thousand other businesses. Democrats could not resist waving this soiled shirt in front of voters and singing "Workmen idle, begging, starving, / Suffering from every ill." Democrats also made a point of emphasizing the best aspects of nominee Samuel Tilden, playing down such handicaps as his poor health from a recent stroke, past railroad deals and tax avoidance, and ties to Tammany Hall. They highlighted his reforming zeal as the prosecutor of the Tweed Ring and even his permanent bachelorhood. They also continued their talk of scandal in the Grant administration, helped by details of the Whiskey Ring's four-million-dollar profit at public expense and the secretary of war's windfall from selling army trading posts, reminding voters that now, more than ever, was the time to "Turn the Rascals Out!"

Rhetoric aside, there was not really that much difference between the two candidates. Both Hayes and Tilden ranked as reformers. Both trusted hard money more than greenbacks and both wanted to see an end to Reconstruction in the South. Despite the similarities, more voters then ever flocked to the polls, a phenomenon that became known as the "Gilded Age paradox."

Hayes, for his part, went to bed election night sure he had lost. He awoke to an historic deadlock. The resolution of it was so controversial and bitter that it could only compare with the 1824 tiebreaker between John Adams and Andrew Jackson, ending in "The Corrupt Bargain." Tilden led by about 250,000 popular votes, but the election turned on contested electoral votes in Louisiana, South Carolina, Florida, plus one in Oregon. The three southern states had each filed two sets of returns, one for Tilden and one for Hayes. The slow filtering in of results gave rise to the expression "Another county heard from." In these states as elsewhere, both parties had engaged in widespread vote-stealing. Republican "Radical Rogues" miscounted votes and doled out money to people, dead and alive, who voted "right." Democrats "Ku-Kluxed" blacks or "bulldozed" them away from polls.

When the deadlock continued an electoral commission was set up and, in a compromise, gave the twenty disputed electoral votes to Hayes, securing his win by just one electoral vote. Democrats ranted about "The Great

Fraud" and "The Crime of '76" and Hayes was belittled as "His Fraudulency." In reality, though, "The Compromise of 1877" gave the party out of power much of what it wanted. The remaining carpetbag governments fell from power when President Hayes pulled out the federal troops propping them up, the federal government backed off on enforcement of the Fourteenth and Fifteenth amendments that had given some equality to blacks, and Hayes placed in his cabinet a former Confederate general and Southern Democrat. It was an uneasy solution to a national crisis. But, as Tilden's manager noted, "I prefer four years of Hayes' administration to four years of civil war."

★ CAMPAIGN OF 1880 ★

Major Candidates   James A. Garfield, 49, Ohio, Republican
Winfield S. Hancock, 56, Pennsylvania, Democrat

Credentials   Garfield was an Ohio state senator (1859–1861), joined the Union Army (1861–1863), becoming a major general, and served in the House of Representatives (1863–1880), acting as House minority leader from 1877.

Hancock, a career military officer, served in the Mexican War (1846–1848) and the Civil War (1861–1865). He became military governor of Louisiana and Texas (1865–1868), took command of the Dakota Territory (1869–1872) and then assumed control of the army's Atlantic Division (1872–1880).

Convention Tickets   When the Republicans gathered in Chicago the "Stalwarts," the conservative faction, were set on "resurrecting" President Ulysses S. Grant, while the "Half-Breeds" or moderates were backing now-senator James G. Blaine. A defeat of the unit rule, which would have required state delegations to vote as a bloc and given the big states to Grant, ended the former president's chances, but it took thirty-six ballots to nominate James Garfield, head of the Ohio delegation, even though he had not consented to being nominated, thus becoming a "draft" candidate. Since Garfield sided more with the Half-Breeds, Stalwart Chester Arthur, the deposed collector of the Port of New York, was readily nominated for the vice-presidential slot on the first ballot.

When the Democrats convened in Cincinnati Samuel Tilden, the 1876 nominee, had not yet announced that he would not be a candidate, but after the first ballot, where the front-runner was General Winfield Scott, Tilden sent word that he was out of the race, and Scott won on the second ballot. The vice-presidential slot went to former representative William English, the only candidate, by acclamation.

JAMES A. GARFIELD

The Greenback-Labor party nominated Representative James Weaver of Iowa and the Prohibition party also put up a ticket.

Campaign Notes Garfield was a campaigner. For his 1866 congressional campaign he had gone 7,500 miles and given some sixty-five speeches. In 1876 he had some out on the hustings for Hayes. He liked voter contact and so, in this campaign, engaged in an early form of "front porch" campaigning by giving a few set speeches to groups that came by rail to his home in Mentor, Ohio.

Hancock did little to promote his own candidacy and did not even get across his own heroic past very well.

Symbols The Republicans used the barge to remind voters of Garfield's humble beginnings as a canal boy. Democrats used the rebus of a hand and a rooster for their candidate Hancock. The elephant and the donkey also got play.

Slogans Republicans applauded "The Canal Boy President," "Purity and Patriotism," "With Garfield We'll Conquer Again," and "From the Tow Path to the White House."

Democrats shouted "Hancock Was Superb!" mimicking General George

McClellan's comment after the battle of Gettysburg, "A Superb Soldier—A Model President," and "Tariff for Revenue Only."

Songs Republicans sang songs of praise like "Jim Garfield of the West" and again waved the bloody shirt in "All Are Ready for the Fray," "When the Johnnies Get into Power," and the bilingual German-American "The Veteran's Vote." A parody titled "Now I Am the Leader of the Democracee" was written to the tune of the Gilbert and Sullivan patter song "When I Was a Lad" from *H.M.S. Pinafore,* which had premiered in the U.S. 1879.

Democrats played up reform once again in "Hancock Is Coming." They also sang about "The Bleached Shirt" of national unity and ridiculed Garfield in "Sir James' Song" to another Gilbert and Sullivan tune.

Paraphernalia Garfield's side wore miniature flag and log-cabin lapel ornaments. Nostalgia for the heady 1840s campaigns brought back the bandanna showing portraits of Garfield and Arthur with the legend "The Union and the Constitution Forever." One decorative ribbon hailed the "Towpathers' Ticket" and another saluted Garfield as "Farmer/Scholar/Soldier/Statesman."

Democrats liked the cloverleaf symbol of Hancock's 2 Army Corps, using it on badges, pins, and tokens. They also had portrait bandannas, a "Little Gem Corps Badge," hand-and-rooster clay pipes, calling cards, and brass pins.

Both candidates got play on movable advertising cards called "metamorphics."

Popular Labels Garfield was the "Soldier's Friend," "Boatman Jim," "Our Boatman," "Farmer Garfield," "the Plow of Ohio," and "the Buckeye Boy."

The Republicans were starting to call their party the Grand Old Party.

Hancock was "The Superb."

Name-calling Garfield was "The Available Man," alluding to his meteoric rise over other more qualified individuals.

Hancock was satirized as "The Democratic Samson" against "The Republican Philistines."

The Press The *Nation* bemoaned that "all the conventions have now begun to treat the platform as a joke."

Spending Republicans spent an estimated $1,100,000 against Hancock's $335,000.

Firsts Garfield was considered the first "draft" candidate.

First time the Republican convention had delegates from every state of the Union.

For the first time, the Republican Convention called only party types and not, as before, people who sympathized with party goals.

Trends   Decisive roles for third parties, following the Greenback-Labor party's showing in the polls.
Garfield's "front-porch"-style campaign.

Vote   With thirty-eight states voting, Garfield won 214 electoral votes and 4,453,295 popular votes (48.5 percent) to 155 and 4,414,082 (48.1 percent) for Hancock and no electoral votes and 308,578 popular votes for Weaver of the Greenback-Labor party.

Benchmarks   One of the closest elections in popular vote in history.
Garfield was a minority president, not receiving a majority of popular votes.

Quote   Garfield on winning the presidency: "I am bidding goodbye to private life and to a long series of happy years which I fear terminate in 1880."

THE presidential election of 1880 has been called one of the most boring and inconsequential of all time. Lacking the volatile issues of the Civil War and Reconstruction, the parties were left with nothing but personal attacks. Republican nominee James Garfield was tarred with the brush of the Crédit Mobilier scandal, having allegedly pocketed $329 in stock dividends from the Union Pacific Railroad's corrupt holding company. Garfield insisted it was "a loan" of $300, which he had repaid, but a House committee judged otherwise. His Democratic opponent, General Winfield Scott Hancock, was accused of shilling for the "lost cause" of the Rebels. Hancock, of course, could boast a "superb" record as a Union Army officer during the Civil War. But accusations were the issues in this campaign.

Handsome and popular, with a record not altogether spotless, "Boatman Jim" Garfield managed his own campaign. Endless advice, though, poured in from party chieftains and supporters, most of it to lie low.

As had become the custom, the key to Republican victory was silence on major issues. The high stakes of party patronage and the close margins of victory characteristic in the Gilded Age made Garfield adopt a rule of thumb: "Say but little, beyond thanks and an occasional remark on the localities through which we pass." But he ended up passing through few, preferring to stay at home in Mentor, Ohio, for most of the campaign. In a foretaste of Benjamin Harrison's 1888 campaign and William McKinley's much grander enterprise in 1896, Garfield waged a "front-porch" campaign. He greeted hundreds of delegations of all types of voters, including suffragettes and prohibitionists, businessmen and Civil War veterans. His wife served them lemonade or stronger waters, depending on their wants, while they picnicked on his property, whistled at his words, and told him of their petitions. Garfield also kept in close contact with county committee chairmen and party regulars. He personally hand-picked the head of the Republican National Committee and the chief fund-raiser, making every effort to forge and sustain close ties to business interests.

Away from Mentor, yet another effort was made to wave the bloody shirt. The *Republican Text Book* was overflowing with bloody-shirt strategy and such songs as the "Conspirators' Cause." One newspaper sneered that putting Hancock at the head of the Democratic party was like putting "a figure of the Virgin on Kidd's pirate craft": It does not change it into an "honest ship."

"Winfield Scott Hancock is a good man weighing 250 pounds" was the ridicule making the rounds. Some were kind enough to add that he had a "record as stainless as his sword." But the truth was that Hancock was not a politician and showed no talent as a campaigner. His acceptance speech, expansive and platitudinous, was said to have a "certain childlike innocence." His remark that the tariff question "is a local issue" sparked outright criticism. Cartoonist Thomas Nast showed Hancock on a speaker's platform whispering to someone: "Who is Tariff, and why is he for revenue only?"

Democrats did their best by hyping Hancock's relatively liberal policies of Reconstruction as the military governor of Louisiana and Texas after the war. They attacked "Old Stalwarts" who waved the bloody shirt. Emphasis was put on the long litany of Republican era scandals, and mileage was made with the "salary grab" act of 1873 whereby Republican majorities in Congress raised salaries of federal officeholders, and congressmen made their own $2,500 annual raise retroactive for two years. On the West Coast, where Chinese immigration was considered a peril, Democrats circulated thousands of copies of a forged letter purportedly written by Garfield endorsing the right of companies to "buy labor where they can get it cheapest." When Republicans denied its authenticity and took out ads showing samples of Garfield's handwriting to compare with the letter, Democrats retorted that a man who lied about $329 from Crédit Mobilier would lie again.

Third parties livened things up a bit, if only by their spirit, revealing how tired and tiresome the two major parties had become. The first sounds of what would become the roar of populism could be heard in the Greenbacks' tuneful warning: "The morning light is breaking, the darkness disappears, Old parties now are shaking with penitential fears; Republicans and Democrats, we've got you by the ears, As we go marching on."

The key states of Indiana and New York decided the 1880 election. The Democrats needed New York's thirty-five electoral votes and either Indiana, or Connecticut and New Jersey. The Republicans needed New York and Indiana. As it turned out, a flood of Republican two-dollar bills bought Indiana, and Democratic infighting lost New York for the Democrats. In New York, Tammany Hall leader John Kelly, who backed an unpopular candidate for mayor, was denounced by fellow Democrats for his "pigheadedness" and for throwing the election away to "gratify his evil temper." So it was that Garfield slipped into the presidency, only to regret shortly that he had ever been so lucky: "My God, what is there in this place that a man should ever want to get into it?'' On July 2 he was shot in the back by a disappointed and deranged office-seeker, as he and Secretary of State James G. Blaine walked arm in arm through the train station in Washington. He died eleven weeks later.

★ CAMPAIGN OF 1884 ★

Major Candidates   James G. Blaine, 54, Maine, Republican
Grover Cleveland, 47, New York, Democrat

Credentials   Blaine helped establish the Republican party in his state, served in the state legislature (1858–1862) and the House of Representatives (1863–1876), acting as speaker (1869–1875). He was elected to the Senate (1876–1881) and became secretary of state (1881).

Cleveland served as a local sheriff (1871–1873), was elected mayor of Buffalo (1882) and was governor of New York (1883–1885).

Tickets   The Republicans met in Chicago. Blaine had tried for the Republican nomination twice before, in 1876 and 1880, but questions about his business dealings had always defeated him. Blaine's main rival for the nomination was competent but undynamic President Chester A. Arthur. Another potential rival, William Tecumseh Sherman, had telegraphed: ''I will not accept if nominated and I will not serve if elected.'' Blaine secured the nomination on the fourth ballot with 541 votes, 130 more than necessary. The vote was made unanimous. The vice-presidential nomination went to Senator John Logan of Illinois on the first ballot.

The Democrats also chose Chicago. Cleveland's appeal was the result both of the fact that he was from the electorally important state of New York and his reputation as an untainted politician. He won on the second ballot with 683 votes. Indiana senator Thomas Hendricks was picked as his running mate. After the Democrats chose their ticket, independent Republicans, nicknamed ''Mugwumps,'' bolted *their* party to support Cleveland.

Campaign Notes   Songs, slogans, banners, flags, and torchlight parades, the political advertising of this age, were used to the hilt in this election. Public participation, especially at the grass-roots level, was enthusiastic and widespread. Parades lasted for hours and elaborate costumes of knightly armor plus plumes and more sometimes cost as much as $150.

Blaine made campaign forays, visiting several states over a period of six weeks and giving, usually brief remarks about four hundred times while Cleveland made only two appearances.

JAMES G. BLAINE

Symbols Blaine's emblems were a white plume, representing his knightly persona, and a pinecone, the symbol of his state of Maine. Cleveland's side had the Democratic rooster and a broom for sweeping the Republicans out of office.

Slogans The Republicans cheered for "Blaine! Blaine! James G. Blaine!" and "The White Plumed Knight from the State of Maine!" Once word was out that Cleveland may have sired an illegitimate son, Republicans taunted the opposition: "Ma! Ma! Where's my Pa? / Gone to the White House. Ha! Ha! Ha!"

For their official slogan the Democrats paraphrased Cleveland himself: "A Public Office Is a Public Trust." They also used "They love him for the enemies he has made." To chide the Republicans they made a slogan of an unheeded postscript on a letter to Blaine: "Burn, burn, burn this letter!" And taking advantage of a Blaine blunder, they cried "Rum, Romanism, and Rebellion."

Songs The Republicans sang for Blaine in "The Plumed Knight" and "We'll Follow Where the White Plume Waves": In "Where Republicans Go" Democrats boomed "They will fret, bye and bye, / They will sweat in the torments below." As for Blaine, Democrats slighted him first by calling a song "Mary Blaine" and then singing "We all do know this knight so bold / Who's feathered well his nest."

Paraphernalia The closeness of the race plus its focus on personalities, especially Blaine's, produced a wealth of items probably rivaled only by the log-cabin–hard-cider campaign of 1840. Photographic images of the candidates were widely used, sometimes with advertisements on the reverse by companies that thought it wise to identify with a political candidate. Blaine's picture, for example, was complemented with an ad for "Perfumed White Vaseline, Chesebrough Manufacturing Company." Set in the Victorian age, the campaign saw many ornate pieces, such as a pair of flower-design frosted-glass dessert plates with images of Cleveland and Hendricks. Ironically, for a nasty campaign, there were few nasty items.

Campaigning for Blaine, some marchers wore papier-mâché suits of armor with white plumed helmets and swords. One medalet showing a knight on a charger was inscribed "We Will Follow Where the White Plume Waves."

Popular Labels Blaine was lionized at the 1876 Republican convention as "The Plumed Knight" and his followers kept that image alive. Cleveland was known as "Grover the Good."

Name-calling To Democrats, Blaine was "Slippery Jim" and "Tattooed Jim." Cleveland's opponents referred to him as "The Beast of Buffalo" and "His Obstinacy."

Curious Fact Blaine and Cleveland were a study in contrasts in more than reputation. Blaine had spent more than twenty years in Washington, D.C.; Cleveland's first trip there was for the inauguration.

The Press *The New York Times* broke its tradition of backing Republican candidates by boosting Cleveland and ridiculing Blaine as a "prostitutor of public trusts, a scheming jobber, and a reckless falsifier."

Firsts The first black elected temporary chairman of a national nominating convention—the Republican.

Trend The coming of age of newspaper cartoonists.

Vote Cleveland received 219 electoral votes and 4,879,507 popular votes (48.5 percent) to 182 and 4,850,293 (48.2 percent) for Blaine and about 360,000 popular votes for third-party candidates.

Benchmarks One of the worst mudslinging campaigns ever.
    The second-closest election in history.
    The first ten-million-vote election.
    Cleveland was elected with less than a popular vote majority.

Quote After the election Blaine wrote to a friend: "I should have carried New York by 10,000 if the weather had been clear on election day and Dr. Burchard had been doing missionary work in Asia Minor or Cochin China!"

B Y 1884 Reconstruction was over, America was exploding westward, big business was booming, and it was open season on campaign madness again. Republicans favored a protective tariff higher than the Democrats', but otherwise there was little difference between the party platforms. It was time for a campaign of pure theater or, as one critic put it, a contest between the "copulative habits of one and the prevaricative habits of the other."

The one was Democrat Grover Cleveland, a Buffalo lawyer who, in three years, had leapfrogged from being his city's mayor to the governorship of New York to presidential candidacy. The other was Republican James Blaine from Maine, an ex-congressman and former secretary of state.

The Democrats went to their convention in July determined to choose a candidate who could not be touched and came away with "Grover the Good." Cleveland was a bit rough around the edges. While a lawyer in Buffalo, he was known to wash down his dinner with beer and then relieve himself out the window of his law office. But he was stoutly honest and as a politician had made many of the right enemies. His campaign slogan, "A Public Office Is a Public Trust," stood in marked contrast to Blaine, a charming, sophisticated, and sometimes funny man who campaigned as the "Plumed Knight" but was also justly known as "Slippery Jim," a dishonest politician.

In fact, just a few weeks before the Republican convention in June, *Puck*, a satirical weekly, published a full-color cartoon of a stripped-down Blaine as "The Tattooed Man." On close inspection, the tattoos were the names of Blaine's questionable business deals and, most especially, the incriminating "Mulligan Letters." A divided party nominated him anyway, hoping that his famed personal magnetism would be the party's talisman.

A statesman who looked the part, Blaine was a veteran legislator and skilled campaigner in his own right. And his partisans soon were successfully poking fun at plodding Cleveland's inexperience and mushroomlike arrival on the political scene. Then, on July 21, the gods seemed to deliver the presidency to Blaine on a silver platter. A banner headline THE TERRIBLE TALE appeared on the front page of the *Buffalo Evening Telegraph*. The story made the shocking revelation that Governor Cleveland had an illegitimate ten-year-old son by Maria Halpin, a widow who had sewn collars for a living.

Some of Cleveland's advisers rushed to Albany, expecting denial. But Cleveland told his associates, "Whatever you say, tell the truth," and that was exactly what he did. Many years before, he admitted, he had cavorted with Halpin and had since supported the child, though he was never sure it was really his. When advisers wrung their hands at the political implications of the affair, he is said to have added, "I don't believe the American people want a gelding in the White House."

Republicans exulted and paraded in costumes of knightly armor, sporting brightly colored plumes and gleefully singing "Ma! Ma! Where's my Pa? Gone to the White House—Ha! Ha! Ha!"

How the campaign might have turned out if Cleveland's amorous proclivities had remained the major issue, no one knows. Just in time, more Mulligan letters turned up new evidence that Blaine had been engaged in some shady bond deals, one with the unheeded postscript: "Burn this letter." Blaine denied wrongdoing, while cartoonists like Thomas Nast pilloried him as a creature drenched in loot, wearing three bedraggled plumes. It was the turn of Democrats to chant: "Blaine! Blaine! Jay Gould Blaine! The Continental Liar from the State of Maine!"

Blaine still had a chance to win the election, but he made two political mistakes on the same day. Tired from six weeks of touring the West and not heeding his advisers, Blaine decided to go to New York City to campaign some more. The Republican candidate met with several hundred Protestant clergymen, among them a Samuel Burchard, who greeted him with "We are Republicans," not the party of "Rum, Romanism and Rebellion." Blaine did not seem to catch the remark and made no reply, but a Democratic party worker did and rushed back to headquarters. Thousands of Catholic votes were lost. That night, Blaine banqueted with two hundred wealthy Republicans at a sybaritic dinner where he spoke about Republican prosperity. The next day, the New York *World* headlined "Royal Feast of Belshazzar Blaine and the Money Kings," and published a cartoon that pictured Blaine at an enormous and sumptuous banquet table dining with plutocrats like Jay Gould and John Jacob Astor while a family hit by the depression looked on, begging.

Cleveland won the election by winning New York by a whisker—1,149 votes—and only 29,214 more than Blaine out of a total of 9.7 million cast for both of them. But it was enough for chortling Democrats to sing: "Hurray for Maria! Hurray for the Kid! / I voted for Cleveland, and I'm damned glad I did."

★ CAMPAIGN OF 1888 ★

Major Candidates   Benjamin Harrison, 55, Indiana, Republican
Grover Cleveland, 51, New York, Democrat

Credentials   For Cleveland, see Campaign of 1884. He was elected president in 1884.

Harrison, grandson of the ninth president, William Henry ("Old Tippecanoe") Harrison, fought in the Civil War (1862–1865), rising to brigadier general, and served as a U.S. senator (1881–1887).

National Tickets   When the Republicans met in Chicago, front-runner James G. Blaine, the unsuccessful nominee in 1884, had already withdrawn from

BENJAMIN HARRISON

the race. Backers of former senator Benjamin Harrison adopted a low profile at first, allowing Senator John Sherman of Ohio to take the lead, but he finally captured the nomination on the eighth ballot. Banker and former New York congressman Levi Morton easily won the vice-presidential nomination on the first ballot.

The Democrats gathered in St. Louis, where there was little question about who the nominee would be. Having won the White House back from the Republicans in 1884, the Democrats were not about to drop the incumbent and Cleveland was easily renominated. The death in 1885 of Vice President Thomas Hendricks created an opening on the ticket, and former Ohio senator Allen Thurman was a shoo-in on the first ballot.

The Prohibition party put up Clinton Fisk of New Jersey, and the Union Labor party also ran a candidate.

Campaign Notes   Alarmed by the Democratic advocacy of lower tariffs, businessmen contributed unprecedented amounts to Republican coffers. In the swing states of New York and Indiana, Republicans spent over a million dollars in the closing days of the campaign, and outright vote-buying was alleged in Indiana.

The Democratic party leaders, unhappy over the controversy Cleveland had generated over the tariff issue, only motivated themselves when there came a Republican ground swell. They pushed the party apparatus on the tariff issue, "educating" the voters about tariffs rather than "moving" the people with inflammatory rhetoric. The aging vice-presidential nominee Thurman took on the active campaigning, while Cleveland stayed on the sidelines.

Symbols Democrats paraded their donkey and waved red bandannas, made popular by vice-presidential candidate Allen Thurman's habitual use of one to wipe his nose after each pinch of snuff.

In addition to their increasingly familiar elephant logo, Republicans appropriated the old Democratic rooster.

Slogans Republicans campaigned on "Tippecanoe and Tariff Too," "Trade, Trade, No Free Trade," "Down with Free-Traders," and "Protection and Prosperity."

Democrats talked up low tariffs with "Don't, Don't, Don't Be Afraid; Only Low Tariff So Don't Be Afraid," and "Unnecessary Taxation Is Unfair Taxation."

Songs Republicans sang "Grover's Veto" about "a fat man" who sat in the president's chair "singing veto, veto, veto" in reference to Cleveland's penchant for vetoing hundreds of pension bills for Civil War veterans. Harrison's own and his family's military deeds were highlighted in "Hip Hip Hurrah, Harrison" and "There Are No Flies on Harrison."

Democrats countered with "His Grandfather's Hat," stirring up images of "Little Ben" running around in William Henry Harrison's military headgear.

Paraphernalia Split logs featuring a picture of Harrison reminded voters that Benjamin was "A Chip off the Old Block" of William Henry Harrison, whose log cabin–hard cider campaign in 1840 won him the presidency.

Democrats won the "battle of the bandannas," as vice-presidential candidate Thurman's trademark inspired over 150 types. Cleveland supporters made their case with hand-held wooden noisemakers featuring a picture of the candidate.

Popular Labels Harrison was "The Soldier's Friend" and "The Log Cabin Candidate / The People's Choice."

Cleveland was "Grover the Good" and "President Veto," a compliment to Democrats.

Name-calling Harrison was "the human iceberg" and "Kid Glove" Harrison.

Cleveland was "The Stuffed Prophet," the "Perpetual Candidate," and "The English Candidate."

The Press The tariff was the talk of the town. The New York *Evening Post* said that Cleveland's declaration of war on the tariff "will serve as the historical record of the transformation of the Democratic party." The *Nation* wrote: "Protection is the Frankenstein of the Republican party."

Spending Republicans reported their costs as $1,350,000, although they raised and spent much more, with $3,000,000 coming in from businessmen alone. The Democrats reported expenditures of $855,000.

Firsts With the introduction of the Australian ballot in several states, the first secret ballots.

Frederick Douglass was the first black to receive a vote for the presidential nomination at the Republican convention.

Trends Transition from Civil War sectional politicians to business-trained political types like Ohio's Mark Hanna and Pennsylvania's Matthew Quay.

Republican party seen as a "millionaire's club."

Vote With thirty-eight states voting, Harrison won with 233 electoral votes and 5,447,129 popular votes (47.9 percent) to 168 and 5,537,857 (48.6 percent) for Cleveland. Fisk of the Prohibition party received no electoral votes but 249,506 popular votes.

Benchmarks Harrison won without a majority (or even plurality) of popular votes.

Cleveland was the fourth incumbent to be defeated.

The last of the "bloody shirt" Republican campaigns.

Quote When Benjamin Harrison finally assumed the presidency, he found that "the party managers had taken it all to themselves. . . . They had sold out every place to pay the election expenses."

FORMER President Rutherford B. Hayes called the election of 1888 "the best and decentest election I ever knew." But "Rutherfraud," who came to power in 1876 in the most disputed election in American history, was probably not the best source. The press consensus was probably more accurate, referring to it as "The Boodle Campaign of 1888," almost wholly financed by big business and choreographed by party "machines" willing to pay five dollars to twenty dollars for votes. The much-heralded Pendleton Civil Service Reform Act of 1883 had put federal employees beyond the reach of party campaign fund-raisers, but not to be outwitted, party chiefs simply looked around for other groups who might be willing to pay to get "their people" into office. It was only natural that politicians would turn to corporate coffers. As the party of prosperity and protective tariffs, the Republicans had much better luck in this regard. Philadelphia merchant John Wanamaker raised more than $3,000,000; he was later made postmaster general.

President Grover Cleveland's refusal to budge on the tariff issue, his insistence that high tariffs were nothing but a tax on the poor that went right into the pockets of corporate chiefs, put the Democrats at a decided disadvantage. The Republicans led a two-pronged attack. On the one hand, they played the tariff issue for all it was worth, equating Cleveland's position to an attack on the entire American way of life, a threat to every man, woman, and child.

The other prong of the Republican strategy was simple: Throw every piece of dirt possible at Cleveland, a bear of a man, knowing that some would stick to such a ponderous and slow-moving target. Cleveland's habit of carefully reading and often vetoing bills that congressmen winked through on behalf of individual constituents—often for the one million veterans of the Civil War—was portrayed not just as a partisan Democratic effort to punish the victors but as a shirker's attempt to get back at those brave men who did not hire substitutes to fight in their place. For his bachelor-days' habit of drinking and talking with cronies late into the night, Cleveland was painted as a slothful boozer. Vicious rumors were circulated that Cleveland beat his new and very youthful wife, his longtime ward whom he had wed in 1886 in a quiet White House ceremony. The rumors were not dispelled even when the First Lady wrote that she wished "the women of our Country no greater blessing than that their homes and lives may be as happy, and that their husbands may be as kind, as attentive, considerate, and affectionate as mine."

Cleveland's opponent Benjamin Harrison, a man of formality and diligence, stayed in Indianapolis, conducting a "front-porch"-style campaign, making more than eighty speeches to 300,000 people. He felt it was safer than going on the road, noting, "I have a great risk of meeting a fool at home but the candidate who travels cannot escape him." He also played it safe in the kinds of things he said, such as "The Republican party has walked upon high paths. It has set before it ever the maintenance of the Union, the honor of its flag, and the prosperity of our people." But all was not lost, because "The Plumed Knight" James G. Blaine went all-out on the hustings for Harrison, carrying forth a single message: "The Democratic Party in power is a standing menace to the prosperity of the country."

In 1884 the Republican Blaine had been defeated in part because, through an indiscretion, he became associated with the cause of anti-Catholicism. In 1888 Cleveland fell into a similar predicament. In response to a letter Republicans had sent to the British minister to the U.S., seeking advice on the upcoming election, he had written that Cleveland seemed by far the better candidate, so far as the British were concerned. This letter was widely published and Cleveland soon became "the English candidate," whom no self-respecting Irishman could support.

Cleveland hardly campaigned at all and sulked in the White House, feeling misunderstood and unappreciated. He made only one public appearance and that was to accept the nomination. But without any party operatives out on the hustings doing the rabble-rousing, back-scratching, and handshaking for him, he couldn't pull in the votes. Rank-and-file party members did not forgive Cleveland for sharing patronage positions with Mugwump Liberal

Republicans, as a reward for their support in 1884. This had squeezed out jobs for Democrats and now, the Liberal Republicans, who had supported Cleveland in 1884, were returning to their own party to support Harrison.

It is often said that Cleveland defeated himself. He had alienated key interest groups like the veterans of the Grand Army of the Republic, because he really believed his own rhetoric that "public office is a public trust," and had gone after waste and fraud. When besieged during the campaign and vilified throughout the press, he pouted; that was his nature, and in 1888 that was his undoing. He did little himself, and others did little for him, to counter the Republicans' portrayal of him as the "Beast of Buffalo." In the end he did not even carry his home state of New York, and that cost him the election. As mayor and then governor of New York, and as president, Cleveland had waged a one-man crusade against New York's Tammany Hall. In 1888 the New York Democratic machine had switched gears and gone into action against its party, vowing "Cleveland will never get New York." And it was right, by 13,000 votes. Though Cleveland won more popular votes, Harrison garnered the crucial electoral votes. Sure of his own righteousness, Cleveland took the news well: "It is better to be defeated battling for an honest principle than to win by a cowardly subterfuge."

★ CAMPAIGN OF 1892 ★

Major Candidates   Benjamin Harrison, 59, Indiana, Republican
Grover Cleveland, 55, New York, Democrat

Credentials   For Harrison, see Campaign of 1888. He was elected president in 1888.

For Cleveland, see Campaign of 1884. He was elected president in 1884 but defeated in 1888.

Convention Tickets   When the Republicans convened in Minneapolis President Benjamin Harrison was not popular with many party leaders, but by tradition an incumbent was renominated, and so he was, easily on the first ballot. Incumbency was not as kind to Vice President Levi Morton. Whitelaw Reid, editor of the *New York Tribune*, was nominated by acclamation to replace him.

When the Democrats gathered in Chicago, front-runner Grover Cleveland was challenged by a short-lived move by New York's Tammany Hall, which pushed the candidacy of Governor David Hill. But Cleveland beat back the challenge and won the nomination on the first ballot. Silverite Adlai Stevenson of Illinois, assistant postmaster-general in Cleveland's first administra-

GROVER CLEVELAND

tion, was selected as the vice-presidential nominee to pacify the Western "soft money" wing of the party.

The People's party or Populists, formally organized in 1891, held their first nominating convention, pairing former Greenback James Weaver of Iowa, an ex-Union general, with James Field of Virginia, a former Confederate major.

Campaign Notes The Republicans stood by tradition and had a private notification ceremony for Harrison. Led by Ohio Governor William McKinley, they went to tell Harrison of his (already known) renomination, listened to his acceptance remarks, and then lunched on lobster, sweetbreads, and sherbet.

Cleveland's managers decided to break precedent with a public ceremony in Madison Square Garden with 18,000 spectators. Cleveland also spoke out on the issue of the day, the GOP tariff, saying it only helped business and hurt the poor and that he wanted a tariff beneficial to both.

Symbols The Republicans had the elephant and Democrats ran with the donkey. Both sides used Harrison's "grandfather's hat," usually depicted as a high hat, to suit their purposes. The Republicans had the hat fitting just right, while the Democrats showed it as way too big.

Slogans Republicans reused "Tippecanoe and the Tariff Too" and "Republican Protection." They tarred Democrats with "Free Trade."

Democrats went with "Four more years of Grover," "A Public Office Is a Public Trust," and "Tariff Reform."

The Populists railed against government "of Wall Street, by Wall Street and for Wall Street."

Songs Pro-Harrison songs were "Just Wait Until November" and "Grandfather's Hat": "Old Tippecanoe, in the forties, / Wore a hat that was then called the *bell;* / His grandson, our leader, now wears it, / And it fits him remarkably well."

Cleveland supporters crooned "Grover, Grover, / Four more years of Grover. / In we'll go, Out they'll go, / Then we'll be in clover." They urged voters to "Turn the Rascals Out" and promised "Cleveland and Victory."

The enthusiasm in this campaign came from the third parties, the People's (Populist) movement of the Plains states. Discouraged by their economic situation, followers sang "The Kansas Fool," in which "The Banker makes of you a tool."

Paraphernalia There was less interest in this Harrison–Cleveland replay than about the initial bout in 1888. As a result there were fewer ribbons, buttons, lapel pins, and banners on display. However, the Republicans did have some protection ribbons in favor of Harrison and woolen tariffs with sheep motifs and others with "American Tin" high-hat ornaments. The Democrats produced ornate tin cards with a spread-winged eagle and oval portraits of Cleveland and Stevenson, with a message against protection for tin.

Populist ribbons advertised "The Issues: Money, Land and Transportation" and "Free & Unlimited Coinage" and "Homes for the Toilers."

Popular Labels Harrison was "The Soldier's Friend."

Cleveland was "Grover the Good" and "Old Grover."

Name-calling Because Harrison was only five-foot-six, Democrats continued to taunt him with "Little Ben" and "a little man in a big chair." He was also "Kid Glove" Harrison and the "White House Ice Chest."

Cleveland was "the Beast of Buffalo," "Old Perpetual," "The Stuffed Prophet," "the elephantine economist of the Mugwumps," and "the same old corpulent Cobden."

The Press The St. Louis *Republic* described the agrarian shift away from the Republican party in very simple terms: "It is Revolution."

Spending Republicans reported spending $1,700,000 to $2,350,000 for Cleveland's side.

Firsts The first time since 1828 that Democrats widely outspend Republicans.

The People's party was the first third party to poll more than a million votes.

Trends Third parties impact public policy.
More professionalism in campaigns.

Vote With forty-four states reporting, Cleveland won 277 electoral votes
and 5,555,426 popular votes (46.1 percent) to 145 and 5,182,690 (43 percent)
for Harrison and 22 and 1,029,846 (8.5 percent) for Weaver. The Prohibition
party polled 264,133 (2.2 percent).

Benchmark Cleveland was the only president to serve a split term.

Quotes The day after the election, Cleveland's wife told reporters: "Mr.
Cleveland's pleasure was not demonstrative. He seemed to be simply in the
enjoyment of a perfect satisfaction."

THE most exciting story was populism and its angry pleas. Cultivated in
the soil of the Plains states, fertilized by the frustration of inflated railroad
rates and storage fees, of mortgage payments with bumper interest rates and
prickly prices fixed by barbed wire and harvester trusts, a movement of
farmers began to be heard. At a time when half of the population still tilled
the land, many who had answered ads to settle cheap homesteads out West
now felt used by the bankers, railroads, and federal government and pinched
by depression-level prices for their crops. They thought a simple and easy
solution was "soft money" and free silver, believing that more money in
circulation would mean higher crop prices and lower debts. They joined
the Greenback party, singing their version of "America": "Land of the
millionaire, / Farmers with pockets bare." And then dreamed up grander
reforms as the Populists of 1892.

Their hellraising was sweet music to the out-of-power Democrats and their
reform-conscious leader Grover Cleveland, who had been exiled from the
presidency in the election of 1888. At first, Cleveland seemed disinterested
in the doings of the Republicans under President Benjamin Harrison, contented with the money he was making as a lawyer in New York City and the
fish he was catching during summers at Buzzards Bay on the Massachusetts
coast. But gradually his ego, easily inflated, became more interested as reports came in of widespread voter unrest. Cleveland himself was watching
the Republicans sink deeper into "the mire" and advised party leaders "Our
policy should be to let them flounder."

Spending money with the greatest of ease, the Republican-controlled "Bil-
lion-Dollar" Congress doled out whatever was necessary to prevent a surplus
and arguments for lowering tariffs from building up. It poured money into a
"God help the surplus" pension program for Union veterans. It increased
moneys for river improvements, coastal defenses and federal buildings, so
much so that within two years more revenue was needed. It then passed the
McKinley Tariff of 1890, which hiked protection and swelled the Treasury
too. But it also swelled anger, of economy-minded Northerners, unpensioned

Southern veterans, and agrarian citizens whose products were generally not protected but who saw prices of their daily needs increase. Democrats then fanned Midwest unrest by sending around door-to-door salesmen who further inflated costs of tinware and such, showing housewives before-and-after prices of the McKinley law. In the midterm elections McKinley and other Republicans were run out of the House, leaving the party with a minority of eighty-eight and the Democrats with hopes for 1892.

The rematch between the undersized Harrison and oversized Cleveland was quiet, to say the least. Because it was still taboo to campaign outright, especially as an incumbent, Harrison had planned a few "speeches" in New York on the way to his summer cottage in the Adirondacks. But when his wife became ill with tuberculosis, the trip was called off and Harrison spent most of his time, until her death two weeks before the election, at her bedside. The trouble was, nobody was anxious to fill in for him. The "Magnetic" James G. Blaine was now too ill to help, and others were not in the mood. To add to the injury, businessmen were cooler now in their support since Harrison had let the Sherman Anti-Trust Act and Sherman Silver Purchase Act slip through Congress.

Cleveland boldly broke tradition by having a public notification ceremony and even more boldly speaking out against the GOP tariff. Of course, he would have been foolish not to take advantage of the opportunity presented by the recent labor strife at the Carnegie steel plant in Homestead, Pa., where owners Andrew Carnegie and Henry Clay Frick had hired Pinkerton men to protect nonunion workers meant to replace union men who refused to go along with a cut in wages. Public opinion turned against Carnegie and Frick, who had used the argument that the steel industry needed protection to keep wages high. "Scenes are enacted in the very abiding place of high protection that . . . demonstrate the falsity that protection is a boon to toilers" noted Cleveland.

But Cleveland was never so bold as to take to the stump. He spent the campaign at his "Gray Gables" cottage at Buzzards Bay, tending to his fishing and his gout, keeping in touch, though, by writing letters to party bosses. When he wrote some letters that were passed to the newspapers, Cleveland was warned about making himself "commonplace." However Cleveland had stand-ins. His running mate Stevenson was whistle-stopping the West, handling the biggest issue—the naming of the highest peak in Washington state either Rainier or Tacoma—like a pro: by not saying which he preferred. And while this was not a big year for torchlight parades and brass bands, Democrats were out on the hustings trying to educate voters about lower tariffs and other reforms. By doing so they cut into the strength of the Populists, who were the fiercest campaigners of all. Presidential candidate Weaver attacked the plutocracy and charged that "the corporation has been placed above the individual."

But Cleveland had stolen Weaver's thunder by also talking about unions being crushed by "those made selfish and sordid by unjust governmental favoritism." His appeal won the workingmen's votes and enough other votes to take the executive as well as both houses of Congress for the Democrats. In a sign of the times, though, businessmen were not terribly upset, figuring they would work something out. Exclaimed Carnegie, "Cleveland! Landslide! Well, we have nothing to fear and perhaps it is best. Cleveland is a pretty good fellow."

★ CAMPAIGN OF 1896 ★

Major Candidates   William Jennings Bryan, 36, Nebraska, Democrat/ Populist
William McKinley, 53, Ohio, Republican

Credentials   Bryan served in the House of Representatives (1891–1895) and was editor-in-chief of the *Omaha World-Herald* (1894–1896).

McKinley served six congressional terms (1877–1883, 1885–1891), becoming chairman of the House Ways and Means Committee (1889), was defeated in the 1890 election because of the McKinley Tariff backlash and then elected governor of Ohio (1892–1896).

Tickets   The Republicans convened in St. Louis. The party had much more trouble with the platform than with the presidential nomination. As passed, the platform came out strongly for gold, causing thirty-four silver Republicans to walk out of the convention. When balloting began, there was no question that William McKinley would win because of the great publicity effort Republican boss Mark Hanna had mounted on his behalf. He took the nomination on the first ballot, receiving 661½ votes, or eight times as much as his closest rival. For vice president the delegates chose New Jersey lawyer and McKinley favorite Garret A. Hobart.

The Democrats met in Chicago with no apparent nominee. Silverites quickly gained control, seating contested silver delegates, William Jennings Bryan among them. Bryan achieved indisputable stardom when he rose to defend the platform's money plank, which he had written. He won nomination on the fifth ballot. Second place was given to Maine shipbuilder Arthur Sewall.

Campaign Notes   Bryan traveled farther (18,000 miles by train), saw more people (five million in twenty-seven states) and gave more speeches (600, or ten to twenty a day) than any presidential candidate before him. Bryan still holds the record for thirty-six speeches in one day between Labor Day and Election Day.

McKinley preferred to receive delegations at home in Canton, Ohio; his campaign was dubbed "The Front Porch Campaign."

WILLIAM MCKINLEY

McKinley was sold in other ways too. About 250 million pieces of literature were printed and distributed, about 50 percent more than in all previous campaigns.

Symbols Bryan was given bouquets of chrysanthemums in the ratio of sixteen white flowers to one yellow to symbolize his stance on silver. The most pervasive symbol was the silver bug that appeared on all kinds of campaign paraphernalia.

McKinley's side sported gold-bug pins, while the candidate himself always wore a red carnation in his buttonhole to bring him luck.

Slogans Bryan's banners read "No Cross of Gold! No Crown of Thorns!," "Sixteen to One," and "We'll Have Our Pockets Lined with Silver."

McKinley's followers chanted "McKinley and the Full Dinner Pail," "Good Money Never Made Times Bad" and "Grand Old Party, Good as Gold."

Songs Populist sentiments filled the lyrics of Bryan's songs as his supporters sang "The Silver Lion Came Tearin' out the Wilderness," "The Silver Song," and "We Want None of Thee."

McKinley's followers paraded to "The Honest Little Dollar's Here to

Stay," "Marching with McKinley to Victory," and "We Want Yer, McKinley, Yes, We Do."

Paraphernalia The 1896 race ushered in what came to be called "the golden age of the political celluloid." Celluloid, developed in 1868, was used to make the campaign button. Over a thousand styles decorated lapels during this election, including slogan buttons, coattail buttons, and candidate-endorsement-with-product-advertisement buttons.

In addition, the most unusual (and short-lived) items produced for both candidates were nude soap babies in boxes with tags reading "My Papa Will Vote for BRYAN" or "for McKINLEY," that looked like babies in coffins and were considered grotesque.

Popular Labels Bryan was "The Peerless Leader," "The Great Commoner" like Henry Clay, "The Boy Orator from the Platte," and "The Silver Knight of the West."

McKinley was "The Napoleon of Protection" and "The Advance Agent of Prosperity."

Name-calling Bryan was called a "demagogue" and an "anti-Christ" as well as a "madman" and a "traitor."

McKinley was known as "Wobbly Willie" and the "prince of straddlers" before he came out foursquare for the gold standard.

The Press The Eastern press was unmerciful in its ridicule of Bryan, referring to him as the "Popocrat" candidate for president.

The *New York Journal*, one of the few major papers to support Bryan, caricatured Mark Hanna as "Dollar Mark," a man of excess who manipulated a pint-sized McKinley.

Cartoons Newspaper political cartoons came of age, and with them more emphasis on daily events than on the general trends and political principles emphasized in magazine cartoons.

Spending By several estimates, Mark Hanna raised about seven million dollars from corporations and wealthy individuals. Together with local and state funds, the Republicans spent about sixteen million dollars, while Democrats spent $600,000.

Firsts Bryan was the first "modern" presidential candidate in terms of aggressively selling himself.

McKinley's campaign, thanks to Mark Hanna, was the first to be professionally run, and Hanna was the first national "boss" of a political party.

Trends Bryan, father of the "stump speech," perfected the art of whistle-stopping—the practice of campaigning from the rear platform of a train.

McKinley's campaign became a blueprint for the mass marketing of a presidential candidate.

Vote   Forty-five states voted. McKinley won with 271 electoral votes and 7,102,246 popular votes (51.1 percent) to 176 electoral votes and 6,492,559 (47.7 percent) for Bryan. Third-party candidates garnered no electoral votes, but received some 300,000 popular votes (1.2 percent).

Benchmarks   Many more people voted than ever before.

McKinley was the first president since Grant to receive a popular-vote majority.

The last of the truly demonstrative campaigns in terms of parades and rallies and their accoutrements.

Bryan's "Cross of Gold" speech was the most memorable ever before a political convention.

Quote   Mayor Tom Johnson of Cleveland summed up the campaign as "the first great protest by the American people against monopoly."

IT was an amazing show. Contrasting character and political style plus a lively bread-and-butter issue made the campaign anything but a contest between Tweedledum and Tweedledee. The public, riveted by the theatrics, voted up a storm. The campaign of 1896 also marked the permanent arrival in American politics of the prominent as well as powerful campaign manager in the person of Cleveland businessman Mark Hanna, who had helped his unprepossessing protégé, Republican William McKinley, in his political career.

Set in the aftermath of a depression that had devastated the South and the West for four years, the campaign quickly became a referendum on keeping the gold standard as a basis for printing money. Those who were hurting wanted the government to coin silver freely and support its price at the ratio of sixteen ounces of silver to one ounce of gold. In campaign parlance, the "gold bugs," mainly Eastern Republicans, were pitted against the "silverites" who were based in the West and were Democratic.

McKinley was a safe choice for the Republicans—"The man without an angle or a tangle," wrote poet Vachel Lindsay. A Civil War veteran and former congressman, McKinley had just finished two terms as governor of Ohio, an electorally important state. His first love was a high protective tariff (the McKinley Tariff of 1890) and he wanted to campaign, as much as he wanted to campaign at all, on that issue.

A thirty-six-year-old forced him to change his mind. William Jennings Bryan, a Western agrarian and a Populist with a golden voice and a bimetallist bee in his bonnet, crusaded for silver in the belief that the poor would have more money and the economy would be better off if the country went off the gold standard. Dashing up the steps two at a time at the Democratic convention, Bryan immediately took command of his audience in rhetoric for the history books: "You shall not press down upon the brow of labor this crown of thorns. You shall not crucify mankind upon a cross of gold!" The next day, on the fifth ballot, Bryan was nominated. He was hailed as the new Moses by the silverites, but conservative Democrats left the party in droves. On top of that, many party leaders refused to endorse Bryan publicly.

On a scale never before attempted, Bryan decided to take his message directly to the people. He maintained a furious pace, sometimes giving thirty speeches a day and addressing crowds of 40,000 without the benefit of microphones. "He preached free silver," said one listener, "as he might have preached Jesus crucified." The Democratic candidate adjusted his clothes and eating habits to the demands of the road. Though a teetotaler, he wore a white neckerchief doused in whiskey to absorb sweat and frequently ended up smelling like a "wrecked distillery." He favored square-toed shoes, instead of the popular pointed look, to avoid stumbling when he boarded trains and wore string ties that he could wash easily. To keep up his energy, Bryan sometimes ate six times a day, wolfing down enormous amounts of food (two or three helpings) at each meal and snacking his way through bags of radishes—all at the risk of nauseating onlookers.

The turnout for Bryan and free silver troubled Hanna more than his candidate. Hanna, now campaign manager, did not want anything to go wrong. He urged McKinley to go on the road, but McKinley refused to budge from his porch. "I might as well put up a trapeze on my front lawn and compete with some professional athlete," he said, "as go out speaking against Bryan." In the end, however, he agreed to have delegations come to him in Canton and said he would speak out for gold.

With help from Hanna and cut rates from the railroads, gold-standard supporters, some 750,000, descended in droves from all parts of the country. They wore gold neckties and gold hatbands and rode gold-trimmed bicycles. Each delegation chairman would read a statement while McKinley smiled and listened "like a child looking at Santa Claus." Then, his mother rocking at his side, McKinley would stand on a chair in his long double-breasted coat with a red carnation in the buttonhole and offer some pithy remark.

By November 3 he and Hanna had outdone Bryan. Where the neat front lawn had been was plain brown earth, looking "as if a herd of buffalo had passed that way." The white picket fence and grape arbor had long since been demolished by souvenir-hunters. The front porch was whittled away too and threatened to collapse on the candidate's head.

Democrats decried the special excursion rates that the railroads charged for the trip to Canton. The Democratic press cartooned Hanna as pig-eyed and bloated, wearing a suit checkered with dollar signs and befriending "The Trusts." Bryanites sang Hanna was "crazy in the head."

Hanna was not crazy, he was crafty. He sold McKinley like patent medicine by sending almost fifteen hundred speakers around the country, mailing out millions of campaign pamphlets and raising millions of dollars from businessmen who feared Bryan's silver fanaticism and wanted a "Full Dinner

Pail" with McKinley. The Bryanites were beaten back by such tactics. Even the wage-earners Bryan courted bolted, many threatened with their jobs if they did not vote Republican. On the Saturday before the election, New York workingmen marched all day singing "We'll hang Billy Bryan on a sour apple tree." Under their breath, their song was something else: "You ask me why 'tis thus / That I make this outward show, / Because my millionaire employer / Says, 'Bryan must go.' " McKinley won decisively, with two million more voters going to the polls than in 1892.

★ CAMPAIGN OF 1900 ★

Major Candidates   William McKinley, 57, Ohio, Republican
William Jennings Bryan, 40, Nebraska, Democrat

Credentials   For McKinley and Bryan see Campaign of 1896. McKinley became president in 1896.

Tickets   The Republicans met in Philadelphia and renominated William McKinley on the first ballot with no opposition. The vice-presidential spot was trickier. Theodore Roosevelt, just forty-one, who had seconded McKinley, was the favorite of Western delegates and the candidate of New York bosses who, for selfish reasons, wanted their "unruly" young governor out of the way. Despite the belief of Ohio senator Mark Hanna, McKinley's campaign manager, that Roosevelt was "unsafe" for Republican business interests and lobbied against him, McKinley threw the choice to the convention. With that, there was no question. Roosevelt was nominated with 925 votes—all but his own New York delegate vote.

The Democrats convened in Kansas City, Missouri, and William Jennings Bryan was unanimously nominated on the first ballot. After a brief contest, Adlai Stevenson, former president Grover Cleveland's vice president, was unanimously chosen for the second spot.

Campaign Notes   McKinley divided his time between the White House and his home in Canton, Ohio, where there were celebrations in the streets for him, but nothing like the front-porch campaign of four years earlier. Like presidents before him, McKinley felt the need to be aloof.

Roosevelt filled in for McKinley to such an extent that he outdistanced Democratic rival Bryan, who held the record for stumping up until then.

Symbols   Republicans cleverly chose the full dinner pail to portray prosperity while serving to identify the party with the workingman. The Democrats

WILLIAM JENNINGS BRYAN

used a three-leaf clover to represent their three main campaign thrusts: anti-imperialism, antitrust, and antigold.

Slogans Republicans fought for "Four More Years of the Full Dinner Pail" and "Let Well Enough Alone." Teetotaler Bryan was unfairly criticized in another: "McKinley drinks soda water, Bryan drinks rum; McKinley is a gentleman, Bryan is a bum."

Democrats cried, "Immediate Freedom for the Philippines," "No Imperialism," and "Equal Rights to All—Special Privilege to None."

Songs "Down with Silver Dollar Bryan, with his promises of wind," Republicans sang in "The Full Dinner Pail," adding "Oh, one good term is deserving of another."

Not to be outdone, the Democrats published a booklet of "Six Red Hot Songs" for the campaign. One was "When Bryan Is Elected; The trusts will be demolished by popular decree."

Paraphernalia This campaign was tame after the big bang of 1896 and marked the beginning of the end of the era of demonstrative campaigns epitomized by the log-cabin–hard-cider ballyhoo of 1840.

Republican objects were high on prosperity and patriotism. Of course, the full dinner pail was ubiquitous, appearing on ribbons, buttons, and banners.

One of the most creative celluloids showed the dinner pail as a working factory, smokestacks and all, with the inscription "Do you smoke? Yes—Since 1896!" Some of the last ornate torchlight-parade lanterns were made for this campaign—dinner pails with cutouts that read "4 Years More of Full Dinner Pail." The "Rough Rider" image of Theodore Roosevelt was used to exemplify patriotism.

The Democrats used items to denounce imperialism and the trusts as well as to boost silver. One celluloid of George Washington was inscribed "Imperialism! Has the Country I Made Free Come to This? Bryan Will Save It."

Popular Labels "Mack and Teddy" starred on the Republican ticket. McKinley was also "The Workingman's Best Friend" and Roosevelt the "Rough Rider" and "TR."

To followers, Bryan was nothing less than "Peerless Leader" and "The Great Orator."

Name-calling McKinley's cautiousness earned him "Wobbly Willie," while Bryan's losing streak won him "Peerless Loser" and Roosevelt's bumptiousness "cowboy."

The Press The sensationalist New York *World* mocked Roosevelt's flamboyant campaign style, commenting "Until Teddy shall actually shoot, stab or lick some of his interrupters it is inevitable that his reputation will shrivel among his kindred spirits."

Bryan's pledge to "stand just where I stood" on silver in 1896 caused the Republican New York *Press* to remark: "Sit down, Mr. Bryan. You must be awfully tired, too."

Spending Bryan's campaign fell far behind once again, filling its national coffers with only about $425,000 to three million in McKinley's chest. The Republicans raised so much that they ended up returning a portion of Standard Oil's contribution.

First The first time a vice-presidential candidate was so active a campaigner.

Trends A downturn in voter turnout.
The falloff in political parades as an art form.

Vote Forty-five states participated. McKinley did better than last time, with 7,219,525 popular votes (52 percent) and 292 electoral votes to 6,358,737 (46 percent) and 155 for Bryan.

Benchmarks The last time voter participation was above 70 percent.
Each party had one woman delegate at the convention.

Quote   Vice president-elect Theodore Roosevelt said he expected to become a "dignified nonentity for four years."

★   ★   ★

PRESIDENT William McKinley loved to shake hands. At White House receptions, sometimes four thousand guests would glide past in the receiving line, McKinley greeting them one by one until he averaged eighteen hundred hands an hour.

McKinley and his invalid wife wanted to be accessible. The president went window-shopping downtown, hopped on streetcars when it struck his fancy, and took the first presidential spin in an automobile, speeding past the White House at eighteen miles an hour.

McKinley's openness set him apart from former Democratic president Grover Cleveland and brought him closer to the people. The economy played favorites too as prosperity returned to the country in 1897. Fields boasted bumper wheat, cotton, and corn, and shortfalls in Europe flung open new markets abroad. Dinner pails were full as workers in smokestack industries stayed overtime to keep up with increased demand.

Democratic fortunes were further tarnished by gold. Its scarcity had been the basis of William Jennings Bryan's earlier silver battle against the Republicans. Now, newly discovered mines and extraction techniques more than doubled production, watering down Bryan's argument and filling to the brim the Treasury's glittery reserves. But Bryan was no quitter. The very night he lost to McKinley in 1896, he announced his campaign for 1900. Having come this far, Bryan was not about to give up silver, but he needed another issue too.

"Wobbly Willie," as McKinley's critics called him for hesitating so, was torn over Cuba. Spain had been mistreating its Caribbean province for years and now local insurgents were asking for America's help. What the administration did not tell the public, two rival New York papers—the *World* and the *Journal*—did, with excess.

Just as things seemed to be getting better, they got worse. Spain said it would offer Cuba self-government and McKinley sent the battleship *Maine* for a "friendly visit" to Havana in early 1898. Then the *Journal* printed a letter home from Dupuy de Lomé, the Spanish minister in Washington, referring to McKinley as "weak" and "yielding to the rabble." And in the dead of night on February 15, the American battleship blew up, killing 260 men on board. "Remember the Maine! To Hell with Spain!" the public cried. Still McKinley did not want to leap. Finally, an investigation blamed "an external explosion" and the president, fearing Bryan's new campaign slogan to be "Free Cuba and Free Silver," asked Congress to act.

By August, four months later, the "splendid little war" was over. That was enough time for Theodore Roosevelt to forge his "Rough Rider" reputation by charging up San Juan Hill in a custom-made Brooks Brothers uniform, his broad-brimmed hat, sporting a blue polka-dot scarf, and intimidating the enemy. Time too for America to put its hands on Puerto

Rico and the Philippines, two other Spanish possessions. The Philippines raised the biggest problem. Cuba was promised self-government, Puerto Rico was annexed in self-interest. But why pay twenty million dollars for seven thousand islands so far away? When the peace treaty was presented to the Senate in January 1899, it was Bryan, of all people, who found the votes for passage.

Bryan was really only helping himself. Now he had his issue: anti-imperialism. When the conventions met almost a year and a half later, there were no surprises. McKinley and Bryan would be opponents once again. The only excitement came with the nomination of "Teddy" as McKinley's running mate. Roosevelt was wanted by the delegates but unwanted by Republican boss Mark Hanna, who considered him a "madman." Afterward, Hanna wrote to the president: "Your *duty* to the country is to *live* for *four* years from next March."

Bryan and Roosevelt were made for each other. They both took to the campaign trail at a dizzying pace. With McKinley intending to stay aloof, Roosevelt told Hanna "I am as strong as a bull moose and you can use me up to the limit." He traveled 21,000 miles in eight weeks while Bryan covered 16,000 miles in five and a half. They were equally biting. Bryan, said Roosevelt, "seeks to sow seeds of malice and envy among Americans." Republicans, preached Bryan, "are now sure that it is both immoral and criminal to oppose forcible annexation." Roosevelt ended up calling Bryan "my opponent" and the fictitious political humorist "Mr. Dooley" remarked: "'Tis Teddy alone that's runnin' and he ain't r'runnin', he's gallopin'."

When imperialism failed to rally the public to his side, Bryan tried trusts and his favorite, free silver. Nothing worked. The Spanish-American War had been popular and the annexation of the Philippines already accomplished. More important, the people as a whole felt prosperous. On election day McKinley enjoyed a greater margin of victory than four years earlier, but the turnout, mirroring the level of excitement about the campaign, was lower.

Six months after his inauguration, McKinley was in Buffalo for the Pan-American Exposition. Eager to shake hands with those waiting in line, even though he had been warned of danger, the president reached out to a twenty-eight-year-old unemployed laborer and anarchist. Before his eyes, the man's hand became a gun. McKinley died September 14. "Now look," barked Hanna, "that damned cowboy is President of the United States."

★ CAMPAIGN OF 1904 ★

Major Candidates Theodore Roosevelt, 46, New York, Republican
Alton B. Parker, 52, New York, Democrat

Credentials Roosevelt was a New York state assemblyman (1882–1884), a member of the U.S. Civil Service Commission (1889–1895), president of the New York City Police Board (1895–1897), and became assistant secretary of the navy (1897–1898). He fought in the Spanish-American War as a lieutenant colonel (1898), was elected New York governor (1898–1900) and vice president in 1900.

Parker was elected surrogate of Ulster county (1877–1885), appointed to the New York supreme court (1885–1889), the state appeals court (1889–1896), the appellate division of the state supreme court (1896–1897), and elected chief justice of the New York court of appeals (1898–1904).

Tickets The Republicans met in Chicago, where Theodore Roosevelt was unanimously selected on the first ballot. His only possible competitor, Mark Hanna, had died four months earlier. Almost as easily, the convention chose by acclamation Senator Charles Fairbanks from the important (but not secure) state of Indiana for the vice-presidency.

The Democrats, with delegates from Florida elected in a public primary, met uproariously in St. Louis and chose conservative judge Alton B. Parker when votes were shifted after the first ballot. Parker ended up with 679 votes; newspaper tycoon and New York senator William Randolph Hearst was runner-up with 181 votes. The nomination was made unanimous. In a real eye-opener, the delegates turned to 81-year-old millionaire Henry Davis for the vice-presidential slot.

The new Socialist party also held a national convention, nominating labor leader Eugene Debs of Indiana along with New Yorker Benjamin Hanford.

Campaign Notes Constrained by presidential precedent from public campaigning, Roosevelt left that to others. Roosevelt stayed in the White House or at Sagamore Hill, his New York home, but acted much like a stage director. He peppered the favorable New York *Press* with story ideas and pinpointed constituencies that needed attention.

Parker did not stump either, preferring to sit on his front porch in Esopus, New York, but few people came by to this outpost.

Symbols The "Big Stick" and the "Teddy Bear" were twin symbols of the Roosevelt years. Parker Democrats, as distinct from Bryan Democrats, wore buttons with a gold background, much as the Republicans had in 1896. By now, too, the donkey and the elephant were generally being used to represent Democrats and Republicans.

THEODORE ROOSEVELT

Slogans Roosevelt's "Square Deal" got top billing with such slogans as "A Square Deal for Every Man." There was also "The Big Stick," "Win with Teddy," "Stand Pat," "Theodore Roosevelt, One and Indivisible," and "Same Old Flag and Victory."

The Democrats came up with "Judge Parker a Noble Man for Our Next President."

Songs "Teddy" was the issue in this campaign and the songs—of both parties—reflected it. At the same time, some of the fun and gusto of nineteenth-century songsters was missing as professional lyricists, more intent on selling sheet music than a particular candidate, got into the act.

Roosevelt's theme music was "A Hot Time in the Old Town Tonight" (which a St. Louis brothel had first put on the map). Otherwise, there was the ragtime "You're All Right, Teddy" and "We Want Teddy Four Years More."

Parker's people sang "Good-by, Teddy, You Must March! March! March!": "Go wash the White House china / and all the linen starch." In "Parker! Parker! You're the Moses Who Will Lead Us out of the Wilderness" they picked up one of Roosevelt's favorite expressions—"deelighted"—and used it against the Republicans: "No more mountain lion shooting, no more wild and wooly fun. . . . Everyone will be *deelighted*, for we have them on the run."

Paraphernalia   In spite of the fact that campaigns were tamer now than they had been in the late nineteenth century, the paraphernalia business was still big. Roughly a thousand different buttons, a hundred varieties of pocket-watch ribbons, and a gallery of posters, penny postcards, and bandannas turned up, as did pipes and playing cards.

Among the Republican items were "Teddy Bear" stuffed animals and buttons, a whistle in the shape of the candidate's toothy grin, a decorative "Rough Rider" serving tray, and "Equality" buttons showing Roosevelt dining with black educator Booker T. Washington, as he had done at the White House in 1901.

The Democrats proved more mean-spirited. In the South one card proclaimed: "The Election of Roosevelt Means Booker Niggerism." A poster of target rings superimposed on a bear was titled "Who Can Kill Teddy Bear?"

Popular Labels   Roosevelt was hailed as "Teddy the Trustbuster," "The Cowboy President," "Peacemaker," and, of course, the "Rough Rider."

Parker was known as "Safe and Sane" and the "Gold Democrat."

Name-calling   To his enemies Roosevelt was, at best, "His Accidency" and at worst "militarist," "imperialist," "usurper," and "political adventurer."

Parker was belittled as "Parker the Silent."

The Press   New York *Sun*, swallowing its past scorn of Roosevelt, declared "Theodore, with all thy faults."

The anti-Roosevelt New Orleans *Times-Democrat* wrote: "The fundamental values of the republic can not survive if this pigmy autocrat be allowed to work his own sweet will through another four years of licensed egotism."

Spending   Even though Roosevelt had proved no friend of big business, corporations did not desert to the Democrats. As a result the Republicans had a war chest of $2,096,000 compared with $700,000 for the opposition.

Firsts   The first landslide election of the twentieth century.

Roosevelt was the first "successor President" to win the presidency in his own right.

The Socialist party made its debut.

First delegates (Democrats in Florida) are chosen by a public primary.

Trends   Voter turnout and campaign participation continue to fall off.

Newspaper journalism plays an important role.

Advertising techniques become popular as a way of selling presidential candidates.

Vote   Forty-five states participated. Roosevelt overwhelmed Parker with 7,628,785 popular votes (57 percent) and 336 electoral votes to 5,084,442 (38 percent) and 140 for his opponent. Socialist Debs won 402,895 popular votes, or 3 percent, but no electoral votes.

Benchmarks   Roosevelt won more electoral votes than any president-elect before him.

The worst major party electoral-vote defeat since 1872.

The biggest popular-vote margin of victory up until then.

Quote   After the election, Roosevelt enjoyed telling his wife "I am no longer a political accident."

THEODORE Roosevelt had "such fun" being president, and it showed. Not yet forty-three, the youngest ever, when he stepped into the presidency after William McKinley's assassination, Theodore Roosevelt was all set to behave. "It shall be my aim," he told the cabinet moments before taking the oath of office, "to continue, absolutely unbroken, the policy of President McKinley." But soon the rambunctious new president was striking "my own note" and making waves where mild-mannered McKinley would have made none.

Roosevelt's zest was legendary, sometimes puckishly so. Once, TR, as he was called, asked a foreign diplomat along on a nude swim in the Potomac, starting a rumor that "the President is really only six years old." And about a month after taking office he impulsively invited the first black, Booker T. Washington, founder of Tuskegee Institute, to lunch at the White House. It caused quite a stir, especially in the South. But Roosevelt said he intended to ask Dr. Washington "to dine just as often as I pleased."

He was always testing his powers as president, daring what recent, more passive presidents had not. But Roosevelt also knew when to pull back. He did not invite the black leader again and his trust-busting, while gutsy, was limited. Above all, Roosevelt treated the presidency as a "bully pulpit" and the press, wooed with access and good copy, was swept along. Barrel-chested and bull-necked, eyes in perpetual motion and gestures too, Roosevelt had so much personality it infected those about him. He enjoyed taking his message to the public, even if startling some listeners with his rather shrill, high-pitched voice. But they liked it when he admonished "the predatory rich" and demanded that "big business give people a square deal." Abroad, the president took a little-known African proverb—"speak softly and carry a big stick"—and turned it into a passport for asserting America's international role.

Despite all this public bravado, Roosevelt still questioned his electoral appeal. He doubted that businessmen would stay with him. But by the time the Republican convention rolled around there was no doubt that Roosevelt was in control. His one faint rival, "Standpatter" senator Mark Hanna, McKinley's famous campaign manager, had died a few months earlier. (Some said it was of heartbreak, since Roosevelt had forced Hanna into an early endorsement of himself.) It was one of the dullest conventions ever.

The Democratic convention, in contrast, was one of the wilder ones. Two-time loser William Jennings Bryan, like Marley's ghost, came to haunt the delegates, but not to be their candidate. He was pleased when they adopted some of his issues and rejected a gold plank but displeased when "Safe and Saners" pushed through their nominee, Judge Alton B. Parker. As if to prove Bryan right, Parker immediately wired the convention that he would take a stand for gold, otherwise offering to withdraw. Delegates accepted Parker, gold and all. Bryan eventually did too.

Parker's resolve made Roosevelt fret that he faced a "formidable opponent." For the most part, the press disagreed, saying that Parker had all "the salient qualities of the sphere" and that his acceptance speech "fell upon his party like a wet blanket."

Neither side came out swinging; a campaign as apathetic as James Monroe's second, it was thought. The Democrats lobbed a few, but nothing worked against the Republican's well-organized campaign. Even big business stayed with Roosevelt—deciding that, after all, Roosevelt was safer, if not saner, than Parker. Finally, at the tail end of the campaign, Parker, taking his lead from the Democratic *World*, accused the trusts of fueling the Republican war chest in return for favors. Roosevelt's dander was up. The charge was "unqualifiedly and atrociously false," he screamed. With no proof, Parker gave up.

Roosevelt was "dee-lighted" with his overwhelming win. "Tomorrow," he said at the time of his inauguration, "I shall come into office in my own right . . . then watch out for me!" But Roosevelt had already softened his "Big Stick" somewhat by reading a statement to reporters the night of his election that he would not run again. He explained that he will have served almost two terms and that that was enough for any president. Not long into his second term, TR changed his mind, telling one friend, "I would cut my hand off right there [at the wrist] if I could recall that written statement."

★ CAMPAIGN OF 1908 ★

Major Candidates   William Howard Taft, 51, Ohio, Republican
William Jennings Bryan, 48, Nebraska, Democrat

Credentials   Taft was appointed Cincinnati superior court judge (1887–1890), U.S. solicitor general (1890–1892), and Sixth U.S. Circuit Court judge (1892–1900). Under President William McKinley became Philippines commissioner (1900–1901), then governor-general (1901–1904), and, under Presi-

WILLIAM HOWARD TAFT

dent Theodore Roosevelt, secretary of war (1904–1908) and provisional
governor of Cuba (1906).

For Bryan, see Campaign of 1900.

Tickets The Democrats met in Denver. Alton B. Parker's huge loss to Theodore Roosevelt had turned Democratic eyes toward William Jennings Bryan,
their now-aging silver prince once again. From Fairview, his home in Nebraska, Bryan was in complete charge. On the first ballot, he won in a walk
with 892½ votes out of 998. It was made unanimous. For the vice-presidential
spot the delegates chose Indiana's John W. Kern, two-time unsuccessful
gubernatorial candidate, by acclamation.

The Republicans convened in Chicago. Although Roosevelt was not a
candidate, he ran the show from the White House. His candidate was Secretary of War William Howard Taft, running against six other candidates and
easily winning with 702 out of 976 delegate votes. His nomination was made
unanimous. Representative James Sherman was voted in on the first ballot
as the vice-presidential nominee.

The Socialists held their second national convention, renominating the
1904 ticket of Eugene Debs and Benjamin Hanford.

Convention Color The Democrats exceeded anything before or since by
their outburst for Bryan. It was partly staged that way. When his name was
merely mentioned, the place erupted. This was unrehearsed at first. Parades

snaked through the hall and state banners went flying toward the stage. Then the spontaneity became something else. Sweaty delegates wondered of each other: "Have we gone over the time yet?" Well over an hour went by before it was agreed that the old record of forty-seven minutes in 1896 had been beaten and the delegates, disheveled and exhausted, stopped.

Campaign Notes Bryan intended to stump less, agreeing with advisers that he would appear more dignified by staying at home and letting people and reporters come to him. But by mid-September he was campaigning just as hard as ever. Making as many as thirty speeches a day, Bryan would often fall down on his bed exhausted and aides would have to throw cold water on his face to wake him up for his next appearance.

Taft initially had no great interest in campaigning and, in fact, spent much more time on the golf course than making speeches until the end of September. Roosevelt admonished him at one point not to allow photographers to catch him on the links. Once Taft got started, he liked the spotlight and even worried about his voice giving out.

Symbols Bryan's followers sported palmleaf fans. Taft, as Roosevelt's hand-picked successor, inherited his symbols—the "Big Stick," sometimes downsized to a wearable toy baseball bat, and even the teddy bear. Taft himself was identified with the possum; there was even a "Possum Klub."

Slogans The Democrats rallied around "Let the People Rule" and "Down with the Trusts." Capitalizing on Taft's girth, they taunted "Nobody Loves a Fat Man" and "330 Pounds—Not Electoral Votes."

Taft was hailed as "The Man of the Hour," his motto was "Smile, Smile, Smile" and his program, like Roosevelt's, "A Square Deal for All." Bryan was pegged as a loser: "If Not Elected First Time, Run, Run Again" and "Vote for Taft This Time—You Can Vote for Bryan Any Time."

Songs Songs were fewer this year and not so catchy. Democrats sang "Billy Bryan Is the Man for Me" and "Line up for Bryan."

Republicans optimistically sang "Get on the Raft with Taft" even though Taft's 330 pounds would have made that difficult.

Paraphernalia Political penny postcards were more popular and satiric than ever. "The Candidates at Exercise," sent out by the Democrats, showed Bryan "The Commoner" pitching hay, next to an insert of Lincoln splitting rails, while Taft "The Pluotcrat" played golf with "29 Million Dollar John." The Republicans circulated "The Nebraska Cuckoo Clock," with Bryan on the clock face and the message "Will Run Every Four Years If Properly Wound."

Popular Labels Bryan was "The Nation's Commoner" and "Billy Boy."

Taft was "Big Bill," "Smiling Bill," and "Good Old Will." Running mate Sherman was "Sunny Jim."

Name-calling   To opponents, Bryan was the "Balding Boy Orator" and the "chameleon candidate," while Taft was "Roosevelt's shadow," "Prince William" to "King Theodore," and a "dodger."

The Press   *The New York Times* ridiculed the Democratic ticket: "For a man twice defeated for the Presidency was at the head of it, and a man twice defeated for the governor of his state was at the tail of it."

Spending   The Tillman Act in 1907 barred contributions from corporations, although stockholders and officers could continue to give, and did. Republicans raised less than in 1896 and 1900, $1,655,518 to $629,341 for the Democrats.

First   The Democratic convention introduced automatic voting machines for balloting.

Vote   With forty-six states participating, Taft went over the top with 7,679,006 popular votes (52 percent) and 321 electoral votes to 6,409,106 (43 percent) and 162 for Bryan. The Socialists won 420,000 popular and no electoral votes.

Benchmarks   Taft was one of the most reluctant candidates in history.
Bryan received the longest convention demonstration ever.
Taft was one of the most reluctant candidates ever.

Quote   As telegraph relayed the news of Taft's victory to Roosevelt at his Long Island home, the President kept exclaiming "We have beaten them to a frazzle."

No one wanted William Howard Taft to be president more than Nellie. Independent and willful, Helen Taft was also frivolous, singing of mint juleps, and daring when she pleased. She was the first white woman to visit the mountainous Luzon region, braving heavy rains and traveling gingerly on horseback, commenting too on the native men's physique and even the colors of their G-string. For the most part, though, Nellie showed a serious side, forming "Drop of Milk" to supply Philippine mothers with supplemental sterilized milk and setting an example of civility toward the island people. But her greatest effort was to come. Nellie had decided that her friendly, oversize lawyer-husband, "Big Lub" to schoolmates, whom she had met at her own "salon" and who had done wonders for the Philippines, should be president. She would get help.

Theodore Roosevelt finally lured Taft back from the Philippines to be secretary of war in the fall of 1903. It was the third "Dear Will" offer the president had made. The other two (seats on the Supreme Court) Taft, now governor-general, had turned down, appealing for more time in his post. The secretaryship suited Nellie just fine "because it was in line with the kind of work I wanted my husband to do." That "work" became more apparent when Taft regretted yet another Supreme Court appointment at his wife's urging. It was crystal-clear one evening at the White House when the Roosevelts were entertaining the Tafts. The president feigned a trance, saying, "I see a man weighing 350 pounds. There is something hanging over his head. I cannot make out what it is. . . . At one time it looks like the presidency, then again it looks like the chief justiceship." Nellie interceded: "Make it the presidency." Taft quietly chose "the chief justiceship."

By January 1908 Taft had little choice. Roosevelt, committed not to run for a "third term," was under pressure to name a successor. His first choice, Secretary of State Elihu Root, declined. "We had better turn to Taft," Roosevelt told his secretary. "He has the experience." Then the president set about arm-twisting. "It's Taft or me," he threatened party conservatives, who had seen fit to name the Panic of 1907 after him. Progressives, eager for more Roosevelt-style reform in industries like meat-packing and thirsty for further land conservation (125 million acres already), he told tartly: "It's Taft—I'm out!" In Chicago, ten thousand Republican conventioneers, not so personally tutored, shouted, "Four—four—four years more!" But Roosevelt held back, Taft was nominated and *The Times* of London declared the convention Roosevelt's "greatest and most striking" victory.

William Jennings Bryan needed only Alton B. Parker's landslide defeat in 1904 to pick up his wares and peddle again. But shorn of silver, a "Boy Orator" no longer, his rich raven hair now receding and grayish, his brazenness past prime, Bryan's allure was more sentimental than real. Yet there was no doubt that he would be the Democrats' standard-bearer a third time. The fifteen thousand spectators and delegates who crowded into Denver for their party's convention were shamelessly smitten with Bryan.

Bryan's newfound popularity came at a price. His issues, such as currency reform and trust regulation, once dazzlingly radical, were now almost dull and mainstream. His thunder stolen, Bryan needed to find new ways to woo voters. He tried turning tables on the Republicans and calling himself the "advance agent of prosperity" but was mocked. He announced that he would not accept campaign gifts over ten thousand dollars and that all donors would be publicized. But when his list of contributors came out in mid-October, the sums were so paltry they discouraged others from backing him.

Before taking the stump, Taft took to the golf links, his favorite pastime, excusing himself that at 297 pounds he needed to reduce before campaigning. When he did get going at the end of September, his speeches were ponderous and full of statistics. Still, the crowds liked him and his smile and were enthusiastic when he said that he stood "shoulder to shoulder" with the president. Roosevelt was not as easy to please, urging from the sidelines "Do not answer Bryan, attack him!" Another time, he wrote "I wish you had some of my bad temper."

Bryan cried foul and said the president "should let his man and me fight it out before the people." Bryan had other troubles too. Even though Samuel

Gompers, head of the American Federation of Labor, had endorsed Bryan, businessmen were doing their best to keep their employees from following the union leader. Bryan's efforts to win Northern Catholics and Southern blacks also fell short.

Taft literally rolled into the presidency (he was 333 pounds by this time), defeating Bryan, who had promised not to run again, more soundly than ever. Nellie, who was never happier in her life, took the occasion of the inauguration to break precedent and take the carriage with her husband from the Capitol to the reviewing stand. Only Taft seemed ambivalent, remarking on his return to the White House after the ceremonies, "I am President now, and tired of being kicked around."

★ CAMPAIGN OF 1912 ★

Major Candidates   William Howard Taft, 55, Ohio, Republican
Theodore Roosevelt, 54, New York, Progressive
Woodrow Wilson, 56, New Jersey, Democrat

Credentials   For Taft, see Campaign of 1908. He was elected president in 1908.

For Roosevelt, see Campaign of 1904. He became vice president in 1900, becoming president on the death of McKinley in September 1901. He was reelected in 1904.

Wilson was professor of jurisprudence and political economy at Princeton University (1890–1902), president of Princeton University (1902–1910), and governor of New Jersey (1911–1913).

Tickets   The Republicans met in Chicago on June 18, after a history making pre-convention primary struggle (see campaign narrative, below). In twelve states, there was now either the direct election of delegates, a preferential vote for president or both.

Taft, whose name was placed in nomination by small-town newspaper editor Warren Harding of Ohio, easily won on the first ballot. For the vice-presidential spot, the convention renominated James Sherman (but Sherman was sick and upon his death the national committee replaced him with Columbia University president Nicholas Murray Butler).

Roosevelt had no intention of staying silent. The day after the Republicans adjourned he announced the formation of the Progressive party, nicknamed the Bull Moose party. It convened; by acclamation the former president was chosen for the presidential spot and California Governor Hiram Johnson as his running mate.

WOODROW WILSON

The Democrats chose Baltimore for their convention, starting June 25. House Speaker Champ Clark of Missouri came to the convention with close to twice as many pledged delegates as likely runner-up, New Jersey governor Woodrow Wilson, but was short of a majority. Eventually, with the help of William Jennings Bryan, who refused to support Clark when the Tammany Hall-backed New York delegation switched its support to him, Wilson won the nomination on the forty-sixth ballot. Indiana governor Thomas Marshall was picked for the second spot.

The Socialists nominated Eugene Debs for a fourth time.

Campaign Notes This election saw an incumbent president take off his gloves and campaign for office. Taft was particularly competitive during the primaries, although he lost eleven of twelve, including his home state of Ohio. After his nomination, Taft gave his acceptance and a few other speeches, but essentially left the stumping and the race itself to Roosevelt and Wilson.

Campaigning from the rear platform of a train, Roosevelt was alternately fiery and folksy, telling children: "Don't crowd so close to the car; it might back up, and we can't afford to lose any little Bull Mooses, you know."

Wilson relaxed as time went by, throwing campaign buttons to crowds and showing an easy humor. Once, looking out on people all around his train, some even perched on the top of boxcars, he began, "Fellow citizens, gentlemen in the pit, and the ladies and gentlemen in the boxes."

Symbols The Republicans had the elephant and sometimes used the possum, a 1908 symbol, for Taft. The Progressive party had the bull moose, and party members waved red bandannas. The Democrats had the donkey and sometimes used a rowboat to promote "Wood-row" Wilson.

Slogans "Tried and Safe" Taft's followers bragged. They also chanted "Washington Wouldn't! Grant Couldn't! Roosevelt Shan't! No Third Term!"

Roosevelt called his program the "New Nationalism" and his party's platform a "Covenant with the People." He campaigned for "A Square Deal All Around."

Wilson's vision for the country was the "New Freedom." Democrats wanted to "Win with Wilson."

Songs "Get on the Raft with Taft" and "Possum Bill" were revived from 1908. New was "Taft the Leader."

In "Teddy, Come Back" Roosevelt's supporters sang "We miss your daring, dashing style." The same point was made in "When Teddy Comes Marching Home," "Teddy'll Swat the Bosses," and "The Moose Is Loose."

"Wilson—That's All!" was already in people's minds as a popular advertisement for a whiskey, so it was only natural that it became the title of a campaign song for the Democratic candidate.

Paraphernalia Overall there was a decline in campaign items, even though the race itself was extraordinarily lively. Parade canes, for example, made a last stand, a sure sign that gloriously extravagant political parades were a thing of the past. Once-popular penny postcards were on the wane as greeting cards in envelopes made the scene. There were also fewer buttons, ribbons and decorative pieces.

Taft buttons read "The sAFesT."

Roosevelt's campaign came up with the "National Progressive" red bandanna, decorated with spectacles, toothy grins, big sticks, teddy bears, rough-rider hats, and bull moose.

Wilson had "Pride of New Jersey" and "For the White House Bound, with a Platform Safe and Sound" buttons.

Popular Labels Taft was known as "Big Bill" and the "Peaceful President."

Roosevelt was called "The Great Hunter" and "Bull Moose," "Rough Rider," "TR," "Teddy," and "The Colonel."

Wilson was hailed as "The Scholar in Politics" and "The People's President" and the "Ultimate Democrat."

Name-calling Roosevelt, the feistiest campaigner, called the president "a fathead who had an intellect a little short of a guinea pig," "apostate," and "a dead cock in a pit."

Taft retaliated by describing Roosevelt as a "dangerous egotist," "demagogue," and "flatterer of the people." To both Republicans and Democrats, Roosevelt was "Teddy the Meddler." Wilson labeled Roosevelt "incompetent as President."

The Press When Roosevelt announced that his hat was in the ring, the conservative *Harper's Weekly* declared "Hate, not hat, is in the ring."

Spending The Republican drive did not live up to expectations, bringing in $1,071,549. The Progressives raised $676,672 and the Democrats $1,134,848, both parties doing better than expected. Parties had to reveal the source of funds under a campaign disclosure law passed by Congress in 1910.

Firsts Wilson was the first presidential candidate to win office by stumping.
Taft was the first president to stump for votes.
The first test for presidential primaries.
Wilson was the first candidate since the Civil War to be born and raised in the South.

Trends The evolution of the modern Democratic party.
More direct public participation in presidential primaries and stumping.

Vote Forty-eight states participated. Wilson won an unprecedented 435 electoral votes—forty states. Roosevelt won 88 electoral votes and six states and Taft 8 votes and two states. In the popular vote, Wilson fell considerably short of a majority, with only 41.9 percent (6,283,019) to Roosevelt's 27.4 percent (4,119,507) and Taft's 23.2 percent (3,484,956). The Socialists managed 6 percent or 900,000 votes.

Benchmarks Wilson won the largest electoral vote to date.
The Socialists won their largest vote ever.
Roosevelt's campaign was one of the most radical in the country's history.
The most spirited third-party campaign ever.

Quote With the election of Wilson, said *The New York Times*, "The people had determined to take the government once more into their own hands."

O NCE fast friends, they were now political enemies, parading their anger for all to see and in the process breaking up a political party that had been in power all but eight of the preceding fifty-two years. There was a time when Theodore Roosevelt had embraced Howard Taft as "you blessed old trump, you big, generous fellow" and told everyone that only Taft could carry out "my policies."

As president, Taft's confidence and geniality were suddenly at risk. Targeted by progressive Republicans, he launched into self-pity about the "hard time" he was having. His easy smile was replaced by irritability and later anger. In part, his wife's stroke just months after he took office made his duties heavy to bear. But Taft also fell short of an image. Even though he excelled in trust-busting and regulatory legislation he compromised on the Payne–Aldrich tariff, yet called it the "best tariff bill" his party had ever passed, and found himself forced to fire noted conservationist and chief forester Gifford Pinchot in a policy dispute. Roosevelt loyalists were up in arms.

Their leader's return from an African safari in June 1910 was a political letdown. Roosevelt announced he would "make no comment or criticism for at least two months." But soon his opinions were in the newspapers and, after the Republicans lost the House in the midterm election, he became more outwardly critical of the administration. Taft seemed at a loss, telling an aide, "If I only knew what the President [as he still called Roosevelt] wanted, I would do it, but . . . he has held himself so aloof."

"The fight is on and I am stripped to the buff!" Roosevelt declared on February 21, 1912, as he threw his hat in the ring and challenged his old friend for the Republican nomination. His game plan was to try to win all of the new presidential primaries and show that he, not Taft, should be the nominee. Surprisingly, Taft shed the incumbent's coat of silence and went head to head with Roosevelt. Roosevelt, he argued, was a "dangerous egotist" and a "demagogue." But Roosevelt stooped lower, calling Taft "disloyal to every canon of ordinary decency" and "a fathead" with an intellect "little short of a guinea pig."

In June, Roosevelt came to the Republican convention in Chicago sporting his Rough Rider outfit under a large sombrero and boasting nine out of twelve primary victories. (Taft won one and Wisconsin Senator Robert La Follette, a progressive like Roosevelt, two.) But that was not enough. Party bosses had seen to it that a critical number of contested delegates were decided in favor of Taft. On the eve of the convention, Roosevelt painted the contest in stark, spiritual tones: "We stand at Armageddon, and we battle for the Lord." It took only one ballot for Taft to secure the nomination. That was all that was necessary too for the formation of a new Progressive party. A few weeks later Roosevelt, saying he was "feeling like a Bull Moose," arrived back in Chicago to become the third party's nominee. Enthusiastic delegates went forth singing "Onward, Christian Soldiers," starry-eyed about their man.

Maybe the Democrats won right then, when the Republicans split in two. Or maybe they also needed the right candidate, one who could compete with Roosevelt on reform but be less threatening than three-time standard-bearer William Jennings Bryan. If that was the case, they were lucky when, on the forty-sixth ballot with Bryan's help, New Jersey governor Woodrow Wilson became their nominee. Pushed into office by party bosses whom he then turned on to accomplish reform, a Gold Democrat who slowly Bryanized his thinking, this former Princeton president, a skilled orator with self-righteous fervor, was perfect for the part. He won friends when he said in his acceptance speech: "There is no indispensable man."

Tutored by the respected Louis Brandeis, "the people's lawyer," Wilson came up with a liberal economic program of "New Freedom" to match Roosevelt's "New Nationalism." A schoolmaster at heart, Wilson lectured his audiences that he wanted to break up the trusts, to restore competition, to favor littleness and "men on the make." Roosevelt argued that trusts were here to stay, that they should be regulated, not "busted." Roosevelt argued too that Wilson's ideas were fifty years late and nothing more than "rural toryism."

The contest came down to the two of them. Taft had all but dropped out, telling his wife "There are so many people who don't like me." Roosevelt took to the stump sooner and stayed out longer, traveling from coast to coast and even to the South. Wilson, who said he was not going to take "swings around the circle" or campaign from the rear platform of a train, changed his mind about both and even enjoyed himself. At one stop, when a man in the crowd shouted "Hello, Woody!," Wilson remarked "At last I feel I have arrived in politics."

On October 14, an assassin's bullet shot through doubled-over pages of a prepared speech and a metal spectacle case to lodge in Roosevelt's chest. Classically, a bloodied Roosevelt gave his speech before going to the hospital. While sympathy surged for the ex-president, voters stayed put. Bookmakers were now offering six-to-one odds in Wilson's favor. On election day the results were quickly known. A lopsided victory for Wilson—overwhelming in electoral votes, only a plurality in popular votes—was enough to give the new president a clear mandate for reform.

For Roosevelt it was a last hurrah. "You can't hold a party like the Progressive party together," he said. "There are no loaves and fishes."

★ CAMPAIGN OF 1916 ★

Major Candidates   Woodrow Wilson, 60, New Jersey, Democrat
                     Charles Evans Hughes, 54, New York, Republican

Credentials   For Wilson, see Campaign of 1912. He was elected president in 1912.

Hughes served as legal counsel for a state investigation of the gas industry (1905) and a federal investigation of the insurance industry (1906), was elected governor of New York (1907–1910) and appointed to the Supreme Court (1910).

Tickets   The Democrats met in St. Louis. There was no contest. Woodrow Wilson was renominated, 1092 to one. Choosing a running mate was even easier. Vice President Thomas Marshall, who had become famous for saying

CHARLES EVANS HUGHES

"What this country needs is a really good five-cent cigar" was voted in—with Wilson's approval—by acclamation.

The Republicans gathered in Chicago. The Progressive party, which still had not returned to the fold, convened separately on the same day about a mile away. Committees from both sides met to reach agreement on a candidate, but when the Progressives insisted on Theodore Roosevelt, the Republicans said no. The parties continued talking to no avail and finally each went ahead with its own nominations. Among seventeen candidates, the Republicans chose Charles Evans Hughes on the third ballot with 949½ out of 987 votes. It was made unanimous. For second place the delegates picked Charles Fairbanks, who had been Roosevelt's vice president.

Campaign Notes   Wilson did not stump for reelection. He made some front-porch speeches from Shadow Lawn, a summer retreat in New Jersey, and some more around the country. He also thought he would follow the maxim "Never to murder a man who is committing suicide slowly but surely."

Hughes surprised many by jumping right into campaigning, kissing babies and shaking as many hands as he could.

Both parties stressed advertising techniques that had become increasingly popular. They used billboards (surpassing the 23,000 for Taft in 1912) and advertisements in newspapers and streetcars. Since rallies were fast disappearing and movies now attracted the crowds, both sides produced films for theater audiences.

Symbols The Democrats were big on the flag, while Republicans featured the elephant and the bull moose together.

Slogans Wilson and the Democrats had a winner in "He Kept Us Out of War." They also used "Peace with Honor," "He Proved the Pen Mightier Than the Sword," and "War in the East! Peace in the West! Thank God for Wilson!" They taunted Republicans with "Wilson and Peace with Honor, or Hughes with Roosevelt and War."

Republicans hailed "America First" and "America Efficient." They mocked Wilson with "He Kept Us Out of Suffrage."

Songs Not surprisingly, Abraham Lincoln's campaign slogan became a Wilson song: "Never Swap Horses When You Are Crossing a Stream." Most adoring was "I Think We've Got Another Washington (And Wilson Is His Name)": "It takes a little while for him to make up his mind, / But he gets there just the same."

The Republicans sang "Charles Hughes, the American": "As Governor of the Empire State, / Honest government you did give." Other hits were "So Long Mr. Wilson" and "The Dizzy Dem-erratic Donkey."

Paraphernalia Buttons were the vogue, with other paraphernalia almost nonexistent. Some for the President were "Woodrow Wilson's Wisdom Wins Without War," "Preparedness/Peace/Prosperity," and "Stand by the President."

An elephant and a bull moose appeared on a button that read "Republicans/Bull Moosers/Get Together." Another highlighted the U and S in Hughes' name. A lapel pin of Hughes wearing Uncle Sam's hat said "It Fits Hughes."

Popular Labels Wilson was "The Man of Peace" and "The Man of the Hour." Hughes was "The Faithful Public Servant" and "The Champion."

Name-calling Roosevelt called Wilson a "pacifist professor," a "damned Presbyterian hypocrite," and a "Byzantine logothete."

Roosevelt was not sparing of Hughes, either, saying privately that he was a "bearded iceberg" and a "whiskered Wilson."

Democrats belittled Hughes as an "animated feather duster" and gave him a new middle name: "E-vasion."

The Press Discussing Hughes, *The New Republic* said it was "very interesting to find a man of rare courage and frankness, of balanced mind . . . wandering around over the country trailing nothing but cold and damp platitudes."

Spending The Democrats reported spending about $2,284,590 compared to $2,441,565 by the Republicans.

First The first election to really impact the world.

Trends The importance of mass advertising in campaigns.
The rise in influence of interest groups.

Vote In a tight race with forty-eight states participating, Wilson won 277 electoral votes and 9,127,695 popular votes (49.3 percent) to 254 and 8,533,507 (46.1 percent) for Hughes. The Socialists had 3 percent, or 585,113 votes.

Benchmarks Wilson is the only two-time minority President.
Women could vote in one-fourth of the states.

Quote Divining the election results, the British ambassador concluded: "The United States does not want to go to war."

FEELING lucky in love and politics, Woodrow Wilson must have relished the rumors circulating in 1916 that if he fell out of a sixteen-story building he "would hit on a feather bed." What light years away from the "intolerable loneliness and isolation" the president felt after the brutal coincidence of his wife Ellen's death and a Serbian student's bullet into history in August 1914!

Only months later Wilson was preoccupied again. This time because of his love for Edith Galt, whom he called "a special gift from heaven." "The President is wholly absorbed in this love affair," adviser Colonel Edward House noted in his diary, "and is neglecting practically everything else." It was the worst of times, too. The war in Europe, which arrayed Germany and Austria-Hungary against Serbia, Russia, Britain, and France in a battle greater than before, was daring America's neutrality. The British had stretched a necklace of mines and ships across the North Sea, preventing American vessels, richly outfitted with commercial goods, from reaching German ports. The Germans, their sleek new U-boats attacking sight unseen in the waters around the British Isles, had maddened many more by sinking the *Lusitania*, a British passenger liner with 128 Americans on board, in May 1915.

Still, Wilson played the pacifist, warning Germany to leave unarmed ships alone. He had caught the public mood perfectly. His romance had not. People could not forget Ellen Wilson so easily. There was gossip of a murder plot and of Ellen's gravesite left untended. A *Washington Post* engagement exclusive made matters worse by mistakenly saying that the president had spent the afternoon "entering" (instead of entertaining) his fiancée. Even those advisers who had wanted the marriage to take place after the upcoming election now favored the earlier date of December 18. They also encouraged the president to come out for women's suffrage to offset any favor he may have lost. He did.

"I am a progressive," Wilson proclaimed to no one's surprise in 1916. "I do not spell it with a capital P, but I think my pace is just as fast as those who do." Wilson had indeed turned heads in the beginning of his presidency by standing watch over Congress until it passed the reforms he wanted. He made periodic visits to the Capitol, sometimes unannounced, to lobby bills to passage. His "New Freedom" victories were swift. In just a year and a half, tariff rates were greatly reduced, a federal reserve banking system and a federal trade commission established, and monopolistic practices further curtailed. Next he started treading in Bull Moose territory, a move he figured would help his party with important interest groups in the general election. He pushed through farm credit legislation, a child labor law, workmen's compensation, and won an eight-hour day for railroad workers, averting a national strike.

Armed with progressivism and the prosperity that the war had brought to American industry, Wilson prepared to meet his Republican challenger, Charles Evans Hughes. But one thing he had not counted on was the pull of peace. At the Democratic convention in June word of Wilson's pacifism caused William Jennings Bryan to weep and delegates to roar their approval. In the end, "kept us out of war" was quietly put into the final draft of the platform. It became the party's most effective slogan.

Theodore Roosevelt, who refused the Progressive party's advances to support Hughes, would have liked the Republican nomination but admitted it would be a mistake "unless the country has in its mood something of the heroic." His strident stumping became legendary. Itching for American involvement in the European war, Roosevelt accused the president of using "weasel words" to stay on the sidelines and said that there should be "shadows enough" at Shadow Lawn, the President's summer retreat, "the shadows of the tortured dead."

Hughes himself was a disappointment. The whiskered, stern-faced, six-year Supreme Court justice tried his best to live down his iceberg reputation. He donned miner's garb to tour a copper mine, mingled with cowboys at the rodeo, kissed babies and pumped hands at ballgames and barbecues, but made only small gains. He antagonized the unions by calling the eight-hour law "labor's goldbrick"; he inadvertently missed an opportunity to meet with Progressive California governor Hiram Johnson in an incident that became known as the "forgotten handshake"; and his positions often seemed contradictory.

"Let Hughes run about the country if he wishes to," was Wilson's thought. He was not going to stump, believing the people wanted the president "at a time like this to stay on the job." Nevertheless, Wilson did pull a few of his own campaign punches, telegraphing a pro-German Irish-American leader who accused him of being pro-British that "I would be deeply mortified" to have support like his, and telling his front-porch listeners that a Republican success would drag the country into "the embroilments of the European war." Just before the election Democrats took out full-page ads in newspapers around the country, reading "Wilson and Peace with Honor? or Hughes with Roosevelt and War?"

To many the contest was not that simple. Wilson did win, but for almost two days the outcome was in doubt. Initially, the East poured in votes for Hughes. Newspapers announced his victory and a large electric sign over the Republican candidate's hotel heralded HUGHES. By Thursday evening the victory was Wilson's as California's thirteen electoral votes, by a margin of less than four thousand votes, fell into the president's column. And songwriters, not missing a beat, came up with a lively new postcampaign tune: "Be Good to California, Mr. Wilson (California Was Good to You)."

★ CAMPAIGN OF 1920 ★

Major Candidates   James Cox, 50, Ohio, Democrat
Warren G. Harding, 55, Ohio, Republican

Credentials   Cox was a newspaper reporter before becoming publisher of the *Dayton Daily News* in 1898. He served in the House of Representatives (1900–1913) and as governor of Ohio (1913–1915 and 1917–1921).

Harding was also a newspaper reporter before becoming publisher of the *Marion Star*. He became state senator (1899–1903), lieutenant governor (1903–1905), and U.S. senator (1915–1921).

Tickets   The Democrats opened their convention in San Francisco with many pretenders but no king. On the first ballot, twenty-four candidates were in the running. Slowly James M. Cox gained until he led on the twelfth ballot. (It took thirty-two more ballots before he was chosen unanimously.) For his running mate, Cox wanted and got Franklin Delano Roosevelt of New York, Wilson's assistant secretary of the navy and a fifth cousin of former president Theodore Roosevelt.

The Republicans met in Chicago, and they too had lacked an obvious front-runner since Theodore Roosevelt's death in January 1919. With eleven hats in the ring, Warren G. Harding, a dark horse from the critical state of Ohio emerged victorious on the tenth ballot from a deadlock resolved in the now-legendary "smoke-filled room" recess. Delegates stampeded Massachusetts governor Calvin Coolidge into second place on the first ballot.

Convention Color   The famous "smoke-filled room" meeting at the Republican convention that led to Harding's nomination was not a secret cabal as the image implies. Called after the first day of balloting when there was no clear winner, it extended into the early hours of Saturday morning. Finally, at

WARREN G. HARDING

about two in the morning, Harding was called for and asked if there was anything troublesome in his past. He left the room, sat by himself for ten minutes, perhaps made a phone call to his mistress Nan Britton, and returned to say "No, gentlemen, there is no such reason." It was then decided that if the deadlock continued support would shift to Harding.

Campaign Notes Cox decided to give Republicans a run for their millions. In September he announced that his Western tour would be "the most strenuous ever undertaken by a nominee for the Presidency"; he covered eighteen states in just twenty-nine days but won no electoral votes. During the entire campaign, he traveled 22,000 miles, gave 400 speeches to two million people, was arrested for speeding, was in a train accident, became hoarse, and was heckled.

Harding waged a "front-porch" campaign just as William McKinley had done in 1896, but was lured away in September and October to give some speeches.

The *Literary Digest* sent out millions of postcards, mainly to middle-class subscribers, in a poll that predicted a huge Republican victory.

Symbols The Democrats used the rooster and the donkey; the Republicans identified with the elephant.

Slogans Democrats vowed a "March of Progress."

Harding boasted "Back to Normalcy," "Let's Be Done with Wiggle and Wobble," and "America First!"

Other Republicans concocted "Cox and Cocktails—Harding and the Home" because of the Democratic candidate's opposition to Prohibition.

Songs Democrats sang "Gov'nor Cox You'll Surely Do": "The man we have has oft been tried, Like Washington, he's never lied."

"Mammy" Singer Al Jolson wrote the official Republican campaign song, "Harding, You're the Man for Us."

Paraphernalia The Democrats dreamed up "Coxsure" and "Americanize America" buttons. They also had Cox–Roosevelt jigsaw puzzles, "Keep Faith with Our Sons, Bring America into the League of Nations" stickers, a newfangled electric sign reading COX for window displays, and a colorful celluloid of Cox and Roosevelt with an eagle, a flag, and sunbeams.

The Republicans showed off Harding mechanical nose-thumbers, "Prosperity/Protection" buttons, "America First" cigar packs, and "America Always First/ Back to Normal/Law & Order" decals. To lure millions of new voters, a Harding ribbon read "Women's First Vote / Vote the Straight Republican Ticket."

Popular Labels "Astounding Cox" or "Jimmie" was up against "Great Handshaker" Harding or "W.G."

Name-calling Cox was belittled as a "puppet" of Wilson and a "bogeyman" who campaigned "like a frontier 'bad man' shooting up the meeting."

To Cox, Harding was a "Happy Hooligan." Others called the Republican nominee a "platitudinous jellyfish," a "puppet candidate," and a "party hack."

Curious Fact Harding's campaign theme—"America's present need is not heroism but healing, not nostrums but normalcy"—was based on a misstatement. Harding either slurred or changed the intended *normality* and the press put down *normalcy*.

The Press After the Cox and Harding nominations, the Providence *Journal* lamented: "The day of supermen is ended in the Democratic as well as the Republican party. From Roosevelt to Wilson we have dropt to two second-rate Ohio politicians."

Spending It was a Republican year, so the Democratic campaign chest suffered. The Democrats had only $1.5 to $2.2 million to spend against $5.4 to $8.1 million for the Republicans.

Firsts   Harding was the first member of the Senate to become president.
The first election to be affected by the Nineteenth Amendment.
The *Literary Digest* poll was the first large-scale poll of electoral preference.

Trends   "Smoke-filled room" entered the language.
Both vice-presidential candidates were active campaigners.

Vote   In an "earthquake" victory with forty-eight states voting, Harding won 404 electoral votes and 16,143,407 popular votes (60.4 percent) to 127 and 9,130,328 (34.2 percent) for Cox. Debs, the Socialist candidate, tallied no electoral votes but drew 919,799 popular votes (3.4 percent). Harding was favored by women, though this newly enfranchised group did not turn out in large numbers.

Benchmark   Harding broke all previous records on popular votes.

Quote   Commented the *New York Post*: "The colossal protest was against Woodrow Wilson and everything that from every conceivable angle might be attached to his name."

SENATOR Warren G. Harding was a model of William McKinley right down to his handshake. Like the former president, Harding made glad-handing an art, once calling it "the most pleasant thing I do." Harding was both a Republican from electorally important Ohio and "presidential-looking." So it was only natural, when Harding captured the Republican nomination, that there be another front-porch campaign.

In a bit of luck or foresight, the Hardings had redone their Greek Revival veranda a few years earlier and now, the arrival from nearby Canton of McKinley's old flagpole added a glorious finishing touch. On July 22, Notification Day, hometown Marion seemed a stage set, with boughs of bunting gracing avenues and gleaming golden eagles staring down from white columns to mark Victory Way, the route from the train station to the Harding home. There the candidate, his wife beside him, waited, impeccably dressed and sporting in his buttonhole McKinley's trademark red carnation. It was 1896 redux, as delegations undulated through the town, this time serenading the object of their affections with "Good Morning, Mr. Har-Har-Har-ding." All the summer long they came.

There was a major flaw, though, in this lookalike campaign. Harding simply did not measure up to McKinley in his political or personal life. Yes, he supported a protective tariff, McKinley's dream come true, but was at a loss to explain why. And, lacking self-confidence, Harding relied more heavily on imagemakers than McKinley had done. Once, when he stumbled delivering a speech, Harding paused, then wryly commented "Well, I never saw this before. I didn't write this speech and don't believe what I just read." But it was in other matters that Harding fell far short, juggling, at times, two mistresses and an illegitimate daughter while telling party leaders that he had nothing to conceal. In fact, after his dark-horse victory at the convention, Harding stopped off at a friend's apartment for a rendezvous with young Nan Britton before heading home.

In a crazy way, Harding was correct. His dalliances were not a campaign issue, even though the Britton affair became known—perhaps because Ohio's governor James M. Cox, the Democratic candidate, was divorced, or because both mistresses and even Duchess, as Harding called his wife, seemed quite content. Not touched either was Harding's slothful Senate record—he had managed to miss two-thirds of all roll-call votes, including one to send the Nineteenth Amendment to the states for ratification. Even his penchant for "bloviating" was considered soothing. How people loved it when the handsome senator said "America's present need is not heroics but healing; not nostrums but normalcy."

The public was weary. President Woodrow Wilson, now paralyzed and propped up in the presidency by his wife Edith, had led the country into "a war to end war" in April 1917. Americans, inspired by George M. Cohan, were soon two million strong "Over There." At home patriotism flourished, along with victory gardens, meatless Tuesdays, and wheatless Wednesdays. But then, fifty thousand Yanks did not return home and the economy lurched into postwar upheaval. President Wilson was another disappointment. At first, hailed in Europe as a hero, children's flowers at his feet and *Vive Wilson* lighting up the Paris skies, Wilson appeared outwitted at the Versailles peace conference. Finally, the League of Nations as his prize, Wilson returned home, only to lose his love's labor in partisan Senate wars—and his health too along the way.

It was probably a mistake for Cox and his running mate Franklin Roosevelt to make the White House their first campaign stop. But Cox, who was not a Wilson man, knew that he could not possibly win the presidency without Wilson's friends.

The die was cast. Cox would come across in the campaign as pro-League, saying "I favor going in." Harding would be anti-League, saying "I favor staying out." Both candidates would wobble and waver within that framework, Cox admitting that he would accept some reservations on League membership and Harding proposing some sort of "association" of nations. Other issues surfaced too. There were rumors of Harding having Negro blood, but the Democrats backed off for fear of adversely affecting the black vote. Cox harped for a while on the Republicans' corporate slush fund, but it backfired when he upped the estimate to thirty million dollars and was susceptible, in turn, to charges of being as "wet as the Atlantic Ocean" for receiving money from liquor companies.

Cox, campaigning with vigor, called Harding a "Happy Hooligan" and bellowed "Every traitor in America will vote tomorrow for Warren G. Harding." Roosevelt, equally energetic, announced "We will drag the enemy off the front porch." Nothing worked. "Cox or Harding? Harding or Cox?" one writer wondered. "You tell us, populi; You've got the vox." Loud and clear, the answer came back: Harding by seven million votes, a record-breaker. The populi, at least those who voted (and less than half did) wanted to go "Back to Normalcy" and forget Wilson. A report from the field to Roosevelt read: "The bitterness toward Wilson is evident everywhere and deeply rooted. He hasn't a friend."

★ CAMPAIGN OF 1924 ★

Major Candidates   Calvin Coolidge, 52, Massachusetts, Republican
John W. Davis, 51, West Virginia, Democrat

Credentials   Coolidge served as a Massachusetts state representative (1907–1908), mayor of Northampton (1910–1911), member of the state senate (1912–1915) and its president (1914–1915). He became lieutenant governor (1916–1918), governor (1919–1920), vice president of the U.S. (1921–1923), and became president in 1923 upon Harding's death.

Davis served as a West Virginia state representative (1899), in the House of Representatives (1911–1913), as solicitor general of the U.S. (1913–1918), and as ambassador to Great Britain (1918–1921), helping to draft the Treaty of Versailles of 1919.

Tickets   The Republicans met in Cleveland, with an obvious front-runner: President Calvin Coolidge, who won on the first ballot. The vice-presidential nomination was more complicated. Former Illinois governor Frank Lowden, who won on the first ballot, did not want it. Two more ballots gave the nomination to Charles Dawes, who had been the first budget director.

The Democrats convened in New York's old Madison Square Garden for an endurance contest that lasted seventeen days. Their forces were divided (see campaign narrative, below). After ninety-nine ballots John W. Davis was way behind, in third place. Finally, the two candidates ahead of him released their delegates—the big winner was Davis—after one hundred and three ballots and a nine-day deadlock. Nebraska governor Charles W. Bryan, William Jennings Bryan's younger brother, won the vice-presidential nomination just barely, with boos audible around the Garden.

A new Progressive party, backed by the Socialists and labor and farm groups, met in Cleveland, choosing Republican senator Robert La Follette for the presidential slot. La Follette picked a Democrat, Senator Burton Wheeler of Montana, as his running mate.

Convention Color   The emotional high point for the Democrats was Franklin Delano Roosevelt's nominating speech for Alfred E. Smith. Stricken by polio

CALVIN COOLIDGE

during the first summer of the Harding administration, Roosevelt on crutches, making a political comeback, not only electrified the convention but bestowed on Smith the "Happy Warrior" label.

Because of its length, the Democratic convention broke all sorts of records—the most soda pop and hot dogs consumed; the most speeches, demonstrations, and fistfights.

Campaign Notes In a throwback to nineteenth-century presidential attitudes, Coolidge thought it undignified to campaign for votes. The tragic death on July 7 of his younger son, Calvin Coolidge, Jr., at sixteen probably increased his reticence.

Davis traveled thousands of miles and campaigned energetically, but found himself tilting at windmills.

New technologies noticeably changed campaigning. The radio, used gingerly, spread candidates' words to more people. Rudimentary "talking pictures" of the three presidential candidates also appeared in movie theaters.

Symbols Republicans revived William McKinley's full dinner pail. Democrats and Progressives used teapots to remind voters of the Harding-era Teapot Dome scandal.

Slogans Coolidgeites claimed the issue was "Coolidge or Chaos." They proclaimed "Keep Cool with Coolidge," "Deeds—not Words," and "Safe with Cal."

Democrats touted "Back to Honesty with Davis" and "Honesty at Home—Honor Abroad." They lectured: "Remember the Teapot Dome" and "A Vote for Coolidge Is a Vote for Chaos."

Songs "Keep Cool and Keep Coolidge" reminded voters of their president's humble heritage. The Republicans also sang "Coolidge and Dawes for the Nation's Cause."

Democrats returned fire with "John W. Davis (Remember the Teapot Dome)" and the "Democratic Victory Song."

Progressives sang "Robert La Follette Is the Man of My Heart."

Paraphernalia Republicans waved "Keep Cool-Idge" fans, drove new autos with "Coolidge" license-plate attachments, sent "Careful Cautious Calvin Coolidge" postcards, and hung "Safe-Sane-Steady" posters.

The Democrats practically ran with Teapot Dome, exploiting the scandal any chance they could get. Celluloids called it "GOP/Your Waterloo" and "Doom" and invited voters to "Take a Kick at the Teapot."

Progressives got into the act with a "C'mon Bob, Let's Go!" button, showing the choice to be between La Follette and a teapot.

Popular Labels Coolidge, a man of few words, was affectionately called "Silent Cal" and "Cautious Cal."

Davis was pitched as "the most Southern Northern man" and "the most Northern Southern man."

La Follette was "Battling Bob."

Name-calling "Sphinx of the Potomac," "jellyfish," and "small-town statesman" were aimed at Coolidge.

La Follette likened Coolidge and Davis to "Gold Dust Twins."

La Follette was a "Red."

The Press *Time* magazine repeated, week after week, "Cal Coolidge sat tight and held his peace."

Spending The national Republican campaign reported it spent $4,020,478 to elect Coolidge, while the Democrats doled out $1,108,836 for Davis' defeat.

First The Republican convention was the first to be broadcast on radio.

Trends The Progressive coalition of farm, labor, and immigrant voting blocs was a precursor of the Roosevelt coalition in the 1930s.

The radio transformed campaigns, decreasing oratory and stump speaking and increasing costs.

Vote With forty-eight states voting, Coolidge's victory translated into 382 electoral votes and 15,718,211 popular votes (54 percent) to 136 and 8,385,283 (28.8 percent) for Davis and 13 and 4,831,289 (16.6 percent) for La Follette.

Benchmarks Coolidge achieved the biggest plurality of popular votes in history to date.

Democratic delegates cast a record number of ballots to choose a presidential nominee.

All-time low voter participation, except for 1824.

Quote "Calvin Coolidge was the issue," said the *Boston Transcript*, "and to the President belongs the victory."

AMERICA lost its innocence as the Twenties roared into place. These were days of jazz at your fingertips and young women with crimson lips and cigarettes. These were nights of secret speakeasies and flapper girls gone free. But the Twenties were more than social mores finding new footing. They were years of readjustment for American doughboys, returning from the excitement of war and the world overseas. They were years of restlessness for wives left behind to do men's work and now asked to return to life as it once was. And they were years of reaction, when Congress clamped a quota of 2 percent on new immigration to protect "natives" from the "huddled masses yearning to breathe free," and a revitalized Ku Klux Klan surged to five million strong, spouting such hatred as "Kill the Kikes, Koons and Katholics."

Grappling with these societal pressures would have been unbearable but for prosperity. It came like a godsend, the effect of expansionary tax policies and a surging, second industrial revolution that turned the recession of 1920–1921 on its heels and made consumers of most everyone. Who would not be dazzled by new products like silk stockings and cigarette lighters, electric sewing machines, and enameled indoor tubs and toilets streaming onto the market?

Business flourished in the White House too, but this business was illicit and the get-rich-quick deals were at the public expense. Though warned, Warren G. Harding—after appointing men of real talent—made room in his cabinet for some of his poker-playing cronies. The results were bittersweet. Charles Evans Hughes as secretary of state achieved an arms limitation treaty among major naval powers and secretary of the treasury Andrew Mellon succeeded in jump-starting the economy. On the other hand, Attorney General Harry Daugherty was implicated in the illegal sale of pardons and liquor permits, while Secretary of Interior Albert Fall took bribes for selling drilling rights to the nation's oil reserves at California's Elk Hills and Wyoming's Teapot Dome. Harding never knew the full extent of the scandals. He died, still loved by the public, his wife at his side, in San Francisco on August 2, 1923.

Vice President Calvin Coolidge was vacationing at his family's simple farmhouse in Plymouth, Vermont. In the parlor, lit by an oil lamp, he placed his hand on his mother's Bible and took the oath of office, administered by his father, a notary public.

The simplicity of the ceremony was seductive to the public. And as the scent of the Harding-era scandals became stronger, fanned by congressional investigations, Coolidge's coolness under fire and penchant for principle were a welcome antidote. This small, spare man, who looked like he was "weaned on a pickle," liked his hair slicked down with Vaseline, and kept his statements short and sweet, restored the people's faith in a Republican administration. Prosperity did the rest.

The Democrats were unprepared; they had expected their ticket to the White House to be through Teapot Dome. Thrown off guard, they convened in late June 1924, following the Republicans' quiet nomination of Coolidge, to make a spectacle of themselves. Urban, anti-Klan, and "wet" (anti-Prohibitionist) forces backing New York governor Alfred Smith battled rural-Southern, Klan-tolerant "drys" favoring Woodrow Wilson's son-in-law William McAdoo. After record-breaking fistfights, demonstrations, and ballots, the delegates turned to a third candidate, Wall Street lawyer John W. Davis. Journalist H. L. Mencken likened the outcome to "France and Germany fighting for centuries over Alsace-Lorraine, and then deciding to give it to England." For many Americans, tuned in on their new radio sets, the uproarious two-week convention was reason enough to vote Republican.

Another reason was that the Coolidges could seem to do no wrong. Grace, called "Sunshine" by the White House staff, radiated the warmth her husband seemed to lack. The president, meanwhile, was photographed in battered hat and overalls working on the family farm. Although his nasal twang now sounded much better over radio, "Silent Cal" did not say much, but when he did it was on a well-worn theme: "The chief business of the American people is business."

Davis became a voice crying in the wilderness. Boldly he broke away from the Democratic platform to condemn by name the Ku Klux Klan and to call for American entry into the League of Nations. The Republicans sidestepped him, leveling their harshest barbs at third-party Progressive candidate Robert La Follette. "Where do you stand," Republican vice-presidential candidate Charles Dawes campaigned, "with the president on the Constitution or on the sinking sands of socialism?" Frustrated, Davis attacked the "vast, pervading silence" of the president. He said he was reminded of Tennyson's poetic line "The dead oared by the dumb, went upward with the flood." The public did not see it that way. Coolidge won with a record popular-vote margin. As journalist critic William Allen White noted, "In a fat and happy world, Coolidge is the man of the hour."

★ CAMPAIGN OF 1928 ★

Major Candidates   Herbert C. Hoover, 53, California, Republican
Alfred E. Smith, 55, New York, Democrat

Credentials   Hoover headed the American Relief Committee in London (1914), the Commission for the Relief of Belgium (1914–1919), the U.S. food administration (1917–1918), was economic adviser to President Woodrow Wilson at the Versailles Peace Conference in 1919 and chairman of the European Relief Council (1920). He became secretary of commerce (1921–1928).

Smith was elected to the state assembly (1903–1915), serving as speaker (1913–1915), became sheriff of New York County (1915–1917), president of the New York City Board of Aldermen (1917), and four-term governor of New York (1919–1920 and 1923–1928).

Tickets   The Republicans met in Kansas City, Missouri. With President Coolidge not running Secretary of Commerce Herbert Hoover won on the first ballot with 837 out of 1,089 delegate votes. Senator Charles Curtis of Kansas was chosen as Hoover's running mate.

The Democrats ventured South to Houston, where New York governor Alfred E. Smith had no competition for first place because his 1924 opponent, William McAdoo, had decided not to run. To balance the ticket, the delegates chose Senate minority leader Joseph Robinson of Arkansas for the vice-presidential spot.

The Socialists nominated editor-pacifist Norman Thomas and labor leader James Mauer.

Campaign Notes   Hoover staged a subdued campaign, never publicly mentioning Smith by name, refusing requests to debate, and maintaining silence on most issues. Still, the campaign was ugly and vicious.

Smith sped around the country, confronting issues such as Catholicism and Prohibition head-on. He made history when his Albany acceptance speech was transmitted via a "strange box-like contraption with a lens on front" to a General Electric plant fifteen miles away.

Both Hoover and Smith had specially designed trains with cars for press conferences, typing and mimeographing, and even a darkroom. The candidates were accompanied by staff, press and publicity aides, reporters, and still and motion-picture photographers.

Radio was widely used by both candidates.

Symbols   Hoover's trademark was a high, stiff white collar, popular fifteen years earlier. Smith had his brown derby and big cigar.

Slogans   Republicans bragged "A Chicken in Every Pot and a Car in Every Garage" and "Let's Keep What We Got: Prosperity Didn't Just Happen."

HERBERT C. HOOVER

"Who But Hoover?" they asked. And headlined HOOVER AND HAPPINESS OR SMITH AND SOUP HOUSES? WHICH SHALL IT BE?

Democrats yelled back "We Want Al," "Good Bye Cal, Hello Al," and "No Oil on Al." They boasted "From the Sidewalks of New York to the White House."

Songs "We're for Hoover" and "Hoover! We Want Hoover" were standard fare, while "If He's Good Enough for Lindy (He's Good Enough For Me)" added a valuable endorsement.

Smith's theme song was "The Sidewalks of New York." Clearly optimistic, composer Irving Berlin came up with "(Good Times with Hoover) Better Times with Al": "Blue skies with Hoover, / Bluer skies with Al."

Paraphernalia Republican owl buttons hooted "Hoo but Hoover" and "Hoo Hoo Hoover"; thimbles touted "Hoover/Home/Happiness"; and posters pitched prosperity with legends like "How About Our Jobs? Vote for Hoover and Keep Our Factories Running."

Democrats decorated license plates, lapels, and buttons with brown derbies, sometimes saying "What's Under Your Hat? Al Smith for President." A moonshine mug inscribed "Al" was a tribute to his "wet" position.

Popular Labels Hoover, "Bert" to his friends, was hailed as "The Chief," "The Great Engineer," "Boy Wonder," and "Assistant President."

Smith answered to "Newsboy Al," "Al," "The Happy Warrior," and "The Brown Derby."

Name-calling   Hoover was derided as a "Herbie come lately" and as "Sir Herbert."

Smith was labeled a "rum-soaked Romanist," "Al-coholic Smith," and "Tammany candidate."

The Press   *The New York Times* said it was a fair contest: "It will not be Hoover the 1928 8-cyclinder Special against the 1896 broken winded donkey."

Spending   Prosperity helped both parties collect record sums and the Democrats almost to rival Republican expenditures. Hoover's national campaign reported spending $6,256,111 compared with $5,342,350 for Smith's.

Firsts   Hoover was the first Quaker president.

Hoover was the first president born west of the Mississippi.

Smith was the first Catholic to receive a major party presidential nomination.

Radio became an important political tool.

Trends   Voters in large urban areas went Democratic.

Vote   Forty-eight states' returns showed a landslide for Hoover, who received 444 electoral votes and 21,391,993 popular votes (58.2 percent) to 87 and 15,016,169 (40.9 percent) for Smith. Thomas, the Socialist candidate, had no electoral votes, but 267,835 popular votes.

Benchmarks   Hoover won the greatest electoral majority to date.

Smith made the biggest Democratic gains among urban voters in almost a century.

One of the nastiest campaigns.

Quote   After the election, humorist Will Rogers commented "You can't lick this prosperity thing. Even the fellow that hasn't got any is all excited over the idea."

★ ★ ★

SUMMERING in the secluded Black Hills of South Dakota in 1927, President Calvin Coolidge and his wife Grace were anything but out of the public eye. In late June, the First Lady and her Secret Service detail, Jim Haley, as handsome as any, left the "Summer White House" at nine in the morning to try yet another trail through the surrounding woods. It would take about an hour, Grace told her husband. Noon came and went and so did lunch, the president too upset to eat. He sent out a search party, but the First Lady

and Haley returned on their own—five hours after starting out. Pacing up and down on the front porch, the president had words with his wife. Coolidge had lost his cool and the press headlined it:
FIFTEEN-MILE WALK IN HILLS CAUSES PRESIDENT ANXIETY AS HE WAITS AN HOUR. Haley was quickly assigned to a new post, making more news. Then, on August 2, his fourth anniversary as president, Coolidge slipped reporters a piece of paper with a simple declaration: "I do not choose to run for president in nineteen twenty-eight." This time "Silent Cal" stayed in character, never explaining why or naming a possible successor.

Antiadministration senators seized the moment to push through a resolution that applauded a two-term presidency and, in effect, locked Coolidge into an early exit. Ironically, it also benefited a man not particularly liked by Coolidge or "Old Guard" Republicans: Secretary of Commerce Herbert Hoover. An engineer and self-made millionaire four times over by the age of forty, Hoover gave up income for volunteerism in London and Belgium during World War I. "Let fortune go to hell" was his credo from then on. As U.S. food administrator under President Woodrow Wilson, Hoover came to symbolize the home-front war effort.

For a time, few knew Hoover's party label, but by 1920, Hoover revealed his Republican registration and was tapped as Warren Harding's, and later Coolidge's, secretary of commerce, bringing savings to government and standardization to products. Still, the "Chief Engineer" was derided as "the Wunduh Boy" by Coolidge and dubbed "Sir Herbert" by traditional politicians who thought he had leapfrogged to the top. But he walked away with the Republican presidential nomination in 1928 anyway and in his acceptance speech boldly stated "The poorhouse is vanishing from among us."

"Al" Smith had fun with such Republicanisms during the course of the campaign. He particularly liked to quote from a flyer headed "A Chicken in Every Pot": "Republican efficiency has filled the workingman's dinner pail and his gasoline tank besides, and placed the whole nation in the silk stocking class." With a twinkle he would ask: "See if you can in your mind's eye picture a man working at $17.50 a week going out to a chicken dinner in his own automobile with silk socks on."

Smith won the Democratic nomination by virtue of being the most popular candidate around, even though loaded with handicaps. He was a Catholic at a time when ties to the papacy were still suspect, from the lower East Side and Tammany Hall-educated when presidents came from upper New York State or Ohio and went to more traditional schools, and positively "wet" when most Americans still stood behind the "dry" Volstead Act. But Smith was four-time governor of New York and could be expected to bring its largesse—forty-five electoral votes—into the Democratic column come November.

But no sooner had Smith snared the nomination than he broke the spell for many Democrats by wiring the convention that he wanted "fundamental changes" in the Prohibition law. In Smith's view, it was mostly a boon for bootleggers, and he was right. "Scarface" Al Capone, forever king of the mob, was taking in sixty million dollars a year from his illicit liquor operations. Still, Southern Democrats called Smith a "rum-soaked Romanist," while Republicans publicly asked "Shall dry America elect a 'cocktail' President?"

Worse were the whispers about Smith's Roman Catholicism, drunkenness, and social eligibility. Letters to the editor reported that Smith was seen "disgustingly tight" or "staggering" with two aides needed to steady him. There were comments too about Smith's earthy accent, changing first to *foist* and hospital to *horspital*, all heard over the *radd-ee-o*, not to mention his wife's unbecoming dress. "My dear, can you imagine the Smiths in the White House?" was a haughty refrain.

Quaker-good Hoover, a straight arrow in high stiff collars, who even smoked "grimly," tried to stop some of the smears. Others he avoided. The election was his for the asking and he knew it. Hoover told his audiences that the "slogan of progress is changing from the full dinner pail to the full garage." He accepted the pitfalls of Prohibition but said it was an experiment "noble in motive." And he labeled Smith's brand of economics "state socialism," arguing instead for "rugged individualism."

Hoover's jaunty challenger, his brown derby set at an undefeated angle, his striped trousers and monogrammed socks the talk of the town, wanted to show that the sidewalks of New York could lead to the White House. He battled hard. In one of the great campaign speeches of all time, his notes scrawled as usual on the backs of several envelopes, Smith stood up in Oklahoma City to denounce the whispered lies as "a treasonable attack upon the very foundations of American liberty."

Smith roused the electorate, but not to himself. Even New Yorkers deserted him. The public seemed convinced that prosperity was a Republican right and with a mighty shove put Hoover into office. It turned out to be the best thing that could have happened to the Democrats. Less than eight months after Hoover's inauguration, on October 29, 1929, one newspaper headline mockingly cried WALL STREET LAYS AN EGG.

So began the Great Depression.

★ CAMPAIGN OF 1932 ★

Major Candidates   Herbert C. Hoover, 58, California, Republican
Franklin D. Roosevelt, 50, New York, Democrat

Credentials   For Hoover, see Campaign of 1928. He was elected president in 1928.

Roosevelt was a New York state senator (1911–1913), assistant secretary of the navy (1913–1920), and governor of New York (1929–1933).

FRANKLIN D. ROOSEVELT

Tickets The Republicans convened in Chicago in somber spirits. The Depression had happened on their watch, putting them on the defensive. Still, they decided not to switch horses. President Herbert Hoover was quickly renominated on the first ballot. Vice President Charles Curtis had more difficulty, but was also renominated on the first ballot.

The Democrats met in Chicago, more confident than they had been in twenty years. Front-runner Franklin Roosevelt, governor of New York, whether or not as a result of a deal between his representatives and those of House Speaker John Nance Garner, won the nomination. Garner got the vice-presidential spot on a voice vote.

Campaign Notes As in 1896, the Democratic candidate drove the Republican to campaign. Roosevelt, who was told by advisers not to stump because it was unnecessary and too taxing, took his own counsel. He traveled 23,000 miles, giving twenty-seven major speeches and thirty-two shorter speeches in all but seven states. It took Hoover until October to campaign. He made about ten major appearances. Along the way he was booed and picketed and his train pelted with tomatoes. "I can't go on with it any more," he told his wife at one point.

While the president wrote all of his own campaign speeches, Roosevelt edited offerings from a host of speechwriters. Much of the input for Roosevelt's speeches came from a number of academic specialists dubbed the "brain trust." Previous presidential candidates had tapped experts, but none as heavily as Roosevelt.

Roosevelt's campaign was the most modern and well-organized yet. An estimated sixty-three million pieces of campaign literature were sent out, especially targeting county and precinct party workers. Roosevelt's campaign also innovatively used preference polls and public relations professionals.

Symbols Hoover had his high, stiff collars, while Roosevelt often sported a red rose in his lapel. The Republican elephant tapered off in use, as did party spirit.

Slogans Republicans asked voters to "Play Safe with Hoover." Hoover assurances—"We Want to Turn the Corner to Prosperity" and "We Now Have Passed the Worst"—were other rallying cries.

Roosevelt was hyped with "Abolish Bread Lines," "Out of the Red with Roosevelt," and "Throw the Spenders Out" banners.

The public came up with its own anti-Hoover slogans: "In Hoover We Trusted: Now We Are Busted," "We Want Bread," and "Hang Hoover."

Songs Those who wanted Hoover again sang of "sailing back again to prosperity" in "Hoover for President, The Hope of Our Nation."

Roosevelt's theme song was "Happy Days Are Here Again" with its sunny forecast: "The skies above are clear again."

Paraphernalia Although down in the dumps over the Depression, Republicans had some fun with campaign material. On buttons, mirrors, stickers, and the like they showed a donkey hightailing it as a GOP elephant pushes a stalled truck labeled "U.S. & Co." The inscription read: "It's An Elephant's Job. No Time For 'Donkey Business.' "

Democrats retaliated with buttons that pictured a donkey bucking an elephant and said, "Kick Out Depression with a Democratic Vote." In an appeal to progressive Republicans, buttons paired "A New Deal / A Square Deal."

Popular Labels Hoover was billed as a "Great Engineer" and a "Great Humanitarian."

Roosevelt was hailed as "Roosevelt the Robust" and "Knight of the New Deal."

Name-calling To detractors, Hoover was "Lord Hoover" and a "fearmonger" who was responsible for the "Hoover Depression."

To Hoover, Roosevelt was a "chameleon on Scotch plaid." To others he was a "Feather Duster," "the corkscrew candidate," a "demagogue," a "Bolshevist," even "Little Lord Fauntleroy" and an "amiable boy scout."

Curious Facts Although Roosevelt had once nominated Alfred E. Smith for president and dubbed him "The Happy Warrior," their relationship had unraveled after Smith's defeat and Roosevelt's political success. In 1932, Smith announced his candidacy twelve days after Roosevelt and fought to the bitter end, refusing to release his delegates to give Roosevelt a unanimous vote.

The Press The *Nation* declared: "Neither of the two great parties, in the midst of the worst depression in our history, has had the intelligence or courage to propose a single fundamental measure that might conceivably put us on the road to recovery."

Spending Both parties had much less money than four years earlier. Hoover's national campaign reported expenditures of $2,900,052, compared with $2,245,975 for Roosevelt's. For both campaigns, the biggest expenditure was radio time.

Firsts Roosevelt had the first modern campaign network.
Roosevelt's brain trust was the first organized use of experts in a campaign.
Eleanor Roosevelt was the first truly politically active candidate's wife.

Trends Voter-preference polls became increasingly popular.
The use of public relations experts rather than party professionals as imagemakers.

Vote Returns from forty-eight states turned around the 1928 outcome. Roosevelt amassed 472 electoral votes and 22,809,638 popular votes (57.4 percent) to 59 and 15,758,901 (39.7 percent) for Hoover. Socialist candidate Norman Thomas won no electoral votes, but 881,951 popular votes or over 2 percent.

Benchmarks The most complete electoral reversal ever from four years earlier.
The last time the Socialists received 2 percent or more of the popular vote.

Quote Returning home to a mother's embrace after his election, Roosevelt exclaimed, "This is the greatest night of my life."

GOVERNOR Franklin Delano Roosevelt had star appeal, when that was still magic and rare, especially among politicians. With legs crippled and useless, clumping forward on eight-pound braces, a cane in one hand, the other in constant search of support, he entranced the American people when life was hardship and nothing more. He came without a plan, communicating confidence and hope only in words like *new deal* and *forgotten man*.

A child of privilege, Roosevelt adopted the political party of his father, a Cleveland Democrat, rather than that of fifth cousin and former Republican president Theodore Roosevelt. Still, he wanted to be president and at twenty-eight ran for the New York state senate, an upstart in a red roadster frightening horses, infuriating farmers, and generally speaking down to voters in an upper-crust Harvard accent. He won anyway and again in 1912. Eight years later a more seasoned Roosevelt barnstormed across the country as the Democratic vice-presidential candidate. The Democrats were defeated in 1920, but Roosevelt, handsome and athletic, stood tall as the party's promise.

All of a sudden, his world turned upside down. Of necessity, pain became Roosevelt's focus, not politics, as he found his legs crippled from polio. "If you had spent two years in bed trying to wiggle your big toe," Roosevelt half-joked to a friend, "anything else would seem easy." Breeziness was part of his charm. He thought he could lick the rip-roaring depression that was suffocating President Herbert Hoover. Hoover, who was being called "our most peevish president," had tried at first to wish the worsening economic crisis away. "The depression is over," he announced when unemployment was four million going on twelve. But he was wrong and the numbers were right. Evictions mounted and the displaced placed their wrath on Hoover, calling their makeshift shanties on the outskirts of towns Hoovervilles, their privies Hoover villas, and newspapers wrapped around their bodies for warmth Hoover blankets. The president felt for these people but never showed it.

Ever the engineer, Hoover did try to make some corrections, granting unprecedented government assistance to certain areas of the economy such as banks, railroads, and rural farm credit corporations. But it was like fiddling while Rome burned, for he held back on direct subsidies to severely hurting farmers and aid to the desperate millions then unemployed. His philosophy remained one of "rugged individualism," which to him meant no federal relief "of individual suffering."

The darkest hour of the Hoover presidency was yet to come. In May 1932, almost twenty thousand World War I veterans, pleading for early payment of bonuses due them in 1945, trailing women and children, set up "Bonus City," the greatest Hooverville of all, within sight of the Capitol. Waiting for the bonus bill to pass Congress and the president to see them, they sang: "Mellon pulled the whistle, / Hoover rang the bell, Wall Street gave the signal / And the country went to Hell!" When neither happened, several thousand returned home courtesy of the government. But more stayed, and tensions simmered in the summer heat. Finally Hoover called out the troops, asking that the bonus army be moved with care. Instead Gen. Douglas MacArthur and his men bore down with tanks, guns, and tear gas on what he called "a mob . . . animated by the essence of revolution." To many, the wonder was that there was not a real revolution. The people were waiting, it seemed, to "Hang Hoover" in November.

Roosevelt, then governor of New York, was easily chosen by the Democrats to run against Hoover. The candidate wanted to win the election on the strength of his personality as well as the plight of the nation. He announced his intention to fly to Chicago to accept his nomination in person, a historic gesture. Ten thousand people greeted him at the airport. His hat was knocked off, his glasses pushed askew, but the rose stayed put in his lapel. Resting his weight on his hands on the rostrum, Roosevelt pledged a "new deal for the American people." The next day a Rollin Kirby cartoon showed a farmer looking skyward at a plane marked "New Deal." The Democrats had their slogan.

Roosevelt dived into campaigning, as much to prove his stamina as to sell himself. He became the white knight battling the black. While Hoover was saying there was a limit to what he could do, Roosevelt declared "We are going to make a country in which no one is left out." He described Hoover's record in terms of the Four Horsemen: "Destruction, Delay, Deceit and Despair."

To some, Roosevelt was a lightweight. Walter Lippmann wrote "He is a pleasant man who, without any important qualifications for the office, would very much like to be President." To others, he was duplicitous, promising panaceas while stating he was going to reduce federal government expenditures "by 25 percent." Hoover also thought he was dangerous and his new deal a new socialism. Should Roosevelt win, he warned, "The grass will grow in the streets of a hundred cities, a thousand towns; the weeds will overrun the fields."

The twelve million unemployed, the ragtag bonus marchers, the failing farmers with their ten-cent corn did not hear. They were listening to Roosevelt on the radio, every one believing him when he said "My friends." On election day a landslide victory underscored what was already known: Roosevelt was their hope for the future. Inauguration day, under black-brushed skies, he found words to reassure them: "Let me assert my firm belief that the only thing we have to fear is fear itself."

★ CAMPAIGN OF 1936 ★

Major Candidates   Franklin D. Roosevelt, 54, New York, Democrat
Alfred M. Landon, 49, Kansas, Republican

Credentials   For Roosevelt, see Campaign of 1932. He was elected president in 1932.
Landon was governor of Kansas (1932–1936).

Tickets   The Democrats met in Philadelphia and happy days were "here again" as party harmony reigned. Delegates did away with the 104-year-old two-thirds rule for nomination and joined the Republicans in requiring a simple majority vote. President Franklin Roosevelt and Vice President John Nance Garner were nominated by acclamation.

ALFRED M. LANDON

By the time Republicans convened in Cleveland, earlier differences had been settled and Alfred Landon was selected on the first ballot. Frank Knox, publisher of *The Chicago Daily News*, became Landon's running mate by receiving all 1,300 votes on the first ballot.

Campaign Notes   Roosevelt did not plan to do much campaigning, but some unfavorable preference polls and heated charges against him caused him to change his mind and almost match his 1932 performance.

The Literary Digest had earned a reputation for correct presidential predictions since 1920. Once again, the *Digest* polled millions of voters and the results, month by month, were for a Landon victory. On October 31, it predicted the electoral count would be 370 to 161. (The *Digest* folded soon afterward.)

The last public encounter between two major party presidential candidates had been in 1912. So, when President Roosevelt invited Landon, as governor of Kansas, to a September conference on drought, it was a big news story. But both Roosevelt and Landon made it strictly business. No political posters were allowed and only pleasantries were exchanged. Roosevelt's side called Landon "a swell guy" and Landon said the president was a "charming gentleman."

Symbols The Democrats had the rose and the donkey, while the Republicans went wild over the sunflower, Kansas' state flower; they also used the elephant more than in 1932.

Slogans Democrats wanted to go "Forward with Roosevelt" and "Follow Through with Roosevelt." "Remember Hoover" they urged and warned that "Sunflowers Die in November."

Landon's side boasted "Life, Liberty and Landon," "Off the Rocks with Landon and Knox," "Save America from Socialism," and "Vote for Landon and Land a Job." To counter Roosevelt's "New Deal," Landon had "The New Frontier."

Songs As in 1932, the Democrats sang up a storm with "Happy Days Are Here Again." They also belted out "Things Look Rosy with Roosevelt" and "Bye-Bye Landon, Goodbye!"

"Oh! Susannah" in many different versions was the Republican favorite. Landon proponent William Randolph Hearst held a national song contest through his newspaper chain, awarding daily ten-dollar prizes and a final thousand dollars to "housemaid" Violet E. Willoughby for her "Landon Campaign Song": "No foolish pride or pomp has he, / No silver tongue in cheek."

Paraphernalia There was an "FDR Is Good Enough for Me" license attachment, a "Happy Days" barrel-shaped bank, and "Man of the Hour," "He Saved America," and "We Rose with Roosevelt" buttons.

Meanwhile, the Republicans dreamed of sunflowers, sunflowers everywhere and so they appeared on buttons and banners, pennants and posters, jewelry (Tiffany & Co. sold a nineteen-petal gold sunflower set with yellow diamonds for $815), and more. Republican items also took aim at the New Deal and Roosevelt. "It's Time to Wake Up" stickers pictured a clockface with the legend: "Every Minute the New Deal Spends $16,894.59." Another sticker of a New Deal worker said: "Let's Vote Him a Regular Job."

Popular Labels Roosevelt was "the Champ," "the Boss," and, by now, "FDR."

Landon was known as "Alf," "the Kansas Lincoln," a "liberal Coolidge," and "the Kansas Coolidge."

Name-calling Roosevelt was belittled as "the New Dealocrat," "Franklin Double-Crossing Roosevelt," and "Frankenstein D. Roosevelt." The New Deal was denounced as the "Raw Deal" and the brain trust as "damned college professors."

Landon was mocked as a "changeling candidate" and "the poor man's Hoover."

The Press *Time* magazine said the campaign "demonstrated to what depths of inanity, bad taste and downright dishonesty American politics can descend."

Spending Attracting funds from big business, the Republicans had a war chest of $8,892,972, compared with $5,194,741 for the Democrats, who received significant amounts from labor.

Firsts Roosevelt was the first president to be inaugurated on January 20, under terms of the Twentieth Amendment.

Roosevelt received the first official endorsement from a labor organization.

The first presidential election in which "scientific" sample polling was used.

Trends More registered Democratic voters than Republican.

Voting patterns reflect class differences.

Large fund-raising dinners became standard.

Vote With forty-eight states again participating, Roosevelt overachieved, netting 523 electoral votes and 27,752,869 popular votes (60.8 percent) to 8 and 16,674,665 (36.5 percent) for Landon.

Benchmarks Roosevelt won the biggest electoral-vote victory since 1820 and a record-breaking popular-vote percentage.

The black vote, Republican since the Civil War, became Democratic.

One of history's most bitter campaigns.

Democrats abolish the two-thirds rule for nomination.

Quote Two days before the election, Democratic National Chairman James Farley wrote down his election prediction for an office pool: LANDON WILL ONLY CARRY MAINE AND VERMONT. 7 ELECTORAL VOTES. (Farley was off by one.)

★ ★ ★

IN a comment reminiscent of France's King Louis XIV's "L'état, c'est moi," President Franklin Roosevelt told brain truster Raymond Moley in 1936: "There is only one issue in this campaign. It's myself and the people must be either for me or against me." On June 27, in his speech accepting renomination as the Democratic presidential candidate, Roosevelt eloquently expressed what being president would mean for him. To a crowd estimated at 100,000, his voice, embellished by loudspeakers and his delivery unshaken by a fall he had suffered backstage, crescendoed, "There is a mysterious cycle in human events. To some generations much is given. Of other generations much is expected. This generation of Americans has a rendezvous with destiny."

Roosevelt was right—he was the issue. But what he did not realize was that his major domestic legacy already lay behind him, in an alphabet soup of Depression-era programs that carried the label *New Deal*. Together, they had sparked bitter constitutional controversies, heightened tensions between the haves and have-nots, and irrevocably recast the nature of government's responsibility toward its citizens. Critics screamed "unconstitutional dictatorship" and "creeping socialism." In a speech remarkable for revealing the depth of anti-New Dealism, former "Happy Warrior" Alfred E. Smith told an audience of white-tied millionaires in early February: "The young braintrusters caught the Socialists in swimming and ran away with their clothes. . . . There can be only one capital, Washington or Moscow." He said he would probably "take a walk" from the Democratic party. It hardly mattered. The Roosevelt Revolution was already branded on the American system.

Though Democrats were sitting pretty as the campaign got underway, Republicans were not without their pretensions. True, their party had been clobbered once again in the midterm elections, and the New Deal Congress had outdone itself dreaming up relief and recovery schemes. Yet New Dealers had been unable to pull unemployment below eight million and a drought, unlike any other, had cast a ghastly dark shadow across the once-fertile Great Plains, adding insult to already injured farmers.

Could the Roosevelt coalition hold together? The Republicans bet not with Kansas Governor Alfred "Alf" Landon. Landon's claim to national fame was the fact that he had been the only Republican governor reelected in 1934. He was also a proven budget-balancer who nevertheless had supported New Deal programs back home.

Landon, affable, courteous and colorless, began the campaign soft sell, taking his "Sunflower Special" train to such sites as Nashua, New Hampshire, where he told his audience: "The American people are aroused at the waste and extravagance of their national Government." In West Middlesex, Pennsylvania, he stated earnestly: "Wherever I have gone in this country, I have found Americans."

Landon was getting nowhere. On his fourth and final tour, he tried fear: "Franklin D. Roosevelt proposed to destroy the right to elect your own representatives, to talk politics on street corners, to march in political parades, to attend the church of your faith, to be tried by jury and to own property." He also went after the new Social Security system, asking if the twenty-six million employees to be covered in January 1937 "are going to be fingerprinted? Or are they going to have identification tags around their necks?"

The Republican National Committee, realizing that Landon needed all the help he could get, sent out over a hundred million pieces of campaign propaganda, some of dubious benefit. Flyers berated New Dealers for supplying "free lunch to hoboes" and "PWA picks, spades, shovels . . . only to lean on." The black vote, a given for the GOP ever since the presidency of Abraham Lincoln, was wooed by having Landon endorsements from Olympic Sprinter Jesse Owens and other high-profile blacks. But that could not compete with the relief many more blacks were getting from New Deal programs.

However, Landon was no voice crying in the wilderness. Smith's "walk" was into the Republican camp. Publisher William Randolph Hearst supported Landon through his fifteen-city newspaper chain with such jingles as: "The New Red Deal with a Soviet seal / Endorsed by a Moscow hand; / The strange result of an alien cult / In a liberty-loving land." Other papers (and almost two-thirds were for Landon) picked up where Hearst left off. The Chicago *Tribune* headlined: MOSCOW ORDERS REDS IN U.S. TO BACK ROOSEVELT.

Roosevelt, a president in his prime, fought back like "the Champ." He swiped at the "economic royalists" and "privileged princes" who, he said, would destroy democracy. He leveled blows at anti-New Dealers: "It was this Administration which saved the system of private and free enterprise after it had been dragged to the brink of ruin." And he challenged his name-callers: "They are unanimous of their hatred of me—and I welcome their hatred."

Cocky, yes, but he thought he had a right to be. Coming into office on the wings of hope, Roosevelt quickly gained public confidence with his soothing "fireside chats" and breakneck achievements in his first hundred days in office. Some of the New Deal creations turned out to be ill-starred, ungainly, or even unconstitutional, but most fit together in such a way as to help those they were intended to, especially the unemployed, farmers, and unorganized labor. With their backing, Roosevelt made a triumphant return to the presidency. No one, said Al Smith, "shoots at Santa Claus."

★ CAMPAIGN OF 1940 ★

Major Candidates   Franklin D. Roosevelt, 58, New York, Democrat
Wendell Willkie, 48, Indiana, Republican

Credentials   For Roosevelt, see Campaign of 1932. He was elected President in 1932 and reelected in 1936.

Willkie, a Wall Street lawyer, became president of the Commonwealth and Southern utility company in 1929.

Tickets   The Democrats met in Chicago amid some confusion. Even though his decision to seek a third term was still secret, Roosevelt won the nomination in one ballot. The vice-presidential nomination, however, was a tug of war. Roosevelt had his mind made up to replace Vice President John Nance Garner with agriculture secretary Henry Wallace of Iowa. Though some objected that Wallace was a former Republican, too leftist, even a "mystic," he still won on the first ballot.

When the Republicans convened in Philadelphia, there were ten candidates, Manhattan District Attorney Thomas Dewey and Ohio Senator Robert

WENDELL WILLKIE

Taft, son of former President William Howard Taft, taking the lead for two ballots. But then, third-place Wendell Willkie made his move and won on the sixth ballot. Senator Charles McNary of Oregon was chosen as his running mate on the first ballot.

Convention Color   At the Democratic convention, when Roosevelt's name was first mentioned, a loud voice rang out from all the speakers: "We want Roosevelt! . . . The world wants Roosevelt." At the end of the speech the voice was heard again, sparking an hour-long demonstration. *The New York Times* discovered that Chicago's superintendent of sewers, was making all the noise from a basement loudspeaker hook-up. "The voice from the sewer" went down in history.

Campaign Notes   Arguing that he was too busy, Roosevelt did not really campaign until two weeks before election day. But throughout the campaign the president got lots of publicity by visiting scores of defense plants and making "nonpolitical" speeches.

Traveling by auto, train, and even airplane, Willkie stumped 30,000 miles, giving 540 speeches in thirty-four states, becoming feistier as polls showed he did better on the attack.

Symbols   Democrats had the donkey, while Republicans had the elephant and something new, a key.

Slogans The Democrats argued "Better a Third Termer Than a Third Rater," "Two Good Terms Deserve Another," "Stick with Roosevelt," and "Carry on with Roosevelt." They attacked the Republicans with "Watch Willkie Wilt" and "Repeat with Roosevelt or Repent with Willkie."

"Win with Willkie," "America Wants Willkie," and "Willkie or Bust" Republicans bellowed. They also chided "There's No Indispensable Man," "No Third Term," "No Fourth Term Either," and "Roosevelt for Ex-President."

Songs Democrats sang "Franklin Roosevelt's Back Again," "Franklin D. Roosevelt Jones," and "Mister Roosevelt, Won't You Please Run Again?"

The Republicans came up with a Willkie version of "On the Banks of the Wabash": "Oh, the moon shone bright one night in Indiana / On a Hoosier lad who had a winning way." They also sang "We're All Going Out to Vote for Willkie."

Paraphernalia One hundred years after the log-cabin–hard-cider campaign made the selling of a candidate an art, Americans went all-out. There were two thousand different styles of campaign buttons, as well as banners and bandannas, posters and postcards, paperweights and pocket knives and more—even a Roosevelt lollipop.

Democrats fought the third-term issue with such buttons as "3 Is a Lucky Number," "No Substitute for Experience," and "Third Term Taboo/23 Skidoo."

Optimistic Republicans dreamed up an elephant inscribed "Life Begins in '40." A key, a play on Will*kie*'s name, was often used on Republican buttons in such ways as "HE WILL (key)" and "THE WILL (key) To WIN." Republicans also used the third-term issue, most originally with "Please Don't Talk 3rd Term" earmuffs. Buttons were harsher: "Dictator? Not For US" and the double-entendre "No Man Is Good Three Times."

Popular Labels Roosevelt was "the Champ," "the Chief," and "FDR." Willkie was "Win" and "Will."

Name-calling Roosevelt was insulted as "that man," "the third-term candidate," "King Franklin," "Dr. Jekyll of Hyde Park," "dictator," "warmonger," and "appeaser."

Willkie was derided as "the simple barefoot Wall Street lawyer," "the rich man's Roosevelt," an "appeaser," a "me-too" candidate, and "the utilities tycoon."

The Press *Newsweek* on Willkie's nomination: "Nothing exactly like it ever happened before in American politics."

Spending The Hatch Act of 1939 and 1940 placed limits of $5,000 on individual contributions to federal candidates and $3,000,000 on national committee yearly income, but these restrictions were easily circumvented. The Democrats reported spending $2,783,654 compared with $3,451,310 for the Republicans.

Firsts Roosevelt was the first and only third-term President.
The first fifty-million vote campaign.
Republicans held the first televised convention.

Trends Personality politics makes party politics less important in the nominating process.

Vote Results from the forty-eight states showed that Roosevelt was up against his strongest opponent yet. He won with 449 electoral votes and 27,307,819 popular votes (54.8 percent) to 82 and 22,321,018 (44.8 percent) for Willkie.

Benchmarks Roosevelt became the only president to serve more than two terms.
Willkie, more than any other presidential candidate, was a creation of the media.
Greatest election for campaign paraphernalia.

Quote If Roosevelt is elected, Willkie charged during the campaign, "you may expect we will be at war by April 1941."

★ ★ ★

WITH World War I a bad memory, America thought it could wait out the new war in Europe. Had it not heard the heavy-soled boots of the German warlords as they pounded neighbors underfoot, eyeing England now? Was it not tuned to the radio words of Edward R. Murrow, sending scenes of pain across the Atlantic? Amazing in hindsight, this campaign was mainly a duel to the finish to stay out of war. Other issues, juicy though they were, never really had a chance.

Heady from his huge second election victory and unhappy with cries of unconstitutionality from the "nine old men" on the Supreme Court, Roosevelt set himself up for a fall. To save the Court "from itself" he proposed to add a new justice for every member over seventy (six) who would not retire. But a coalition of Republicans and conservative Democrats shouted down this "dictator bill" and Roosevelt was accused by members of his own party of "court packing."

While the Court eventually tilted more liberal, and one conservative septuagenarian retired, allowing Roosevelt a justice to his own liking, the incident left a bad taste. A sudden, sharp so-called Roosevelt Recession and the president's unsuccessful "purge" of party enemies in the midterm elections added to his troubles. With deficit bills still climbing and not enough to show for it, New Deal critics were out in force, claiming the U.S. really stood for "unlimited spending." As this chapter closed on the Roosevelt presidency, another opened.

Roosevelt's decision to run again was foreign-born. The Nazi–Soviet pact, the German march on Poland and, after a deceptive lull, the rapid-fire taking of Norway, Denmark, Belgium, and finally France, drew to a close Roosevelt's private debate. A week before the nominating convention, the president told national chairman James Farley that he would be available. Farley was opposed. Eleanor Roosevelt, who found out next, replied "I do not believe in it." In his acceptance speech, Roosevelt credited his "conscience," but the editorial press, vastly opposed to him, blamed a "Messianic complex" and "dictatorial tendencies."

The Democrats' third-term gamble was no match for the Republicans' risk. The GOP took a candidate created for them by the media and made a real race of it. Roosevelt, an aging "champ" now, would be facing Wendell Willkie, youthful, combative, and iconoclastic. Willkie was a Wall Street lawyer who ended up president of one of his big utility clients, the Commonwealth and Southern Company.

The media came in for a closer look. *Time* put Willkie on its cover July 31, 1939, adoring him in a nonpolitical way: "An Indiana crackerbox debater in store clothes . . . more publicly articulate than any big businessman today." The next month politics was the talk, with Arthur Krock of *The New York Times* describing him as the "darkest horse" but the one to follow. *Fortune, Life, Look* fell in line. Willkie, having voted Democratic as late as 1938, was now a full-fledged Republican. He had never held political office or entered any primaries, but that did not seem to matter. Delegates at the convention, overwhelmed with "Willkie clubs," "Willkie amateurs," and Willkie himself (he came two days early), became convinced that this boyish businessman with unruly hair, eager arguments, and pocketfuls of good press was the fresh face they were looking for. Still too green for some, Willkie acknowledged his nomination saying: "And so, you Republicans, I call upon you to join me."

Nothing stopped Willkie. He traveled more miles than William Jennings Bryan in 1896 and spoke to people who had never seen a candidate before. His voice gave out, but he did not, hoarsely charging that the "third-term candidate" thought he was "indispensable." He made mistakes, many of them. He called Cicero, Illinois, "Chicago" and when corrected, blurted out "All right, then to hell with Chicago." He boarded his campaign train declaring "I am opposed by the most ruthless gang of buccaneers in history." He was heckled, booed, and pelted with eggs.

Willkie persisted, saving his biggest guns for Roosevelt's handling of the European theater. He first lashed out at the president as "the great appeaser" who sold "Czecho-Slovakia down the river." He moved on to American preparedness, claiming that New Deal mismanagement had "failed to build us a defense system." Then he tried fear, as Herbert Hoover and Alfred Landon had done before him. Willkie painted Roosevelt as a warmonger who had made "secret treaties" that would mean "wooden crosses for sons and brothers and sweethearts." "If you elect me," he pledged, "no American boy will be sent to the shambles of the European trenches."

Willkie won one: He succeeded in luring the president into the ring. Roosevelt had said that he did not have the "time nor the inclination" for political debate, but by mid-October he had had enough: "I am an old campaigner and I love a good fight." He pointed to the "cash-and-carry" plan that sent American war materials to Britain and declared it would never have gotten through Congress if "left to Martin, Barton and Fish." Audiences loved the rhythm of the three Republican names, chorusing it back to him. And Roosevelt promised what he had promised before but left out "except in case of attack," giving it greater impact: "I shall say it again and again and again: 'Your boys are not going to be sent into foreign wars.' " Hearing what they wanted, the voters elected the "old campaigner" in a third decisive victory.

★ CAMPAIGN OF 1944 ★

Major Candidates Franklin Delano Roosevelt, 62, New York, Democrat
Thomas E. Dewey, 42, New York, Republican

Credentials For Roosevelt, see Campaign of 1932. He was elected president in 1932 and reelected in 1936 and 1940.

Dewey was U.S. attorney for the southern district of New York (1932–1933), special prosecutor of organized crime (1935–1937), district attorney of New York County (1937–1938), and elected New York governor in 1942.

Tickets The Democrats convened in Chicago in the same convention hall they had used to nominate President Franklin Roosevelt in 1932 and 1940. Unlike four years earlier, Roosevelt's intentions were clear. He would accept renomination as a "good soldier," and he won handily on the first ballot. The vice-presidential spot was much more tricky, since Roosevelt was effectively dumping Vice President Henry Wallace, who had a wide following but was too liberal for most delegates. Party bosses, with Roosevelt's approval, settled on Senator Harry S. Truman of Missouri, who won on the second ballot.

The Republicans also met in Chicago, where harmony was the password as two leading contenders dropped out in favor of Thomas E. Dewey even before the first ballot. When Governor Earl Warren of California would not run for vice president, Ohio's governor John Bricker, one of those who had stepped aside for Dewey, was every delegate's choice.

THOMAS E. DEWEY

Convention Color Truman balked at running for vice president and was called the "contrariest Missouri Mule." Roosevelt barked "Tell him if he wants to break up the Democratic party in the middle of a war, that's his responsibility." Truman caved in: "I'll have to say yes."

Dewey, who officially announced his candidacy only during the convention, broke Republican tradition by coming in person to accept his nomination instead of waiting for a formal notification ceremony.

Campaign Notes In his acceptance speech Roosevelt said that he would not campaign "in the usual sense" in "these days of tragic sorrow." But he did make one famous "speech about Fala" (see the campaign narrative, below) plus five others geared to the campaign.

Dewey campaigned the usual way, by train. But unlike stumpers before him, he did not disclose his route and rear-platform appearances were a rarity. His prepared speeches, given at local meeting halls and in auditoriums, were really meant for radio audiences.

Symbols Roosevelt's dog Fala got into the act, along with a V-for-victory symbol and the donkey. The Dewey campaign made efficiency a Republican symbol along with the elephant.

Slogans The Democrats, borrowing from Abraham Lincoln's wartime campaign, used "Never Swap Horses While Crossing a Stream." They also liked

"Ev'rything's Gonna Be Rosy with Roosevelt," and "We Are Going to Win This War and the Peace That Follows."

The Republicans favored "Time for a Change," "Dewey or Don't We?," and "Win the War Quicker with Dewey and Bricker." Also popular was the anti-Roosevelt saying "Back on Relief with the Commander-in-Chief."

Songs Democrats warbled "He's the People's Choice" and "My Friend Franklin": "He's as high above his rival as the top of the steeple, / They say everyone's against him, / Ev'ryone except the people."

Republicans celebrated their candidate's past in "Yankee Dewey Dandy": "He busted gangs and jailed the mobs / And cleared out every phony." In "Republican Battle Hymn" they jeered: "A horse that's run twelve years should be retired to pastures green." They also belted out "A Dewey, Dewey Day."

Paraphernalia With war making materials short, campaign items were way off. The best Democratic fare was handmade, a black Scottish terrier lapel pin with the message " 'Fala' " Me to the Polls."

Republicans turned out promotional "Dewey the Racket Buster—New Deal Buster" and wartime "Mothers/Sisters/Wives/Sweethearts" buttons.

Popular Labels Roosevelt was hailed as "the Boss" and "the Champ." He called himself "Dr. Win-the-War." Truman, after the way he was selected for the vice-presidential slot, was known as "the second Missouri Compromise."

Dewey was "the Racket Buster," Bricker "an Honest Harding."

Name-calling Roosevelt was belittled as a "dictator" and "Santa Claus to the World." His administration was "tired old men" and World War II "Roosevelt's War."

Dewey was called a "little man" by Roosevelt and "The Great Prosecutor" by other Democrats who wanted to recall to mind the failings of "The Great Engineer" Herbert Hoover. Too many people to mention take credit for saying Dewey was "like the groom on the wedding cake." His followers were "Dewey-eyed Republicans."

The Press *The New York Times*, against Roosevelt in 1940, changed in wartime: "Mr. Roosevelt has a large first-hand knowledge of the problems that will arise in the making of the peace."

Spending With the Hatch Act ceiling of $3,000,000 on national campaign expenditures, the Democrats reported spending $2,169,077 to $2,828,652 for the Republicans although some estimates skyrocket to $7.4 million and $13.5 million respectively.

Firsts   Roosevelt was the first and only fourth-term President. The first election influenced by political action committees.

Trends   The election marked a shift from U.S. isolationism. Republican effort to win back black vote.

Vote   This was the closest of all the Roosevelt elections. With forty-eight states reporting, the president received 432 electoral votes and 25,606,585 (53.5 percent) to 99 and 22,014,745 (46 percent) for Dewey.

Benchmarks   The second American election in the middle of a major war. The last time the South went Democratic in a big way.

Quote   Commented a Republican newspaper: "Without a doubt the desire to play it safe was the determining factor in the election."

"H AS the Old Master still got it?" *Time* asked for the country at large as the campaign got underway. The president, once so fit and dazzling even with his infirmity, was now sometimes scary to look at. His shoulders slumped, his neck was shrunken inside suits like costumes too large, and his eyes seemed painted on purpose with dark circles and tiredness. But he had his good days, and September 23 was one of them. There was some comment when he was wheeled into place on the dais for the International Brotherhood of Teamsters banquet and then again when he did not try to rise to speak, but his performance made up for everything.

He talked about his age, but only for a moment, saying that he was "actually four years older" from the last election, "which seems to annoy some people." He accused Republicans of wooing labor just before election day, but not otherwise. He ridiculed Republicans in Congress for voting against war preparedness but now changing their views. "I am too old for that," teased Roosevelt. "I cannot talk out of both sides of my mouth at once." But he saved the best to last, defending his Scottish terrier against charges that his rescue once cost millions of taxpayer dollars. Roosevelt intoned "These Republican leaders have not been content with attacks on me, or on my wife, or on my sons . . . they now include my little dog Fala." The audience burst into laughter and *Time* concluded "The Old Master still had it."

From then on, someone said, it was "a contest of Dewey versus Fala." Thomas Dewey, a youngster in political years, a Clark Gable without the romance, had managed to capture the Republican nomination by the sheer size of his reputation as a crimebuster in New York, convicting once-untouchables Waxey Gordon and Lucky Luciano.

That was the easy part. From the outset of the campaign, Dewey did not allow himself much wriggle room. A believer in the social agenda of the New Deal such as collective bargaining and unemployment insurance, and out to win the independent vote, Dewey tried constructive criticism. Fellow Republicans chided "me-tooism."

"The military conduct of the war is outside this campaign," Dewey declared in his acceptance speech. Frankly, there was little fault to find. Ever since December 7, 1941, and Roosevelt's war cry—"a date that will live in infamy"—Americans had let go their much-loved isolationism and thrown themselves into fighting.

Victory took time. In the first half of 1942 in the Far East, the Japanese were on a winning streak, taking the Aleutians, cutting the Burma Road, and causing the administration to order proud general Douglas MacArthur out of the Philippines. Finally, Japan's conquest was checked in carrier-based aircraft battles off Australia and Midway Island. On the Soviet front, the Russians stopped the Germans in icy Stalingrad, September 1942. Two months later American and other Allied forces, under the command of likable Gen. Dwight D. ("Ike") Eisenhower, successfully invaded North Africa and then started on the "soft underbelly" of Europe through Sicily. September 1943, Italy surrendered. On D-Day, June 6, 1944, the Allies began the liberation of France that ended in August. Even Republican journalist William Allen White wrote of Roosevelt "We, who hate your gaudy guts, salute you."

With the New Deal and the war pretty much out of range, Roosevelt's health was Dewey's best target. But there was no proof. The president's physician had stated "He's perfectly O.K." So Dewey only hinted, charging in his acceptance speech that the administration had "grown old and tired and quarrelsome in office." After Roosevelt's "Little Fala" speech Dewey began more direct attacks: "He asked for it. Here it is!" He raised the Red menace. Roosevelt is "indispensable," Dewey argued, "to Earl Browder, the ex-convict and pardoned Communist leader." (Browder was urging Communists to support Roosevelt this time.) He recalled the ten million still unemployed in 1940, amounting, he said, to a "Roosevelt Depression." And he claimed that Roosevelt's "own confused incompetence" had lengthened the war. "It's time for a change," Dewey concluded.

Roosevelt got back to campaigning on October 21, as much to prove that he was still up to it as to answer attacks. That day for four hours and fifty-one miles, a cold rain falling, Roosevelt toured New York City in an open car. Wearing the navy cape and weathered hat of his three previous campaigns, he became drenched, waving to Jewish garment workers in Manhattan, Italian and Irish immigrants in the Bronx, and Brooklyn's blue-collar unionists, two million in number. Several days later he told a crowd of one hundred thousand how strange it was that "quarrelsome, tired old men" have built a military machine "which is fighting its way to victory." Finally, he reminded his listeners that war had been forced upon the country, but under the circumstances, he would make the same decisions "again, and again, and again."

Roosevelt won what he called "the meanest campaign" of his life by a comfortable margin, yet it was the closest of his four. Dewey obviously would have done better if the war had not been going so well. As it was, a month after the inauguration Roosevelt met Winston Churchill and Joseph

Stalin at Yalta to discuss the future problems of peace. Then on April 12, FDR died. All of a sudden, a man who had made his way up in politics with the backing of a big-city machine yet stayed clean, whose claim to fame was an investigation of waste in government right in the middle of war, who was described as shrewd but "plain as an old shoe," was president. "I feel as if the moon and all the stars and all the planets have fallen upon me," Harry S. Truman confessed.

★ CAMPAIGN OF 1948 ★

Major Candidates Harry S. Truman, 64, Missouri, Democrat
Thomas E. Dewey, 46, New York, Republican

Credentials Truman served in World War I, rising from lieutenant to major (1917–1919), was elected Jackson county judge (1922–1924) then presiding judge of the county (1926–1934), U.S. senator (1935–1945) and vice president in 1944.

For Dewey, see Campaign of 1944; he was the Republican presidential nominee in 1944.

Convention Tickets The Democrats met in Philadelphia in a sorry state (see campaign narrative, below). Truman was the fallback, after World War II hero Gen. Dwight D. Eisenhower rejected an early move to nominate him. When balloting began, Mississippi's delegation and part of Alabama's walked out, upset over civil rights in the party platform, and Truman won on the first ballot. When Truman's choice for vice president, Supreme Court Justice William Douglas, was not interested, the delegates selected Senate Minority Leader Alben Barkley of Kentucky by acclamation.

The Republicans convened in Philadelphia with a sizeable number of television viewers. As four years earlier, Thomas E. Dewey was the front-runner because of important primary victories, but with seven hats in the ring, he still had to fight hard and won on the third ballot. Dewey's and the convention's choice for vice president was California governor Earl Warren.

The Progressives, a pairing of liberal Democrats and Communists, nominated Henry Wallace for president, and the second spot was given to Idaho's guitar-playing senator Glen Taylor.

The States' Rights or Dixiecrat party met three days after the Democratic convention to nominate South Carolina governor Strom Thurmond for president and Mississippi's governor Fielding Wright for vice president.

Campaign Notes Truman, according to his own accounting, traveled 31,700 miles and made 352 speeches on the record "and about the same number that were not."

HARRY S. TRUMAN

"Whistle stop," which came to identify Truman's style of campaigning, more or less originated with Republican senator Robert Taft. He criticized the president in June for "blackguarding Congress at every whistle station in the West."

Dewey traveled almost 9000 miles on his "Victory Special," making 107 speeches. Practically every poll showed Dewey winning. Pollster Elmo Roper gave Dewey 44 percent to 31 percent for Truman on September 9 and then stopped polling because Dewey "is almost as good as elected."

Symbols Truman's side sported plastic whistles for the whistle-stop campaign; they also used the donkey. The Republicans had the elephant and efficiency, which cartoonists symbolized by showing Dewey as an automated adding machine. The Progressives, with so many folksingers in their ranks, had the guitar and banjo. Dixiecrats surrounded themselves with Confederate flags.

Slogans The people egged Truman on with "Give 'em Hell, Harry" and "Pour it on 'em, Harry." Other boosters said "Phooey on Dewey" and "Don't Tarry—Vote Harry."

The Republicans yelled back "Save What's Left," "Truman for Ex-President," "H-Club—Help Hustle Harry Home," "Dewey is Due in '48," "To Err is Truman," and "IGHAT" or "I've Got Hatred Against Truman."

The Progressives chanted "One, two, three, four / We don't want another war."

Dixiecrats declared "Save the Constitution—Thurmond for President."

Songs The Democrats played the "Missouri Waltz" again and again even though Truman privately hated it. They were also wild about an adapted version of "I'm Just Wild About Harry."

The Republicans pounded their message home with "What Do We Do on a Dew, Dew, Dewy Day?" and "Date in '48."

Progressives had their own singing vice-presidential candidate plus folksingers Pete Seeger, Woody Guthrie, and scores more who flocked to their cause. "I've Got a Ballot," "Stand and Be Counted," and "The Wallace–Taylor Train" were in their repertoire.

Paraphernalia Truman's past was glorified in comic books, a first ("Harry Truman, Like So Many Other Americans, Sailed for France to Fight for Freedom") and his present in posters: "Secure the Peace/Elect Harry S. Truman." Democratic buttons read "We Did It to Dewey Before and Will Do It Again."

Republican buttons stole the jackass from the Democrats and used it to fill out such legends as "I'll bet my —— on Dewey" and "Keep Your —— off the Grass / It's Dewy."

The Progressives came up with an eye-catching "Wallace for President" button, showing a silhouette of Roosevelt and Wallace smiling broadly.

Popular Labels Truman was called "the average man's average man," "Whistle Stop Harry," "The Man from Missouri," and "The Man of Independence."

Dewey was "the Racket Buster."

Name-calling Anti-Trumanites labeled the president "High-Tax Harry," an "Accidental President," a "squeaky-voiced tinhorn," "the worst president, a Missouri jackass," and a "nasty little gamin."

Dewey was a "city slicker." Truman said G.O.P. stood for "Grand Old Platitudes" and "Gluttons of Privilege."

Wallace was "Pied Piper of the Politburo."

The Press The *Detroit Free Press* on Truman: "a game little fellow" who "went down fighting with all he had."

Spending The Democrats reportedly spent $2,736,334 to $2,127,296 for the Republicans.

Firsts The Republican party renominated a defeated (in 1944) presidential candidate.

The first integrated inaugural.

Trends   Primaries become more important.

Whistle-stop campaigning entered the campaign lexicon, and campaigning became big-time.

Civil rights became a vibrant campaign issue.

Vote   As the returns from forty-eight states slowly came in, they defied all the polls. Truman won 303 electoral votes and 24,179,345 popular votes (49.6 percent) to 189 and 21,991,291 (45.1 percent) for Dewey and 39 and 1,176,125 for States' Righter Thurmond. Wallace received no electoral and 1,157,326 popular votes.

Benchmarks   The biggest political upset in history.

The closest election in thirty-two years.

Truman's campaign represented the high point of old-fashioned presidential barnstorming.

Truman proved that a Democrat could win without a Solid South and without New York, but he won without a majority of popular votes.

Quote: It was widely observed that Dewey had "snatched defeat out of the jaws of victory."

PRESIDENT Harry Truman, his dander up, his spectacles glittering, and his polka-dot bow tie like a playful companion, took off around the country, refusing to believe newspapers, experts, and straws in the wind. On the first day of October, with George Gallup's poll predicting a landslide defeat for him and oddsmakers betting fifteen to one against him, the president beamed optimism. "I am trying to do in politics what Citation has done in the horse races," he told a whistle-stop crowd in Lexington, Kentucky. "I propose at the finish line on November 2 to come out ahead." As if on cue, Citation, always a slow starter, finished eight lengths ahead in the Gold Cup race at Belmont Park the next day.

"You can't make a soufflé rise twice" quipped Alice Roosevelt Longworth when New York's governor Thomas Dewey wanted a second run as the Republican presidential nominee. Nobody paid much attention. Dewey's loss to President Franklin Roosevelt in 1944 was written off as unavoidable in wartime and his showmanship during the primary season made him unstoppable. Besides, people talked about a "new Dewey," more personable and fun-loving, yet a fighter. He came to the convention with front-runner status.

It was not all Dewey's fault that he became so smug. His previews were terrific. The *New York Post* suggested that the Democrats "might as well concede the election to Dewey and save the wear and tear of campaigning." Colored invincible, Dewey quickly took to the high road, avoiding any hands-on combat with his opponent.

Truman was down but not out. His "accidental" presidency had not been easy. To end the war and save American lives, Truman had dropped two atomic bombs on Japan. Critics charged that he never looked back. The Cold War started on his watch. The residue of the Second World War—high taxes, high prices, and high spending—was laid at his feet. His approval rating, starting off at 87 percent, was 32 percent by November 1946. In the midterm elections, Republicans came up with the winning slogan—"Had Enough?"—and the Democrats lost control of both houses of Congress. Truman's tougher talk with Russia led to the Truman Doctrine that meant anti-Communist aid to Greece and Turkey and the Berlin airlift. It also caused the disaffection of former vice president Henry Wallace and the formation of the Progressive party. Truman's tougher civil rights proposals caused "Dixiecrats" from thirteen Southern states to fly the Confederate flag again under the banner of a states' rights party. In this setting Truman began the "loneliest campaign."

What a contrast they made! Truman, a hellion on wheels, yelling at Republicans in his Missouri twang and homespun slang, conducting the whistle-stop campaign of the century on a train named only "The Trip of the President." And Dewey, a persona of pinstripe politeness, so smoothly and efficiently running for office that he was called a machine with a cellophane cover, trying "to prevent anything from rocking the boat" or, actually, the "Dewey Victory Special."

Give-'em-Hell Harry ran against "that no-account, do-nothing, Eightieth Congress" more than against Dewey. In Dexter, Iowa, he told eighty thousand farmers and friends that it was the Republican Congress that did not provide enough storage space for their bumper crops and that they would suffer for it. He said it his way, identifying the GOP as "gluttons of privilege who had stuck a pitchfork into the farmer's back." He wooed the labor vote, warning that under Republican rule "you men of labor can expect to be hit by a steady barrage of body blows." "Give 'em hell, Harry," came the familiar cry. Truman protested that he did not mean to give the Republicans hell, that he only spoke the truth and they "think it's hell."

Truman did make his share of mistakes. "I like Old Joe," he said about Stalin as the Iron Curtain fell. And he likened Dewey to Adolf Hitler as a "front man" for others. But Dewey made the bigger blunder, blurting out when his train backed up by mistake that he had a "lunatic" for an engineer. Truman had a field day, telling his audiences what "wonderful train crews" he had. More devastating was the angry message written by railroad workers on yards of dusty boxcars: "Lunatics for Truman."

Dewey, for the most part, held himself above the fray. Like stanzas from "America the Beautiful," his favorite speeches were about "the fertile plains" and "sheer majesty" of America. "America's future," he would say, "is still ahead of us."

As Truman's campaign lengthened its lead with crowds much bigger than Dewey's, the only thing the press conceded was "the president's growing entertainment value." Truman could not have cared less. When *Newsweek* reported that not one of fifty leading political experts picked him to win, he scoffed "Not one of those fifty fellows has enough sense to pound sand in a rathole." He called all the polls against him "sleeping polls," meant to lull the public into not voting. On the brink of the election when *Life* referred to Dewey as "The Next President" and *Kiplinger Magazine* ran a cover on "What Dewey Will Do," Truman was telling his crowds that "the tide is beginning to roll." He was right and they were wrong. The day after the election he returned to Washington holding aloft the *Chicago Tribune*'s early edition headline: DEWEY DEFEATS TRUMAN. A huge sign on the *Washington Post* building greeted him: MR. PRESIDENT, WE ARE READY NOW TO EAT CROW WHENEVER YOU ARE READY TO SERVE IT.

★ CAMPAIGN OF 1952 ★

Major Candidates Dwight D. Eisenhower, 62, Kansas, Republican
Adlai E. Stevenson, 52, Illinois, Democrat

Credentials Eisenhower, a brigadier general when the U.S. entered World War II, rose to general, became supreme allied commander in charge of the D-Day invasion in December 1943, and a five-star general in December 1944. Resigning from the army in February 1948, assumed the presidency of Columbia University (1948–1950) and was appointed supreme commander of NATO (the North Atlantic Treaty Organization) (1951–1952).

Stevenson served as senior adviser to the first U.S. delegation to the United Nations and was elected governor of Illinois (1949–1952).

Convention Tickets The Republicans met in Chicago divided in their loyalties between conservative Senator Robert Taft of Ohio and Gen. Dwight Eisenhower, the candidate of moderate and liberal factions. On the first roll call among five candidates, Eisenhower led with 595 votes to 500 for Taft and the rest trailing. Swiftly, states started switching and the final tally put Eisenhower far over the top. Senator Richard M. Nixon of California, Eisenhower's choice, was nominated by acclamation for the second spot on the ticket.

The Democrats also convened in Chicago. For the first time in sixteen years, the party did not have an incumbent running. While Senator Estes Kefauver of Tennessee arrived with the most pledged delegates, sentiment was with Illinois governor Adlai Stevenson, who had repeatedly ruled himself out. Stevenson won on the third ballot, when Kefauver put him over the top with Tennessee's delegates. For vice-president, Senator John Sparkman of Alabama won by acclamation.

DWIGHT D. EISENHOWER

Convention Color Eisenhower's managers were masterful users of the new nationwide medium—television. They accused Taft of trying to "steal" the nomination during the contested-delegate fight and, after Eisenhower's nomination, managed a public peace between the nominee and Taft—all in the glare of television lights.

Campaign Notes Eisenhower traveled by train, plane, and motorcade to forty-four states, covering more than 30,000 miles and making 228 speeches. He even went South, unheard of for a Republican presidential candidate, into every state but Mississippi, campaigning harder there than any presidential candidate since Stephen Douglas.

Little was left to chance in Eisenhower's campaign. Advance men lined up media coverage; cheerleaders were recruited to toss tons of confetti and telephone callers to get the crowds out. An advertising firm was hired to draw up an overall "campaign plan" that pinpointed voters who needed to be reached and how to reach them.

Eisenhower's wife Mamie was a class act on "Look Ahead, Neighbor," the campaign train. She passed out buttons from the rear platform of the train, half-singing "I've been working on the railroad."

Stevenson preferred the plane, traveling almost as many miles as his opponent, visiting thirty-two states and delivering 203 speeches, but there was no master campaign plan.

Symbols While the elephant was the official symbol, the "Republican cloth coat" became an unofficial symbol after Nixon's "Checkers speech." Democrats had the donkey and after Stevenson unwittingly bared a hole in the bottom of his shoe and it was captured in a photograph, his holed shoe was used to counteract his highbrow image.

Slogans "I Like Ike" was a winner for the Republicans. They also used "K1C2"—"Korean War, Corruption and Communism"—and variations like "Let's Clean House with Ike and Dick."

Democrats retaliated with "You Never Had It So Good," "Don't Let Them Take It Away," "Peace with Honor," and "I Like Ike but I Am Going to Vote for Stevenson."

Songs "I Like Ike" was turned into song by Irving Berlin: "Makes no deals, / His favors can't be curried / And Uncle Joe [Stalin] is worried / 'cause "we like Ike."

The Democrats liked to remind voters "You never had it so good" in "Don't Let Them Take It Away."

Paraphernalia "I Like Ike" turned heads on nylon stockings, bow ties, bubble-gum cigars, hand-lotion packets, and more. Buttons came in many different languages: "J'Aime Ike," Me Gusta Ike," "Mi Piace Ike," in Hebrew, Morse code, and Braille.

Stevenson's side copycatted somewhat, using "I Like Adlai," "I Say Adlai," and "I'm Madly for Adlai" on nylons, bandannas, ashtrays, and the like. Stevenson's famous sole was shown off on buttons, doorhangers, and lapel pins with such legends as "Walk to Victory with Stevenson."

Popular Labels Eisenhower was "Ike," "Man of the Hour," "the General," and "Mighty Tower Eisenhower."

Stevenson was the "Reluctant Candidate" and the "Thinking Man's Candidate."

Name-calling "The Extremely General Eisenhower" and "the phantom candidate" critics called Eisenhower.

Stevenson and his advisers were labeled "eggheads." Nixon attacked Stevenson as "Adlai the appeaser," a "Ph.D. graduate of Dean Acheson's Cowardly College of Communist Containment," and a "dupe of Hiss."

The Press *Newsweek* said "the campaign ended in vituperation, mudslinging, and mutual recriminations. For millions of voters, Election Day came none too soon."

Spending On a par with 1928, the Republicans reported spending $6,608,623 to $5,032,926 for the Democrats. But estimates reach $80 million with all costs taken into consideration.

Firsts   The first television campaign.
Eisenhower became the first presidential candidate to rely on an advertising firm to help him get elected.

Trends   A two-party system in the South.
From now on, the elected president has won the New Hampshire primary.
Ticket-splitting became common.
Specialized, big-time money raisers.

Vote   The returns from forty-eight states showed an impressive win for Eisenhower, who received 442 electoral votes and 33,936,234 popular votes (55.1 percent) to 89 and 27,314,992 (44.4 percent) for Stevenson.

Benchmarks   The most emotional campaign since 1896.
The last major whistle-stop campaign.
One of the few times voters did not vote their pocketbooks.
One of the biggest increases in turnout ever.

Quote   The day after the election, newspaper headlines screamed IKE IN A LANDSLIDE.

FOR "reluctant" candidates, Dwight Eisenhower and Adlai Stevenson kicked up quite a storm, but that was about the end of the similarity. Eisenhower, the darling of America ever since Allied D-Day forces under his leadership scrambled ashore at Normandy, was such a familiar figure that even the man on the street thought it right to call him "Ike." Stevenson, on the other hand, was like a well-kept secret. Taking over the governorship of Illinois at forty-nine, he was so unknown at the start of the campaign that crowds used to cheer his campaign manager instead. Of course, television, a new player in the game, quickly changed that, as it did so many things.

For a while, it looked as though the campaign would pit President Harry Truman against his nemesis in Congress, Senator Robert Taft—"Mr. Republican." The cast quickly changed. In January 1952, Truman's approval rating was 25 percent and shaky. Although his Fair Deal had raised the minimum wage and expanded Social Security, Truman's gains were swept off the front page by scandals about gifts of freezers and a mink coat to Truman cronies in Washington.

There was bad news on the foreign front, too. In 1949, the West's China hope, Generalissimo Chiang Kai-shek, was forced to retreat to Formosa, leaving the mainland under Communist control. In 1950 North Koreans in their Soviet-made tanks crossed the line, the thirty-eighth parallel demarcation between North and South Korea. Truman used the United Nations, not Congress, to wage war and took the unpopular step of firing Gen. Douglas MacArthur, who wanted to take the conflict to China's door. While Truman talked containment, American boys kept dying. At home, Republican senator

Joseph McCarthy was painting the town red, charging Communists in the State Department. On March 29, 1952 at the Jefferson-Jackson Day dinner, Truman, following his own advice about getting out of the kitchen "if you can't stand the heat," said he would not run again.

The Republicans had already concocted a campaign formula: "K1C2"—"Korea, Communism and Corruption." Now they needed a candidate. Eisenhower's Republican credentials and availability, announced in time for the New Hampshire primary by suitor Senator Henry Cabot Lodge, spoiled the well-laid plans of Senator Taft. Any lingering misgivings Eisenhower had were wiped away by a film of fifteen thousand supporters at a Madison Square Garden rally, staged after a prize fight, who shouted "We like Ike." He won New Hampshire and almost took Minnesota as a write-in candidate in the "Minnesota Miracle." In June, now a civilian, Eisenhower came home to clinch the nomination.

Stevenson, whose eloquence left Democratic delegates demanding his candidacy, only said yes on the fourth day of the convention. One of the reasons Stevenson had resisted outright overtures from Truman was that he wanted to run on his own, not on Truman's record. But Truman nixed that idea and said that he too would whistle-stop.

Eisenhower started slowly, but soon his advertising firm advised him to "Attack, Attack, Attack!" and party pros urged him to make peace with the right wing. Swing he did at the "top-to-bottom" mess in Washington, at the "corruption such as makes us hang our head in shame," and at the price of Democratic full employment—"dead and mangled bodies of young Americans" in Korea. He said he would "find the pinks" in government and politically embraced two private enemies, senators William Jenner and Joseph McCarthy, who had called his friend, Gen. George Marshall, a "traitor."

Television softened the blows and made Eisenhower's likability available for all to see. Fifty spot commercials added a sense of intimacy as Eisenhower answered questions from carefully selected "ordinary" citizens. And television helped the Republicans out of a jam. On September 18, the *New York Post* headlined: SECRET NIXON FUND. Eisenhower considered dropping Nixon unless he came out "as clean as a hound's tooth." Nixon had his say in a televised speech, arguing that the $18,000 was only used to fight Communists and the like, that his family's worldly possessions were such things as his wife's "respectable Republican cloth coat" and, yes, a dog named Checkers, a gift that "the kids love" and "we're gonna keep it."

Stevenson set out to "talk sense to the American people" in well-turned phrases. He used wit often. When a platform under Eisenhower collapsed, Stevenson quipped, "I've been telling him for two months that nobody could stand on that [Republican] platform." And he too got lots of licks in, calling the Republican campaign a "systematic program of innuendo and accusation" and Eisenhower aides "gutter counselors." But he failed miserably on television, writing oratory, not sound bites, and often continuing on long after the camera shut off.

Five words ended the campaign early. On October 24, Eisenhower announced in Detroit: "I shall go to Korea." Democrats labeled it a grandstand play, but the people loved it, believing that the man who worked wonders on the European front could work an end to the war in Asia. They voted him in overwhelmingly. On inauguration day, after taking the oath of office, Eisenhower turned and gave his wife a kiss, the first ever at an inaugural. A new era had begun.

★ CAMPAIGN OF 1956 ★

Major Candidates   Dwight D. Eisenhower, 66, Kansas, Republican
Adlai E. Stevenson, 56, Illinois, Democrat

Credentials   See Campaign of 1952. Eisenhower was elected president in 1952, and Stevenson was the Democratic presidential nominee.

Convention Tickets   The Democrats met in Chicago. After a terrific struggle in the primaries between Adlai Stevenson, the 1952 nominee, and Tennessee Senator Estes Kefauver, Kefauver withdrew. Stevenson breezed through on the first ballot with 905½ votes to 210 for New York governor Averell Harriman and 80 for Senate majority leader Lyndon Johnson. In an untraditional move, Stevenson left the choice of the vice-presidential nominee to the delegates, and they chose Kefauver over Massachusetts Senator John F. Kennedy.

The Republicans convened in San Francisco. There was nothing but affection for President Dwight Eisenhower who seemed in the pink, despite a heart attack the year before and major surgery in June. He was renominated on the first ballot with all 1,323 votes. Vice President Richard Nixon also won unanimous backing.

Convention Color   As soon as Stevenson threw the nomination for vice president to the convention, it was historic. It became more so when the vote showed that Kennedy, a Catholic, did extremely well in the South. Ever since the defeat of Alfred E. Smith for the presidency in 1928, it was thought that a Catholic could not win there.

Campaign Notes   Stevenson set out to visit as many states and shake as many hands as possible even though he disdained handshaking as not thoughtful enough, and ended up traveling three times as much as Eisenhower. He met trouble with negative feelings about his divorce. It seemed that more people were raising the issue in this campaign than in 1952, saying "If a man can't run his family, he has no business trying to run the country."

ADLAI E. STEVENSON

Even though Eisenhower did not need or want to exert himself, he ended up traveling 14,000 miles and visiting thirteen states. Virginia, Texas, Oklahoma, and Tennessee were added to his itinerary when they seemed to be up for grabs. He motorcaded in a bubble-domed limousine and flew in the Columbine III.

Once again, the Eisenhower camp was more masterful with television than Stevenson's. Republican admen talked sponsors into shortening popular programs by five minutes to allow time for campaign commercials.

Symbols Republicans had the elephant and golf tees. The Democrats had the donkey and a new broom—a Stevenson prop to show what he was going to do in Washington.

Slogans The Republicans ran on "Peace, Progress, Prosperity," "Keep America Strong with Ike," "For the Love of Ike, Vote Republican."

The Democrats were out to "Get the Country Moving Again," "Give 'em Hell, Adlai" and "FEF—Forget Eisenhower Forever," shouting all the way "Nervous about Nixon" and "Nix on Nixon."

Songs "Sweetheart of the GOP" was composed for Mamie, while Irving Berlin's "I Like Ike" was modernized as "Ike for Four More Years."

The Democrats sang back "We're Madly for Adlai" and "Believe in Stevenson." Broadway greats, Frederick Loewe and Alan Jay Lerner wrote "Adlai's Gonna Win This Time" to the tune of "Get Me to the Church on Time."

Paraphernalia Bumper stickers came into vogue but required commitment since the easy-to-remove vinyl type did not appear until the 1970s. On Republican cars, they carried such messages as "I Like Ike," "I Still Like Ike," or "I Like Ike Even Better." There were also "I Like Ike" sunglasses, a humongous "I Like Ike" button, and golf tees packaged in "We're Fore Ike" wrappers.

Democratic cars passed by with "I Say Adlai" and "We Believe in Steve" bumper messages as well as such anti-Eisenhower quips as "Ben Hogan for President. If we're going to have a golfer, let's have a good one!"

Popular Labels Eisenhower was "Ike," "Man of the Hour," "the General," and "Mighty Tower Eisenhower."

Stevenson was "The Man from Libertyville" and the "Thinking Man's Candidate" who espoused a "New America."

Name-calling "Part-time leader," "administration without heart," and the "Cadillac Cabinet" were Democratic digs at Eisenhower and his staff. Nixon was "Tricky Dick."

Stevenson was tagged as a "country-club, tweedy snob," "a real lemon," the "issueless candidate," and a candidate who was after the "momma vote."

The Press According to the Chicago *Daily News*: " 'Tis a strange campaign. Ike and his team will stick to the high road, while Stevenson . . . will campaign on a lower level than he did four years ago."

Spending The Republican national campaign reported spending $7,778,702, while the Democrats shelled out $5,106,651.

Firsts The first time since 1848 that a president won without bringing along at least one house of Congress. This happened only four times in history.

Full disclosure of presidential ailments.

The Democrats completely opened up the vice-presidential nomination.

Trends Catholics vote for the incumbent.

The importance of primaries dwarfs conventions in the nominating process.

Television spending outdistanced outlays for radio.

The airplane was the chief mode of travel.

Vote Carrying forty-one of the forty-eight states, Eisenhower had 457 electoral votes and 35,509,472 popular votes (57.6 percent) to 73 and 26,022,752 (42.1 percent) for Stevenson.

Benchmarks Eisenhower scored the biggest triumph since Franklin Roosevelt's 1936 trounce of Alfred Landon.
Eisenhower became the oldest president yet.
The last significant farm vote for a Democrat.
The last significant black vote for a Republican.

Quote Walter Lippmann on Eisenhower's victory: "Since there was a great contented majority behind him, he did not have to admit there was any issue to debate."

MAMIE Eisenhower came to the White House with pink as a passion. The presidential bedroom ached pink from the new king-size bed with its pink pincushion headboard, pink sheets and covers to the pink slipcovered chairs, pink monogrammed wastebasket and generous bowl of "Mamie Pink" carnations. Each day until about noon Mamie herself was a vision in pink. She loved a pink bow in her hair, a pink nightgown, a pink satin bedjacket or housecoat, and pretty pink spiked slippers. When the Textile Color Institute asked and got her permission to introduce a "Mamie Pink" for household furnishings it became the hottest shade of the decade. Mamie, this First Lady in Pink, was perfect for her part in the Fabulous Fifties.

"Just between us girls," she would write to make a point. "Ike runs the country, I turn the porkchops," she would answer to probing questions. *Housewife* would be all right to list as her occupation. Mamie fit a mood of change back to women feeling good about themselves. The postwar blues that instigated *Life*'s 1947 photo essay on "The American Women's Dilemma" had dissipated as America scrambled to new suburbs on new highways, had more babies and more disposable income, watched more television and longed to belong.

Everything seemed normal now in the White House (the "Pink Palace" to staffers), especially when it was learned that "Ike" and Mamie enjoyed eating their dinner on TV trays in front of the tube, watching favorite shows like "I Love Lucy" and "What's My Line?". The fact that Ike liked to goof off some days and play more than a little golf only got highbrows enraged and complaining about a "part-time President." Most others thought he deserved it. Eisenhower made governing look easy when everyone, including himself, knew it was anything but.

"I shall go to Korea" was Eisenhower's winning line in 1952. He followed through with a three-day visit and a warning to North Koreans and their Chinese backers that the United States would not be inhibited "in our use of weapons." Whether it was caused by Eisenhower's derring-do or Soviet leader Joseph Stalin's timely death, as Democrats claimed, a truce was signed in July 1953, in effect putting an end to the enormous bloody toll in American dead and wounded, and the president got credit. "Eight millionaires and a plumber" Eisenhower's cabinet was called sarcastically, but it was the businessmen in the group who got the tax rate down and military spending reduced. Secretary of State John Foster Dulles' comments in print about the "necessary art" of taking the country to the "verge of war," denounced as "brinkmanship," were offset by the president's own atoms-for-peace and open-skies efforts to defrost the Cold War. Luckily, "low-blow Joe" McCarthy, who had tarred scores of innocents with the label "Red," self-destructed on television when he tried to make the army heel. Even the midterm return of the House and Senate to Democratic control had a silver lining. Eisenhower got along well with the Sam Rayburn–Lyndon Johnson leadership.

But would Ike run again? The decision seemed to settle itself when, on the night of September 24, 1955, in Denver, the President, his chest hurting, woke Mamie. She was told to wrap herself around him to quiet him. It worked. But twelve hours later the world learned that Eisenhower had had a heart attack. On November 11 Eisenhower came back to Washington, headed for his farm in Gettysburg and three weeks of rest. Four days later Adlai Stevenson announced that he would try again for the Democratic nomination. Eisenhower, who was making a remarkable recovery, made up his mind at Gettysburg. "He faced the sheer, god-awful boredom of not being President," an aide said later. The country found out late the following February.

By that time Stevenson was in a fierce primary fight with Tennessee senator Estes Kefauver. From New Hampshire, where Kefauver in his coonskin hat pulled a rabbit out of another by winning in spite of Stevenson's establishment support, to California, where Stevenson, uncomfortably costumed in a tasseled denim jacket, red string tie, and ten-gallon hat, got back at him for good, they battled so long and hard that Stevenson had some of the wind knocked out of him for the major race. He told aides that he wanted to focus on foreign policy for the fall campaign, that he found domestic issues boring now. Charging the administration with "Pollyanna politics" and "deception," he proposed that America unilaterally stop H-bomb tests and end the peacetime draft. Eisenhower criticized the testing ban as a "theatrical national gesture" and the draft idea as "incredible folly." Many others wondered if Stevenson understood the world out there. Or the nation's mood.

Eisenhower, saying he would leave the "yelling" to the opposition, talked about "the glow of happiness" that he saw everywhere and that people should vote "happy." In contrast, Stevenson made his listeners feel uneasy. "I ask your support not in the name of complacency but in the name of anxiety," he said. "I ask your support not because I say all is well. . . . I ask your support not because I offer promises of peace and prosperity but because I do not."

When the world went mad again just before the election, with Britain and France invading Egypt to regain the Suez Canal and the Soviets crushing "liberation" in Hungary, the public sought Eisenhower's reassuring embrace. And when Stevenson, two days before the election, raised the fear that Eisenhower, who had gone through major surgery in June but liked to brag "I feel fine," would not survive four more years, it only backfired. "Eisenhower Wins In A Sweep," headlined *The New York Times*. Ike, too, was perfect for his part in the Fabulous Fifties.

★ CAMPAIGN OF 1960 ★

Major Candidates John F. Kennedy, 43, Massachusetts, Democrat
Richard M. Nixon, 47, California, Republican

Credentials Kennedy served in the navy during World War II (1941–1945), most notably as skipper of PT-109, became a member of the House of Representatives (1947–1953) and then a United States senator (1953–1961). He wrote the Pulitzer Prize-winning *Profiles in Courage* (1956).

Nixon became a member of the House of Representatives (1947–1950), a United States senator (1951–1953), and vice president under Dwight D. Eisenhower (1953–1961).

Convention Tickets The Democrats convened in Los Angeles. Senator John Kennedy, having chased Senator Hubert Humphrey out of the race in the primaries, came to the convention with more delegates than any other candidate and won on the first ballot. To woo the South, Kennedy chose Senator Lyndon Johnson of Texas as his running mate.

The Republicans met in Chicago. They too had a front-runner, Vice President Richard Nixon, who also won on the first ballot. The vice-presidential slot went to United Nations ambassador Henry Cabot Lodge, with all delegates voting in favor.

Campaign Notes Kennedy traveled to forty-four states, covered some 44,000 miles, and gave about 120 major speeches. Nixon chalked up about 65,000 miles, gave 150 major speeches, and—in the last week of the campaign, by taking a 7,000-mile jaunt to Alaska—fulfilled his campaign pledge to visit each of the fifty states. Both were spent by election day.

The candidates' wives were major players too. Pat Nixon spoke out on the new role for women, saying "they have emerged as volunteers for a cause they believe in." Jacqueline Kennedy, a former reporter, wrote a weekly "Campaign Wife" column, syndicated by the Democratic National Committee. She addressed medical care for the aged, the need for 140,000 classrooms, and "the issue uppermost in every woman's mind is peace."

By one count, Kennedy made 220 campaign promises, including a Peace Corps, higher teachers' salaries, and "to seek 80 million jobs by 1982." Toward the end of the campaign Nixon tried to catch up, promising a manned flight around the moon and to send Eisenhower to Eastern Europe.

Symbols Democrats played up Kennedy's heroism with PT-109, while Republicans used pictures of Nixon's "kitchen debate" with Soviet Leader Nikita Khrushchev to show their candidate's heroics. Donkeys and elephants were used too.

JOHN F. KENNEDY

Slogans   Kennedy preached "Let's Get America Moving Again," "A Time for Greatness," and "Leadership for the '60s." Kennedy boosters bragged "All the Way with JFK," and could not resist "Nix on Nixon."

Nixon countered "Peace Without Surrender," "Experience Counts," "We Never Had It So Good," and "Keep America Strong."

Songs   Democrats adapted the new, popular song "High Hopes" for their campaign: "K–E–Double-N–E–D–Y / Jack's the nation's favorite guy."

Republican favorites were "Buckle Down with Nixon," "Here Comes Nixon," and "Click with Dick."

Paraphernalia   There were Kennedy sponges, ice cream bars, and straw boater hats. The candidate's "youth," both an asset and a liability, was highlighted on "Youth for Kennedy" buttons. Democrats also reproduced an unflattering photo of Nixon with the tag line "Would You Buy a Used Car from This Man?"

Republicans emphasized "Experience Counts" and "No Substitute for Experience" on bumper stickers, posters, and buttons. Other buttons broadcast "Man of Steel" and "Ike's for Dick and So Am I."

Anti-Kennedy materials, such as "Nix—On Kennedy" buttons, "Sorry Nik [Khruschchev] / I Like Dick" tabs and "Remember PT-109/Like Who Gets a Chance to Forget" bumper stickers also made the rounds.

Popular Labels Kennedy was "JFK," "Jack," and "Man of the '60s." Nixon was "Dick."

Name-calling Kennedy was a "boy," accused of a "barefaced lie" with "too much profile and not enough courage."

Nixon could not shed his reputation as "Tricky Dick," "Slippery Dick," or "Dick the Ripper."

The Press James Reston of *The New York Times* wrote: "In sum, Mr. Kennedy gains as these debates go on even if he does no more than stay level with the vice president."

Spending The Democratic national committee doled out $9,797,000, matched by $10,128,000 for the Republicans.

Firsts Kennedy was the first Roman Catholic elected president.

Nixon was the first candidate to stump all fifty states.

Kennedy was the first to win the nomination through the primaries.

The first presidential debates were held.

Trends Handpicked advisers take over from party pros.

Polling plays a bigger role in strategy.

Vote The nip-and-tuck election brought more people out to vote than ever before, helped by the addition of two states to the union in 1959. Carrying just twenty-two states, Kennedy had 303 electoral votes and 34,226,731 popular votes (49.7 percent) to twenty-six states, 219 electoral votes and 34,108,157 popular votes (49.5 percent) for Nixon. (Mississippi's and most of Alabama's delegates went to Virginia Senator Harry Byrd.)

Benchmarks Kennedy was the youngest elected president.

Kennedy won by the smallest popular percentage margin in history and without a majority of popular votes.

Television became the dominant medium in campaigning.

Image and sex appeal were factors as never before.

Democrats adopt the strongest civil rights plank yet.

Quote Kennedy on his victory: "It was TV more than anything that turned the tide."

JOHN F. Kennedy wanted the presidency maybe more than he had a right to. He was considered too young, too politically untried and, above all, too Catholic. And he was a loner, voting with a liberal bent but really voting his own way. His father, Joseph Kennedy, a "Daddy Warbucks" when it came to politics, was rumored to have bought and bartered his son's success.

But none of this mattered when father and son sat down together in the library of their white house in Hyannis Port, three weeks after the 1956 election and four months after the younger Kennedy almost won the Democratic vice-presidential nomination. They had switched their sights to first place on the ticket in 1960 and the son, playing devil's advocate, was raising all the possible obstacles, especially the part about being Catholic. "Just remember, this country is not a private preserve for Protestants," said the father. Other Catholics will be proud that you are running and "that pride will be your spur." "Well, Dad, I guess there's just one question left. When do we start?"

Richard Nixon thought he deserved the presidency maybe more than he had a right to. As Dwight Eisenhower's vice president he had won high marks for filling in during the president's illness, ably but without bravado; for troubleshooting in South America, where he was spat upon and stoned but did not lose his temper; and for finger-pointing and lecturing Soviet chairman Nikita Khrushchev at a "typical American house" exhibit in Moscow but making it no more than a "kitchen debate." When New York's brand-new governor, Nelson Rockerfeller, felt like challenging Nixon in the primaries, he quickly discovered that the party's doors were "locked, barred and closed" to anyone but the vice president and gave up. Only Eisenhower was somewhat of a wild card, hedging on whom he would support.

Kennedy's game plan was to convince party leaders of his vote-getting prowess through the primaries. Minnesota senator Hubert Humphrey, whose liberal enthusiasm had propelled him from the mayoralty of Minneapolis to the Senate, would be his rival. Other senatorial greats of the day like dynamic Lyndon Johnson and distinguished Stuart Symington were willing to wait for the convention. The first match-up was in Humphrey's neighbor-state Wisconsin, but that made no difference when the Kennedy clan and extras descended to campaign. Both candidates spent $150,000 in the state, but Humphrey felt like a "corner grocer running against a chain store."

With his primary victories, Kennedy dominated the Democratic convention and, with his credentials, Nixon had no competition for the Republican nomination. In his acceptance speech Kennedy, exhausted now from the year-long effort, sounded so, and his "New Frontier" theme lacked sparkle. Nixon, watching from Washington, felt he could beat Kennedy on television, if it came to that. As it was, Nixon's words of acceptance added up to probably his best-delivered campaign speech: "When Mr. Khrushchev says our grandchildren will live under Communism, let us say his grandchildren will live in freedom."

As the campaign began in earnest, Kennedy's strategy was to win back the Democratic voters who had switched to Eisenhower and leave the religion issue until later. But early on, the Reverend Norman Vincent Peale charged that a Catholic president would be under "extreme pressure from the hierarchy of his Church." Addressing Baptist ministers in Houston, Kennedy successfully snuffed out the issue, saying "I believe in an America where the separation of Church and State is absolute." He never made another major speech on religion, but his Houston triumph was taped and 300 prints quickly circulated. Meanwhile, Nixon's course was to erase his old "Tricky Dick" image. He wowed the South with political politesse. Both candidates also got their digs in. Nixon, who hammered Kennedy on his youth and inexperience, liked to refer to his own "experience in talking with Mr. Khrushchev, even if it was just in the kitchen." Kennedy, pointing to such things as the "missile gap" with Russia, Fidel Castro's takeover of Cuba, and the Soviet's first-in-space Sputnik, retorted that Nixon's experience was more in "policies of retreat, defeat and weakness."

The "great debates" were a turning point in America's perception of two candidates, both good-looking, both bright, both able to excite legions to their side. The first televised encounter, watched by an estimated seventy million people, defined differences that never faded from the screen. Kennedy, tanned and rested, was handsomely in command. He had done his homework and it showed and Nixon ended up arguing "Our disagreement is not about the goals of America but only about the means to reach these goals." Nixon, eight pounds underweight due to a knee infection wore his shirt collar too loose and his drawn face, covered lightly with Lazy Shave, was the worse for a shadow of a beard. And it was Kennedy, not Nixon, who heeded a producer's advice: "Play to your cameras. That's where the votes are."

Nixon never recovered, even though he did better in the next Quemoy–Matsu foreign policy debate and two more, even though Eisenhower was now his biggest backer ("His counsel has been invaluable to me") and even though he came out swinging harder. After the first debate, Kennedy's crowds quite visibly multiplied, as he was christened with star quality and his charm and eloquence became more apparent. He helped himself too by telephoning his concern to Coretta Scott King when her husband was arrested during a restaurant sit-in and jailed on a trumped-up technicality. When Nixon did nothing, Martin Luther King's father remarked, "I have a suitcase full of votes and I'm going to take them to Mr. Kennedy and dump them in his lap." Kennedy scarcely won with the black vote, the Catholic vote, and the industrial city vote. On a frosty inauguration day, power passed from the oldest man yet to serve in the presidency to the youngest ever elected. Kennedy, skillfully now, spoke for the ages: "And so, my fellow Americans, ask not what your country can do for you. Ask what you can do for your country."

★ CAMPAIGN OF 1964 ★

Major Candidates   Lyndon B. Johnson, 56, Texas, Democrat
Barry Goldwater, 55, Arizona, Republican

Credentials Johnson was elected to the House of Representatives (1937–1949), a United States senator (1949–1961) and vice president under John F. Kennedy (1961–1963). November 22, 1963, the day of Kennedy's assassination, Johnson became president.

Goldwater was elected to the United States Senate in 1952 and wrote *Conscience of a Conservative* in 1960.

Convention Tickets   The Democrats convened in Atlantic City on August 24 and it was LBJ all the way; he was nominated for a term of his own by acclamation. Like a circus ringmaster, Johnson then took over and introduced his surprise choice for his running mate Senator Hubert Humphrey. Humphrey was also chosen by acclamation.

By the time the Republicans met in San Francisco, Arizona senator Barry Goldwater had locked up 300 delegates through state conventions alone and other major contenders had dropped out (see campaign narrative, below). A last-minute effort by Pennsylvania governor William Scranton, a moderate, to try to stop Goldwater fizzled. With seven hats still in the ring, including that of Margaret Chase Smith of Maine, Goldwater won decisively on the first ballot. For second place on the ticket, Goldwater chose Representative William Miller of New York.

Convention Color   Emotionalism ran high at the Republican convention. Scranton's aides started things off by sending a scathing letter to Goldwater in a futile effort to force a debate between the two candidates. It said that Goldwater's managers treated delegates like "a flock of chickens whose necks will be wrung at will" and that "Goldwaterism has come to stand for a whole crazy-quilt of absurb and dangerous positions." New York governor Nelson Rockefeller, booed and blasted with cowbells and trumpets while speaking against extremists, "kooks" to him, upped the frenzy by snapping "This is still a free country, ladies and gentlemen."

Goldwater whipped up delegates with his acceptance speech: "Extremism in the defense of liberty is no vice! And let me remind you also that moderation in the pursuit of justice is no virtue."

Campaign Notes   Johnson wanted to "stay presidential." For a while, he did just that, but he also wanted every vote and so at the end of September he hit the trail, covering 60,000 miles in forty-two days.

Goldwater chalked up 75,000 miles, the distance of three trips around the

LYNDON B. JOHNSON

earth. At one point he wondered of his strategists if he could give up all the traveling but was firmly told, "You can't; it's always been done this way."

Symbols The Democrats had the donkey and Johnson's Stetson, while the Republicans had the elephant and Goldwater's black-rimmed glasses.

Slogans "Come, let us reason together" from the prophet Isaiah, "All the Way with LBJ," and "USA Likes LBJ" were favorites of the Democrats.
   One of Goldwater's favorites—"In Your Heart You Know He's Right"—prompted Johnsonites to reply "In Your Guts You Know He's Nuts."
   Goldwater's followers also used "We Want a Choice, Not an Echo" and "You Know Where He Stands—Vote for the Man You Can Trust."

Songs The Broadway hit tune "Hello, Dolly" became "Hello, Lyndon": "You're still glowin', you're still crowin', / You're still goin' strong."
   The Republicans had "Go with Goldwater": "You know where he stands / Clap your hands and go with Goldwater!" They also used "The Battle Hymn of the Republic."

Paraphernalia Message T-shirts made the scene, essentially replacing now-passé political bandannas. Johnson's pictured two kids, a gleeful donkey, and the legend: "If We Had Our Say / We'ed Vote For LBJ."

Goldwater T-shirts pictured Goldwater, a jet (he was a jet pilot), and the legend: "Go with Goldwater." Cans of "Gold Water, The Right Drink for the Conservative Taste" hit the spot for some.

Popular Labels Johnson was "LBJ," "Great Guided Missile," "Preacher Lyndon;" "Great Manipulator," and "Dynamic Texan."

"Barry" Goldwater or "Mr. Conservative" was also "AuH₂0," the chemical term for gold water.

Name-calling Johnson was lampooned as a "Great Wheeler Dealer," "crook," "scheming wire-puller," and "the phoniest individual that ever came around."

Goldwater was attacked as "trigger-happy," a "raving, ranting demagogue," and "extremist."

The Press The *Saturday Evening Post*, Republican up until then, editorialized: "Goldwater is a grotesque burlesque of the conservative he pretends to be. He is a wild man, a stray, an unprincipled and ruthless jujitsu artist like Joe McCarthy."

Spending The Democrats spent roughly half as much as the Republicans, or $8,757,000 to $16,026,000.

First Johnson was the first Southern, Democratic presidential nominee since James Polk in 1844 and the first president from a Confederate state since the Civil War.

Trends Conventions become the focus of demonstrators.

A Republican voting preference among white Southerners.

Vote Returns from fifty states and the District of Columbia were loud and clear for Johnson, who received 486 electoral votes and 43,129,566 popular votes (61.1 percent) to 52 and 27,178,188 (38.5 percent) for Goldwater.

Benchmarks Johnson's electoral vote sweep was the best since 1936.

Johnson's popular vote margin was the best to date.

A promised great issue debate fizzled into one of the silliest, most boring and mindless of campaigns.

Quote Said Emmet John Hughes in *Newsweek*: "The grand combat of 1964 was a rather ghastly waste of time."

PRESIDENT John Kennedy, bantering with his brother Robert and other friends in the Oval Office, would tease "Say, whatever became of Lyndon Johnson?" It always got a laugh. Such was the nature of the vice-presidency that even a dynamo like Johnson, Kennedy's "Riverboat Gambler," could be lost sight of. Yet Johnson was not left out in the Kennedy administration. He consoled Berlin right after the building of the wall, oversaw efforts to reach the moon and start a Peace Corps on earth, and was present at cabinet meetings. Still, Johnson felt like a bystander to history, waiting his turn. And the Kennedys' easy grace and glamour that made Camelot the romantic comparison also made this Texas hill-country boy uncomfortable.

Then on November 22, 1963, the day America wept, Johnson got what he wanted, but it was all wrong. In a cold, bloody, cowardly act, Kennedy was killed by a drifter in Dallas, a city he came to court. The silence was deafening. Kennedy's vision and eloquence had made America feel young and spirited again. He had won and lost in the presidency. The fiasco of the Bay of Pigs invasion was offset by making Russia blink in the Cuban missile crisis. He was not able to prevent East Berlin from being sealed off, but did stem the loss of hope by standing at the wall and saying *"Ich bin ein Berliner."* He used clout to roll back steel prices, making business angry, but then proposed a whopping cut in corporate taxes to stimulate the economy. He stumbled, at first, in civil rights, causing Martin Luther King to cite "tokenism," but regained all favor with the strongest-yet civil rights bill. In Vietnam Kennedy increased the number of advisers from 1,000 to 16,000, but insisted "In the final analysis, it is their war . . . the people of Vietnam against the Communists." His thousand days were too short.

Johnson meant to make up for that, immediately picking up with his mantle the Kennedy agenda. It helped healing and it helped him when, four days after the assassination, Johnson went to Congress and reminded his comrades of the fallen President's words at his inauguration: "Let us begin." Back at the controls, more powerful than ever, Johnson maneuvered the tax and civil rights bills to passage, managed to get medical care for the aged and food stamps for the poor, announced his goal for a "Great Society," and eased relations with the Soviet Union. By June 1964, the Gallup poll gave him 81 percent of the vote against Arizona senator Barry Goldwater.

Goldwater, the conscience of conservatives, never had as much drive for the Republican nomination as his right-wing followers. In April, asked about the movement to nominate him, Goldwater said he had given up trying to stop it. The primaries were riddled with his shoot-from-the-lip statements. In New Hampshire, Goldwater said NATO commanders should have the option of using atomic weapons and suggested that Social Security be made voluntary. In California he half-joked that maybe "we could saw off the Eastern Seaboard and let it float out to sea." Other times he quipped: "Let's lob one into the men's room of the Kremlin." The London *Economist* observed that Goldwater "has alienated some of his own admirers by scaring the daylights out of them." But there was no one else. New York governor Nelson Rockefeller lost an early lead when he divorced and remarried and lost out completely when his son was born, drawing attention back to his marital tale, three days before the California primary. Goldwater was an easy target, but Johnson wanted all the votes of all the people to prove his legitimacy and to prove that he was loved, and so he fought.

The campaign was a free-for-all with no direct hits. "Mr. President, You're Fun," *Time* wrote after a Texas weekend with Johnson where he careened around his ranch at the wheel of a Lincoln Continental at up to 90 miles an hour, sipping beer from a paper cup. The Republicans made a film for national television called *Choice* that interestingly featured a car like Johnson's, speeding madly along country roads, as beer cans were tossed out of the driver's window. It also showed race riots, striptease artists, and close-ups of Bobby Baker, Johnson's Senate aide who was now under investigation. But Goldwater pulled it before airtime, saying it was "a racist film." The Democrats did little better with their most powerful shot: a sixty-second television spot of a pretty little girl picking petals from a daisy, counting "one, two, three . . . nine." Startled, she hears the voice of a man counting down. The screen goes black and a mushroom explosion appears. Johnson is heard: "These are the stakes . . ." It ran only once before being protested off the air.

On the road, Goldwater kept thrusting, saying that "low-yield atomic weapons" could be used to defoliate the forests of Vietnam, that he would get out of the United Nations if Red China got in, and that freedom includes "the freedom *not* to associate." "To Lyndon Johnson," he claimed, "running a country means . . . buying and bludgeoning votes." In one speech by a *New York Times* count, Goldwater used such trigger phrases as *nuclear weapons*, *push the button*, and *mass destruction* almost twenty-six times in the same amount of minutes.

Johnson played it presidential at first, handling such matters as a skirmish in August between American and North Vietnamese boats in international waters. But by the end of September he went to the people with his "Uncle Cornpone" hat and talked a blue streak: "Let's keep a smile on your face, let's keep faith in our heart." He also talked fear: "In the nuclear age, the President doesn't get a second chance. . . . If he mashes the button—that's it." Above all, he talked peace: "We are not about to send American boys nine or ten thousand miles away from home to do what Asian boys ought to be doing." The morals charge against a senior Johnson aide in mid-October did not have time to impact before Nikita Khrushchev's ouster and Red China's first nuclear explosion made people long for continuity. Of his landslide victory, Johnson said "It is a mandate for unity."

★ CAMPAIGN OF 1968 ★

Major Candidates   Hubert H. Humphrey, 57, Minnesota, Democrat
Richard M. Nixon, 55, California, Republican

Credentials   Humphrey was mayor of Minneapolis (1945–1949), helped found Americans for Democratic Action (1947), was elected to the U.S. Senate (1949–1965), lost to John F. Kennedy in the 1960 presidential primaries, and was elected vice president to Lyndon Johnson in 1964.

For Nixon, see Campaign of 1960. He lost his bid for governor of California in 1962.

Convention Tickets   The Democrats convened in Chicago. The forces of Vice President Hubert Humphrey were dominant, even though Humphrey had not entered any of the primaries. Before the first roll call, the century-old unit rule was eliminated, allowing diversity in a state's votes. Humphrey won the nomination on the first ballot. Humphrey's choice for the second spot was Maine senator Edmund Muskie, who won on the first ballot.

The Republicans met in Miami Beach amid controlled calm. Former vice president Nixon was out front, but nipping at his heels were New York governor Nelson Rockefeller and California governor Ronald Reagan. On the first ballot and after votes switched, Nixon won. Nixon took a lot of people by surprise by asking Maryland governor Spiro Agnew to be his running mate and the delegates went along.

The American Independent party never held a convention. Its founder, former Alabama governor George Wallace, simply declared himself a third-party candidate in February and late in the campaign chose retired air force general Curtis LeMay as his running mate.

Convention Color   Later, after an investigation, what happened "Bloody Wednesday" at the Democratic convention was called a "police riot." Provoked by some of the 10,000 Yippies, Mobilization ("Mobe") marchers, and other demonstrators who poured into Chicago, shouting obscenities, throwing rocks and bags of urine, part of the city's police force, a might of 11,000, went berserk. They took after the longhairs with nightsticks, Mace, and brute force. Protestors chanted "The whole world is watching."

Campaign Notes   Hecklers were everywhere, and each candidate coped or did not. Humphrey was so appalled at the transference of Johnson hate to him, as in such chants as "Dump the Hump" and "HHH Nominated by Chicago Gestapo" signs, that sometimes he was reduced to tears. Nixon was pestered by hecklers demanding "Why Don't You Debate?" and an end to "Doubletalk."

HUBERT H. HUMPHREY

Symbols Humphrey's initials HHH and Nixon's arms raised high with his hands in victory signs became symbolic. Wallace's followers raised the Confederate flag.

Slogans Democrats rallied around "Who but Hubert?", "Some Talk Change. Others Cause It," "Viva Humphrey," and "A Man for the People."
   Republicans liked "Nixon's the One" until they replaced it with "This Time Vote Like Your Whole Life Depended on It."
   Wallace ran on "Stand Up for America" and "Let the People Speak."

Songs The Democrats did not come up with a winner, although "Battle Hymn of the Republic" was used.
   Republicans had "Nixon's the One."
   For Wallace there was "The George Wallace Waltz."

Paraphernalia Double-knits not only modernized the clothing industry, they put a snag in the popularity of lapel pins and political-pin jewelry because of the damage they did. Disposable stickers took their place: "If I Had a Button It Would Say Humphrey–Muskie."
   Nixon had hand-held clickers saying "Click with Dick," telephone dialers, and "Nixon's the One" bumper stickers, bubblegum cigars, and matchbooks.

Wallace buttons and bumper stickers bragged "Wallace—Yes! / Busing—No!"

Popular Labels Humphrey was "the Happy Warrior" and "HHH."

Nixon was "The New Nixon" and "old pro" who preached to "forgotten Americans."

Name-calling Humphrey was derided as "Hubert the Happy."

Nixon took licks as "Richard the Silent," "Richard the Chicken-Hearted," "Tricky Dick," "The Shadow," and "Brand X." His running mate was "Spiro Who?"

Wallace and LeMay were "the bombsy twins," while Wallace alone was "charlatan" and "demagogue."

Spending The Democratic national committee reported spending $11,594,000 to $25,402,000 for the Republicans. The big difference was big donors, with Nixon garnering $8 million from 285 individuals.

Firsts Nixon was the first presidential candidate since William Henry Harrison in 1840 to win after a previous electoral defeat.

Channing F. Phillips was the first black officially nominated for the presidency by a major party at a national convention.

Trends Spot commercials become big.

Mass media advertising is used.

Opinion analysis is in vogue.

Vote With fifty states and the District of Columbia voting, Nixon won 301 electoral votes and 31,785,480 (43.4 percent) to 191 and 31,275,166 (42.7 percent) for Humphrey and 46 and 9,906,473 (13.5 percent) for Wallace.

Benchmarks Nixon made one of the most successful political comebacks in history.

Nixon won with less than a majority of popular votes.

Wallace won more popular and electoral votes than any other third-party candidate.

The primaries had less impact than in any recent election.

Quote Nixon on election night: "Having lost a close one eight years ago and having won a close one this year, I can say this: Winning's a lot more fun."

AFTER his giant election victory in 1964, "Landslide Lyndon" Johnson had a mandate and he ran with it, shoving through a compliant, "hip-pocket Congress" so many "Great Society" programs that only Franklin Delano

Roosevelt and his congressional New Dealers were rivals. There was also a war in Vietnam. By slow, almost secretive steps the number of United States forces had risen from 3,500 in February 1965 to 285,000 in June 1966. In January of that year, in his State of the Union message, Johnson said America could have it all—guns *and* butter: "I believe we can continue the Great Society while we fight in Vietnam."

By early 1968 Johnson's "mandate for unity," worn like a badge of honor, was in shreds. Race riots, "white backlash," and the Tet offensive had made a mockery of his two-fisted approach, stamped him as a grotesque kingly caricature in cartoons and caused his approval rating to plummet to 35 percent. While hordes of college students protested "Impeach LBJ" and "Drop LBJ ON North VIETNAM," others plodded through the snows of New Hampshire, shorn of their long hair and trademark jeans, looking "clean for Gene" as they tried to woo voters to Democratic "dove" Senator Eugene McCarthy. This children's crusade caught fire when, just two days before the primary, *The New York Times* reported that Gen. William Westmoreland had asked for another 206,000 men to add to the 550,000 already in Southeast Asia. McCarthy did not win, but he came close enough to pierce Johnson's invincibility. With that, New York senator Robert Kennedy, also dovish, entered the race and Johnson did the unthinkable. On March 31, speaking from the White House, he told the public that he had turned down Westmoreland's request, talked nostalgically about "what we won when all of our people united," and said that he would not accept his party's nomination "for another term as your President."

As if America fell from grace, a spectacle followed so irrevocable and so sad that there was no sense to make. In the setting sun on Thursday, April 4, a rifle shot killed Martin Luther King, Jr., the country's most influential black leader, and ripples of fear and anger erupted in riots in hundreds of American cities. On the night of the June 4 California primary, when Kennedy bested McCarthy and rallied his followers "On to Chicago," knowing that he was now Vice President Hubert Humphrey's main challenger for the nomination, he also took a simple shortcut through the kitchen of a Los Angeles hotel. He was shot three times; front-page pictures the next day showed him on the floor, bleeding and dying.

The times called for more than the usual political rhetoric, yet Humphrey did not seem to understand. Carried away by the announcement of his own presidential bid, a typically ebullient Humphrey spoke about "the politics of happiness, the politics of purpose and the politics of joy . . . all the way from here on out." But it could not be. Humphrey saw that for himself in his Chicago hotel room, when he watched the "kooks and rioters," as he called them, outside the Democratic convention hall and lambasted "that instrument" for televising the chaos to America. As the convention ended, "United with Humphrey" posters were disposed of and Humphrey privately thought "I'm dead."

Early September polls showed that Humphrey was running about ten points behind Republican candidate former vice president Richard Nixon and roughly the same margin ahead of wild-card candidate former Alabama governor George Wallace. Nixon had done so much for himself by his "forgotten Americans" acceptance speech that, for the first few weeks of the campaign, it seemed that nothing could touch him. He campaigned cocoonlike, going from organized rallies to organized television interviews where panelists, including one black, had been preselected by his campaign staff and the audience was instructed to rush up to Nixon at the end, cameras running, to congratulate him. Even Humphrey's taunts of "Richard the Silent" when Nixon refused to debate and his threat "to put a blow torch to his political tail and run him out into the open" did not rouse the Republican candidate from his set, successful course.

Wallace, best known for defiantly and theatrically standing in the schoolhouse door to bar blacks from the University of Alabama in 1963, gradually lost interest in his "segregation forever" cause, but kept his white, rural, lower-income backers who liked the way he talked about *them* and *us*. Humphrey called him "the apostle of fear and racism" and Nixon belittled the "third-party kick." But Wallace was as high as 20 percent in the polls until he picked as his running mate retired air force general Curtis LeMay, who had once advocated bombing North Vietnam "back to the Stone Age" and now said he would use nuclear weapons whenever "necessary."

In the major leagues, a vice-presidential candidate was doing damage too. Nixon's well-packaged campaign was coming unraveled through off-the-cuff remarks of Spiro Agnew. He said Humphrey had been "soft on communism" and "if you've seen one city slum, you've seen them all." He referred to a Japanese reporter as a "fat Jap."

Belatedly Humphrey tried to become the central character. Criticized by Nixon as Johnson's yes man, trotting "meekly behind his master," the vice president stepped away from the administration's Vietnam policy on September 30: "I would stop the bombing of the North as an acceptable risk for peace." The next day he made fun of Nixon's "perfumed, deodorized, detergentized campaign." The "new Nixon," the calmer, more compassionate Nixon, was finally on the defensive. He went whistle-stopping, à la Harry Truman, lambasting Humphrey as the man with the "loosest tongue in the nation" who made "the fastest switch of position ever seen in American politics." Johnson switched too. On October 31, five days before the election, he told the nation that he had ordered a halt to all bombing. One reporter wrote that Johnson had given Nixon "a trick" and Humphrey "a treat" for Halloween. Polls showed the two candidates only two to three percentage points apart. Nixon won by an eyelash, claiming victory by saying one sign "touched me the most" during the campaign: "Bring Us Together."

★ CAMPAIGN OF 1972 ★

Major Candidates Richard M. Nixon, 59, California, Republican
George S. McGovern, 50, South Dakota, Democrat

Credentials For Nixon, see Campaign of 1960 and 1968. He was elected president in 1968.

McGovern was a member of the House of Representatives (1957–1961), director of the Food for Peace program under President John Kennedy (1961–1962), and was elected a United States senator in 1962.

Convention Tickets The Republicans met in Miami Beach and, after one floor fight requested by President Richard Nixon for the look of an open convention, Nixon was renominated on the first ballot. Vice President Spiro Agnew was also renominated on the first ballot.

The Democrats, also in Miami Beach, tried for the most open convention ever and got the good with the bad. The long, unstructured convention nominated South Dakota senator George McGovern, who won on the first ballot. McGovern settled on Missouri senator Thomas Eagleton for the vice-presidential nominee, but in early August replaced him (when it turned out he had been hospitalized for psychiatric problems) with Sargent Shriver, the first director of the Peace Corps.

Convention Color The Republican and Democratic conventions were a study in contrasts, showing in microcosm how different America could be. There were so many young, long-haired, blue-jeaned delegates at the Democratic convention it looked "like the cast of *Hair*" to one older delegate. Also, with so many more minorities and women, fewer party leaders made it as delegates; only 30 of 255 Democratic members of the House were represented. The Republican convention had Middle America.

Campaign Notes Richard Nixon, as other incumbents before him, wanted to stay presidential and not tour the country. He sent surrogates, most successfully—his wife Pat and daughters Tricia and Julie, and Tricia's husband, Ed Cox. Nixon's own first campaign trip was to the Texas ranch of secretary of the treasury Texas governor John Connally for a "Democrats for Nixon" barbecue. But mainly he waited for the last three weeks of the campaign and then visited only the big states.

McGovern's campaign plane, the Dakota Queen II, lifted off the ground the Sunday before Labor Day with an exhausted candidate who had already been on the road for a year and a half, and a campaign schedule almost as ambitious as Nixon's fifty-stater in 1960. Once McGovern got going, his campaign was so geared to media events and markets that the traveling

RICHARD M. NIXON

press complained about "fuselage journalism"—darting from one event to another, not getting a real feel for McGovern's interaction with the people.

Symbols   Republicans had Nixon's victory salute and a dove. The Democrats liked the dove even more than their opponents.

Slogans   Nixon campaigned on "Four More Years," "Now More Than Ever," "Stand Pat with Nixon," and "Nixon's the One." Opponents shouted "Would You Buy a Used War from This Man?"

McGovernites challenged "Right for the Start," "Come Home, America," and "Make America Happen Again." His opposition chanted "Hanoi Needs McGovern and Fonda."

Songs   The Republicans dusted off "Nixon's the One" while Frank Sinatra adapted "The Lady Is a Tramp": ". . . the Quaker and the Greek / They make this Italian want to whistle and stamp."

Democrats identified with folk songs of the 1960s such as Bob Dylan's "When the Ship Comes in."

Paraphernalia   Anything that identified Nixon with the presidency was all right with the Republicans. There were white coffee mugs with "Re-elect the President," bumper stickers with "Right On, Mr. President," and an ornate "The President" poster, showing a smiling Nixon framed by pictures of him negotiating with the Chinese and Soviets, addressing the convention, and walking on the beach in suit and shoes.

McGovernites liked to picture their campaign as having grass-roots and small-donor appeal with buttons bragging "I Am a Grassroot" and "Buck Nixon/(I Did!)." Their candidate's various plans to redistribute income were hailed on "Robin McGovern" buttons and his push for peace on dove jewelry and McGovern/Shriver dove lapel pins and a strident "Come Home & Stop Killing Little Babies" button.

Popular Labels Nixon liked to be called "The President."
McGovern was "the prairie populist" and "the people's candidate."

Name-calling Nixon retained his reputation as "Tricky Dick." Agnew was "The Mouth That Roared."
McGovern was "The Goldwater of the Left," "soft and weak."

The Press *Time* wrote: "After a month of false starts and wheel spinning, the McGovern campaign is definitely on the move—backward."

Spending The Republicans spent twice as much as the Democrats, $61,400,000 to $30,000,000.

Firsts Eagleton became the first vice-presidential nominee since 1860 to withdraw after an adjourned convention.
The Solid South went soundly Republican.
Shirley Chisholm was the first black woman presidential candidate.

Trends Turnout stays below 56 percent and voter independence grows, reflecting the diminished role of parties.
The importance of primaries in giving unknowns a chance in the presidential sweepstakes. Almost half the states had primaries now.

Vote Nixon won in a nationwide landslide with returns from fifty states and the District of Columbia giving him 520 electoral votes and 47,170,179 popular votes (60.7 percent) to 17 and 29,171,791 (37.5 percent) to 1 (an elector from Virginia) and 3,671 for Libertarian John Hospers. McGovern won only Massachusetts and the District of Columbia.

Quote "Let's make the next four years the best four years in America's history," said Nixon on election eve, his last words to the public as a candidate for office.

★ ★ ★

Too early on Watergate and too late on Vietnam, George McGovern in 1972 was left without an issue against President Richard Nixon. Paraded as a Robin Hood for tax proposals that would hit the rich and help the poor, the Democratic presidential nominee never recovered from proposing in his primary campaign the utopian idea (some said crackpot scheme) of giving every American $1000, just for, well, living. Meant as a broad-brush attack on poverty, it scared the daylights out of blue-collar workers, usually Democratic to the core, who knew that it meant their taxes would jump. Pitched as a Pied Piper of the young, he ended up disappointing them and getting no kick from their first-time votes by dropping Thomas Eagleton as his running mate on the basis of past mental problems. *Time* called McGovern's campaign "The Hard-Luck Crusade."

The president was low in the polls in 1971, a summertime approval rating of 49 percent, because peace had not come to Vietnam—or to America, for that matter. He still had 200,000 troops there, albeit down from 549,500 on taking office and being reduced slowly in stages, a timetable strictly held to. But to compensate almost, not wanting the United States perceived as "a pitiful helpless giant," Nixon announced in April 1970 that American and South Vietnamese troops would attack Communist supply lines in Cambodia. That action raised backs, mostly of students, who demonstrated in Washington and died, two protesting and two standing by, at Kent State University. In June 1971, the "Pentagon papers" leaked and the whole sordid story of escalation in Vietnam became public.

Nixon, as always phoenixlike, extricated himself from his domestic problems, which also included an economy now under wage and price controls to curb inflation, by going abroad. In 1972 he got himself invited to both Mainland China and the Soviet Union, substituting détente for the Cold War, and in the process opening the way for diplomatic relations with the Chinese and signing an arms limitation pact and "the great grain deal" with the Soviets. He also announced that he was reducing the number of troops in Vietnam to 69,000 even though ongoing peace talks had stalled.

Nixon expected a tough reelection fight, worried that three possible Democratic candidates—senators Edward Kennedy, Edmund Muskie, and Hubert Humphrey—were unbeatable or that maverick George Wallace would steal his antibusing thunder in the South. But the fates had their own design. On July 18, 1969, Kennedy drove his 1967 Oldsmobile off the Dikes bridge at Chappaquiddick. He swam to safety, but Mary Jo Kopechne, also in the car, drowned. In February 1972 Muskie strode into New Hampshire for the primary, almost a favorite son. But when he chose to defend his wife against attacks in the *Manchester Union Leader*, melting into tears, that scene was juxtaposed on television the next night with pictures of President Nixon and Chinese premier Chou En-lai toasting each other and feeding goldfish. Muskie won New Hampshire, forty-eight to thirty-seven for McGovern, but it was considered a defeat. In California, McGovern won decisively over Humphrey, who left the race. And on May 15 in a Maryland shopping center, a man bent on killing anybody who would make him famous, shot campaigner

Wallace, paralyzing him from the waist down. That left the Democratic nomination to McGovern. Nixon later remarked "The election was over the day he was nominated."

But one would never have known it from the way Nixon's men went about securing victory. They set up the Committee to Re-Elect the President—CREEP—to conduct the campaign outside regular Republican channels. CREEP raised hundreds of thousands, much of it laundered, from corporate sources, dangling ambassadorships and protection in return, and kept on its payroll the likes of E. Howard Hunt and G. Gordon Liddy, soon to become infamous. A "Red Seal Security" office within the Internal Revenue Service, on orders from Chief of Staff H. R. Haldeman (often at the instigation of Nixon himself), combed through the tax returns of McGovern and his staff and "enemy" newsmen looking for dirt. Then, on June 17, following a call from a Watergate security guard police discovered five agents of CREEP in the offices of the Democratic National Headquarters. The next day, the *Washington Post* ran a front-page story on a "Plot to Bug Democratic Party Office." (*The New York Times* put it on page thirty.)

McGovern, his campaign hobbled and in disarray after the Eagleton affair, went for the jugular. In early August he said the break-in was "the kind of thing you expect under a person like Hitler" and demanded that the president's involvement be examined. In October he called the Nixon administration "the most corrupt in the history of the United States." But around the same time, polls showed that three-quarters of the public thought Watergate was "just politics."

McGovern did not get far on Vietnam, either. When Nixon ordered the bombing of Hanoi and the mining of Haiphong harbor for "world peace," the American people backed his actions. Even likely target Vice President Spiro Agnew, known for denouncing the press as "nattering nabobs of negativism," did not give McGovern an issue, keeping his rhetoric on the high road during the campaign.

Finally, the press started to close in on the real story of direct White House involvement in Watergate. On October 10 a banner front-page headline in the *Post* revealed: FBI FINDS NIXON AIDES SABOTAGED DEMOCRATS. On October 25, Haldeman, specifically, was named. The White House retorted "shabby journalism." Before more needed to be said, Henry Kissinger, Nixon's national security adviser, stole the spotlight, saying "peace is at hand." Peace was not really that close, but McGovern looked even less desirable. After Nixon's landslide victory, Watergate came back. "I am not a crook," the president protested in 1973. On August 8, 1974, he resigned.

★ CAMPAIGN OF 1976 ★

Major Candidates Gerald R. Ford, 63, Michigan, Republican
James Earl Carter, 52, Georgia, Democrat

Credentials Ford served in the Navy during World War II (1942–1946), was elected to the House of Representatives (1949–1973), becoming Minority Leader (1965–1973). Appointed vice president under the Twenty-fifth Amendment in 1973, he took over as president upon Richard Nixon's resignation in 1974.

Carter served in the U.S. Navy (1946–1953), was elected a Georgia state senator (1963–1967) and governor of Georgia (1971–1975).

Convention Tickets When they convened in Kansas City the Republicans were split between former California governor Ronald Reagan and President Gerald Ford. Both broke tradition and arrived in town three days early to round up delegates, but Ford narrowly bested Reagan on the first ballot. For his running mate Ford chose Kansas senator Robert Dole, who won on the first ballot.

When the most unified Democratic convention since 1964 opened in New York new party rules had eliminated winner-take-all primaries and required delegates to announce their presidential preference before the primary. Jimmy Carter, who came bearing the most delegate votes, won the nomination on the first ballot. He selected Minnesota senator Walter Mondale as his running mate.

Eugene McCarthy, with Lester Maddox, ultraconservative former governor of Georgia, ran on the Independent ticket, calling for a reduced military, protection of natural resources, and challenging the domination of the two major parties.

Campaign Notes Ford's "Rose Garden strategy" or "no-campaign campaign" kept him at the White House until the end of October. Ford's campaign concentrated on eight large industrial states (New York, New Jersey, California, Illinois, Ohio, Pennsylvania, Texas, and Michigan), figuring he needed to win five of them to win the election. He took four.

Carter focused on thirteen large states with 291 electoral votes. Based in his hometown of Plains, Georgia, Carter began his campaign at 5:00 A.M. every morning. His chartered plane was dubbed "Peanut One" and his campaigners were the "Peanut Brigade."

Symbols Republicans used the Model T, the Statue of Liberty, and the flag.

The peanut and Carter's toothy grin were popular images. Carter wore lucky red ties and his wife Rosalynn often wore a Carter-green coat.

GERALD R. FORD

Slogans   After Watergate, Republicans hailed Ford as "The Man Who Made Us Proud Again" and spoke of "Feeling Good About America" and "Peace, Prosperity, and Public Trust."

Democrats praised Carter as "A Leader, for a Change" and "A New Generation of Leadership." Voters were urged to "Vote Grits and Fritz in '76."

Songs   Republicans liked "Hail to the Chief" and the Michigan fight song. Ford commercials used "I'm Feeling Good About America."

Democrats sang "We Shall Overcome." The country-rock favorite "Why Not the Best?" was played at election-night celebrations. Carter's favorite was "Amazing Grace."

Paraphernalia   Many Ford campaign buttons and posters promoted "President Ford '76" and jewelry and T-shirts used Model-T symbols. Local Republican groups sometimes focused more on Carter, with buttons saying "Don't Settle for Peanuts," "Carter Hasn't Shown Me Anything but His Teeth!", and "In His Heart, He Knows Your Wife."

Democrats pushed a "New Generation of Leadership" and "The Best for America's Third Century." Watergate-reminder buttons read "Remember the Bugging, Vote Carter." The peanut showed up on mirrors, T-shirts, scarves, jewelry, belt buckles, whistles, and buttons with "Peanut Power" and "I'm Nuts About Carter."

Popular Labels   Ford was "Jerry," "Mr. Nice Guy," and an "insider."
   Carter was "Jimmy," a "real Southerner," an "outsider," and a "soft-drawling peanut farmer."

Name-calling   Ford and Dole were called "The Sominex Team" and "Dull and Dole."
   Carter was called "Jimmy Who?," "Wee Jimmy," and a "Yankee from Georgia."

The Press   After Carter's *Playboy* interview, the *Chicago Sun-Times* headlined SEX, SIN, TEMPTATION—CARTER'S CANDID VIEW while the *Washington Star* ran CARTER ON SIN AND LUST: I'M HUMAN . . . I'M TEMPTED.

Spending   The Federal Election Campaign Act Amendments of 1974 placed a $1,000 limit on individual contributions and $5,000 on organizations per candidate per contest. The amendments also set up public funding of presidential campaigns with each receiving $21,820,000 in federal funds—less than half of what was spent in 1972. There was no limit on the number of PACs (political action committees) that could contribute to a candidate.

First   Barbara Jordan was the first black and the first woman to present a keynote address at a convention.

Trends   The rise of the South in political and cultural influence.
   Face-to-face debates become de rigueur.
   Mushrooming of PACs.

Vote   Carter was narrowly elected, carrying twenty-three states and the District of Columbia with 297 electoral votes and 40,827,394 popular votes (50.1 percent). Ford carried twenty-seven states with 241 electoral votes and 39,145,977 popular votes (48 percent). McCarthy received 745,042 popular votes.

Benchmark   Carter's victory represented the South's final political reunification with the North.

Quote   After the election, Carter said "The only reason it was close was that I as a candidate was not good enough as a campaigner. But I'll make up for that as president."

★   ★   ★

OUR long national nightmare is over." When Gerald Ford spoke those words, minutes after taking the presidential oath without pomp or circumstance on August 9, 1974, and not long after Richard Nixon had retreated to California, giving a last victory salute, nobody knew what to expect. Watergate had twisted a nation's trust in government into distrust and now Ford (who stepped into the vice presidency when Spiro Agnew was forced out for having taken bribes, and, with Nixon's resignation, was the country's first appointed president) wanted to close the most sordid chapter in American history.

He was perfect for the part, in some ways. A "congressman's congressman," Ford had friends on both sides of the aisle. His immediate response to the seizure of the American merchant ship *Mayaguez* by Cambodian gunboats offered a needed boost to national morale. People liked the fact that he was unpretentious and that he said "Truth is the glue that holds government together."

Yet Ford fell short, when he went back on statements made to a congressional committee that he would neither pardon Nixon nor seek election if he became president, and his honeymoon with the press and public was over for good. The former football star fumbled too, devising a "Whip Inflation Now" campaign with millions of unwanted WIN buttons that struck even Ford as "too gimmicky" and too late. When he refused to give bailout money to New York City, the *New York Daily News* headline screamed FORD TO CITY: DROP DEAD. Still in July 1975, Ford stated that he wanted to be the Bicentennial President, hoping to discourage other Republicans. But soon, out of the West rode Ronald Reagan, the dreamboat of conservatives and former governor of California, who threw his Stetson into the ring, running "against evil incarnate as embodied in the buddy system of Washington."

"Jimmy *Who* Is Running for *What*?" mocked the *Atlanta Constitution* as soon as home-state governor Jimmy Carter announced his candidacy in December 1974. When Carter declared, he was unmentioned in public opinion polls. But he did have, in his files, a 1971 *Time* cover story on him with the slash: "Dixie Whistles a New Tune." Carter had won *Time*'s favor, not by his conservative gubernatorial race, coming out against busing and for George Wallace, but by his inaugural words: "The time for racial discrimination is over." In 1976, the press again would focus on the fresh face of this former peanut farmer.

"Hello, I'm Jimmy Carter and I'm running for president," "I'm not a lawyer, I'm not a member of Congress," and "I've never served in Washington." "I'll never tell a lie." In the South he would add: "Isn't it time we had a president without an accent?" Carter entered thirty primaries, winning more than half. His big break was a little win at a little dinner, packed with supporters, in Iowa. The next day *The New York Times*' front page read CARTER APPEARS TO HOLD A SOLID LEAD IN IOWA. He did win, by coming in second to "uncommitted" in the Iowa caucuses, and went on the network morning news shows. He managed 28 percent of the vote in New Hampshire, topping congressman Morris Udall and the rest, and made the covers of *Time* and *Newsweek.* He squeezed out George Wallace in Florida and was labeled a winner even though he later lost in New York and, in an interview, upheld "ethnic purity" in neighborhoods. This smacked of racism to some, but Martin Luther King's father rallied to Carter's side and all was forgiven. Throughout, Carter presented himself as a "born-again Christian Baptist Sunday School teacher" who would restore trust. When he won the nomination in July, *Time* wrote "One could almost hear shouts of 'Hallelujah!' "

Ford was still fighting the game of his life with Reagan. He started out strong, winning the New Hampshire primary and others in the East despite Reagan's assault on his foreign policy as nothing more than "the rights to sell Pepsi-Cola in Siberia." As the contest moved into conservative country Reagan had clout and a big California victory. Reagan broke his lucky streak by the preconvention announcement of his choice for vice president, Pennsylvania's liberal senator Richard Schweiker. It only hurt and Ford was nominated on the first ballot.

Carter started high in the polls, but polls can be as ephemeral as images and Carter's novelty was becoming detrimental. His own consultants were finding a "weirdo factor" and a worry that he was "fuzzy on the issues." Carter continued to call Ford an "appointed president." The president, still saddled with the pardon, was staying close to the White House.

In September, the October issue of *Playboy* hit the stands with Carter's views on a range of subjects. Only one stood out: sex. Carter had tried to explain how he dealt with his religious beliefs: "I've looked on a lot of women with lust. I've committed adultery in my heart many times. This is something God recognizes I will do." He offended more people by using the words *screw* and *shack up*, and still more by including Lyndon Johnson with Nixon as "lying, cheating and distorting the truth." "*Playboy* killed us," said Carter Pollster Pat Caddell. His figures had Carter dropping ten points to even with Ford and then Ford ahead.

The debates became more important. Ford won the first by being in control, while Carter acted nervous and tentative. The second went to Carter when Ford made the implausible remark that there is "no Soviet domination of Eastern Europe." Carter responded: "I'd like to see Mr. Ford convince Polish-Americans that they are not under Russian domination." Carter bested Ford in the third debate, too. The president, now on the campaign trail, critiqued Carter: "He wavers, he wiggles and he waffles and he shouldn't be president of the United States." The voters felt otherwise, but not by much. The new president humbly took office: "Your strength can compensate for my weakness." Then he walked to the White House.

★ CAMPAIGN OF 1980 ★

Major Candidates   James Earl Carter, 56, Georgia, Democrat
Ronald W. Reagan, 69, California, Republican

Credentials   For Carter, see Campaign of 1976. He was elected president in 1976.

Reagan served in the U.S. Army during World War II (1942–1945), was elected California governor (1967–1975), and made an unsuccessful bid for the Republican presidential nomination in 1976.

Convention Tickets   The Democrats convened in New York City where, despite his incumbency, Carter was challenged for renomination by Senator Edward Kennedy of Massachusetts. But Carter forces defeated a rules challenge and Carter won the renomination on the first ballot. Vice President Walter Mondale was also renominated.

Republicans met in Detroit, optimistic about November. Reagan was the front runner, having won twenty-four of thirty-four primaries, and received the nomination on the first ballot. When negotiations with former president Gerald Ford fell through Reagan selected his strongest opponent during the primaries, Texan George Bush, who had been director of the Central Intelligence Agency and United Nations ambassador, as his running mate.

Republican congressman John Anderson of Illinois, who lost to Reagan in the primaries, decided in April to run on a National Unity ticket with former governor of Wisconsin Patrick Lucey as his running mate.

Campaign Notes   Both campaigns started off with gangbuster media events, but Reagan gained the edge. Carter went back to the South for a Labor Day picnic in Tuscumbia, Alabama, with Southern-fried fixings, balloons galore, a band to play "Hail to the Chief," and popular singer Charlie Daniels as a draw. Unfortunately, much of the television commentary that night was over aerial shots of people leaving the grounds, after the lunch and entertainment. Reagan, looking his silver-screen best, stood in Liberty Park, New Jersey, with Polish leader Lech Walesa at his side and, behind him, the Statue of Liberty and a shining blue sea. Lady Liberty had never failed Americans, he said, "but this administration has failed the working men and women."

Symbols   Carter preferred the image of statesman and so the peanut all but disappeared. Carter did, however, wear his "good luck" red ties.

Reagan's Stetson reinforced his image as a Westerner.

Slogans   "Stand by the President" and "Leadership and Strength" Carter's followers shouted.

JIMMY CARTER

Reaganites promoted change with "Let's Make America Great Again," "Together—A New Beginning," and "Win One for the Gipper."

Songs The Democrats liked "Hail to the Chief," "There's Gonna Be a Great Day," and "Happy Days Are Here Again."

Republicans sang "God Bless America" and "This Land Is Your Land."

Paraphernalia Democrats portrayed Carter statesmanlike on buttons reading "National Solidarity/Re-elect Our President," and "Leadership and Strength/Carter '80." Opponents sported T-shirts with the legend "Why not an actor—we've had a clown for 4 years."

On buttons and posters, Reagan was depicted as a virile Westerner, wearing his Stetson, and—true to life—younger than his age. Other signs declared "Reagan Country." Anti-Reagan items, usually the product of independent groups, included buttons saying "Reagan for Shah" and "Send Reagan Back to Central Casting."

Popular labels Carter was "Jimmy."

Reagan's was "Dutch," a nickname from youth, or "the Gipper," from a movie he made.

Name-calling Carter's attacks on Reagan produced a "meanness" charge and he was attacked as a naive appeaser.

Reagan's avoidance of hard questions earned him the nickname "The Great Deflector." Carter implied that his opponent was a warmonger, a mad bomber, and trigger-happy.

The Press As the election approached, *Time* wrote: "The chance grows that the 1980 election will be swung by the decisions of an erratic government in Iran or by ephemeral images on TV."

Spending The second presidential election with public funding saw each campaign receiving $29,400,000.

First For the first time, women voted at a higher percentage rate than men.

Trends The American public becomes more conservative.

Media attention to Iowa and New Hampshire primaries magnifies, the latter considered the most important before the actual election.

Vote Reagan won big, taking forty-four states and 489 electoral votes and 43,904,153 popular votes (50.7 percent) to forty-nine electoral votes and 35,483,883 popular (41 percent) for Carter, who carried six states and the District of Columbia. Anderson, who cut into Carter's vote a bit, won no electoral votes but 5,720,060 popular votes (6.6 percent).

Benchmarks The only defeat for an incumbent since Herbert Hoover's in 1932.

Reagan was the oldest president-elect.

Quote Said *The New York Times*: "On Election Day, Mr. Carter was the issue."

Jimmy Carter, the peanut farmer who became president through a pardon and prayer, and the primaries, of course, who had the winningest smile this side of Paradise, retreated to Camp David in July 1979, his approval rating at a near-record low of 29 percent. For ten days, Carter met with business and religious leaders, politicians, and then with a local family in their living room to find out why there was a national malaise. On July 15, he televised his findings, taking some blame, but essentially pointing to the audience, saying there was "a crisis of confidence . . . that strikes at the heart and soul of our national will."

To many, it seemed that Carter was almost shrinking in size in the presidency even as the world was spinning further out of control. Early on, he had pinpointed as a major cause of inflation the country's dependence on foreign oil. He proposed a "moral equivalent of war" crusade and asked

Congress to pass an energy package. As usual, "outsider" Carter only got some of what he wanted. He made more headway when lush Iranian oil supplies dried up after the shah fell from power in January 1979, but by then long pump lines and high pump prices had tarnished his smile. Early too, Carter ridiculed an "inordinate fear of communism" and in June 1979 embraced Soviet leader Leonid Brezhnev at summit talks. But the Soviets showed how fearsome they still were by bloodily replacing Afghanistan's government with one more to their liking in December 1979. His brother's links with Libya, called "Billygate," were also an embarrassment. Carter did have major achievements, such as securing approval of the Panama Canal treaties and forging the Camp David accords between Israel and Egypt. But rising prices and unemployment kept the domestic focus on pocketbook issues.

And then there were the hostages. Exactly one year before the election, radical Iranian students seized the American embassy in Teheran and those inside. They wanted the exiled shah returned. Carter answered with economic sanctions and covert negotiations. Three days after the hostage-taking, Senator Edward Kennedy formally announced that he would challenge the president for the Democratic nomination. "I'll whip his ass," Carter said.

Carter did win, because it was natural for a country to support a president under siege and because Kennedy made too many mistakes. In an interview with TV's Roger Mudd, Kennedy could not articulate his personal reasons for wanting to be president. At other times he appeared to be running interference with the administration at the wrong time, saying the shah "ran one of the most corrupt regimes" in history and that Carter's policies should be questioned. Carter did try, through a "Rose Garden strategy," not to campaign. But after a rescue mission failed in the desert of Iran the president went to the people and won the needed delegates. At the convention, cameras running, Kennedy eluded Carter, who traipsed after him, for a final victory salute. Carter looked, said an aide, like a "puppy dog."

In the Republican arena, former actor and California governor Ronald Reagan, campaigning "to get government off our backs" and playing the front-runner, skipped a debate before the Iowa caucuses. Preppy, more moderate George Bush, with a laundry list of credentials, did debate, win the caucuses, and claim that he had "Big Mo." But in New Hampshire Reagan stole that back, and probably the nomination with it, when Reagan aides, unbeknownst to Bush, invited all the other Republican contenders to join in a debate originally meant to be between just him and Reagan, sponsored by the *Nashua Telegraph* and paid for by the Reagan campaign. As Reagan and the rest trooped onstage, Bush appeared to sulk in silence, while *Telegraph* editor Jon Breen ordered Reagan cut off. "I'm paying for this microphone, Mr. Green," Reagan snapped (almost getting the name right). Liberal Republican John Anderson of Illinois decided to make a third-party run. His followers soon fell off, however, and he was charged with being a "spoiler."

The campaign seesawed in favorites as the two major candidates made troublesome remarks. Reagan initially sparked doubts about his political judgment by calling the Vietnam war "a noble cause" and then saying that Tuscumbia, Alabama, site of Carter's Labor Day rally, was the birthplace of the Ku Klux Klan (it was not). Carter showed a mean streak, saying the election will help to decide "if we have war or peace" and, later, "whether Americans might be separated black from white, Jew from Christian." As the end neared, Carter donned red hand-tooled cowboy boots to protect him from Republican "horse manure right before an election," while Reagan hyped support from dove Eugene McCarthy to prove "I don't eat my young." In a more serious vein, Reagan asked "why fifty-two hostages have been held hostage for a year now," sensing public patience with America's humiliation was wearing thin.

By October 28, the date set, both sides wanted to debate. Onstage Reagan looked more relaxed, even walking over to shake hands with Carter before the debate. He also deftly sidestepped some of the president's tough comments by quipping "There you go again." Carter made the one big mistake of the evening, answering an arms-proliferation question by mentioning "a discussion with my daughter Amy," then eight, in which she agreed the arms issue was important. In closing, Reagan won. "Are you better off than you were four years ago?" he asked. "Is it easier for you to go and buy things in the stores. . . . Is there more or less unemployment . . . ?" The answers came back in votes on election day. The only surprise turned out to be how well Reagan had done.

The former actor had once said that politics was like show business: "You begin with a hell of an opening, you coast for a while, and you end with a hell of a closing." As if scripted, word came, on the day of Reagan's inauguration, that the fifty-two hostages in Iran had flown to freedom. It *was* a hell of an opening!

★ CAMPAIGN OF 1984 ★

Major Candidates   Ronald W. Reagan, 73, California, Republican
                      Walter F. Mondale, 56, Minnesota, Democrat

Credentials   For Reagan, see Campaign of 1980. He was elected president in 1980.

Mondale was first appointed, then elected, Minnesota state attorney general (1960–1964), was first appointed to the Senate (1964) when Hubert Humphrey was elected vice president and subsequently elected for his own terms (1965–1977), and then served under President Jimmy Carter as vice president (1977–1981).

Convention Tickets   In an atmosphere as triumphant as Dwight D. Eisenhower's renomination by acclamation in 1956, the Republicans met in Dallas

RONALD W. REAGAN

to celebrate the renomination of President Ronald Reagan. Reagan faced no opposition and, in a break with tradition, he and Vice President George Bush were unanimously renominated together in a single roll-call vote.

The Democrats convened in San Francisco and, even though new rules allowed delegates to switch their commitments, Mondale had the nomination locked up, after a bitter primary contest in which eight Democrats battled for their party's nomination, and won on the first ballot. One week prior to the convention, Mondale made history by choosing as his running mate the only woman ever to be on a major party ticket, New York representative Geraldine Ferraro.

Campaign Notes   Reagan, as was the prerogative of incumbents, chose not to campaign until the end. In the final week, Reagan was his busiest, taking a five-day, eleven-state tour that was specifically designed, with victory certain, to garner all fifty states for the president. He went to New York, Massachusetts, Pennsylvania, and even a surprise stop in Mondale's home state.

Mondale started swinging at the Democratic convention: "Mr. Reagan will raise taxes, and so will I. He won't tell you. I just did." Then taking wing on "The Louisville Slugger," he logged more miles and made more speeches than any previous candidate for the presidency. He too had a big final week, traveling twenty-one cities and giving twenty-two speeches. Traditional events worked well, as 50,000 lined Chicago's streets for a torchlight parade and 100,000 rallied in New York's garment district, matching John F. Kennedy's 1960 turnout in numbers and enthusiasm.

Symbols   Republicans hyped national symbols like the flag to portray patriotism, while Mondale, like Jimmy Carter before him, often wore a red tie.

Slogans   Republicans had the monopoly on slogans, as well as optimism. They bragged "America Is Back, Standing Tall," and "Leadership That's Working." They also revived "Win One for the Gipper."

Democrats had no identifiable slogans except, of course, "Vote for Mondale–Ferraro."

Songs   Republicans liked "America the Beautiful" and the upbeat "I'm Proud to Be an American" and "God Bless the U.S.A."

Democrats belted out "New York, New York" for Ferraro, as well as "Celebration" and "Here Comes the Change of the Tide." They used Crosby Stills Nash & Young's "Teach Your Children Well" for their most effective advertisements.

Paraphernalia   Reagan was once again featured as youthful and Western in a Stetson and denim shirt. Heart-shaped pins carried the message: "America loves Reagan." A plethora of anti-Reagan items went from simple slogans like "Dump Reagan" and "Ronbuster" to "Send Him Back to Hollywood," "Impeach the Leech, Put the Button Out of His Reach," even "Jane Wyman Was Right."

The majority of Democratic items were red, white, and blue and often pictured Mondale and Ferraro. "Mondale's Got the Beef" buttons were holdovers from the primary contests. Ferraro's nomination created a wealth of items, some much more favorable to Ferraro than her running mate.

Popular Labels   Reagan was called "The Great Communicator," "The Great Rhetorician," and "the Gipper."

Mondale's nickname was "Fritz" or "Fighting Fritz."

Name-calling   Reagan was the "Teflon-coated President" and the press talked about a "drool factor."

Mondale was "The Great Depressor," "the man who dares to be cautious," and "Norwegian Wood."

The Press   The *Wall Street Journal* noted: "The Democrats go into the campaign on a wing and a prayer. The wing, new and untested, is Rep. Geraldine Ferraro; the prayer, old and familiar, asks Democrats to come home to the liberalism of their fathers."

Spending   The campaign-spending-law allocation was increased to $40,400,000 for each candidate. Republicans spent $25 million on advertising and the Democrats doled out $20 million.

Firsts   Ferraro was the first woman and first Italian-American to appear on a major party ticket.

The Rev. Jesse Jackson was the first black candidate to reach a major party convention with a sizeable bloc of delegates.

Trends   The Democrats look for a new type of Democrat, not of the New Deal generation.

More voters label themselves Republican, especially among voters under twenty-four.

Vote   Reagan, in his last political race, got his "hell of a closing" by winning in forty-nine states with 525 electoral votes and 54,158,802 popular votes (58.4 percent) to thirteen and 37,443,559 popular votes (41.6 percent) for Mondale, who won only his home state of Minnesota and the District of Columbia.

Benchmarks   Reagan carried forty-nine states for only the second time in history; Richard Nixon did it in 1972.

Reagan received the most electoral votes ever, but his electoral margin was exceeded by Franklin Roosevelt in 1936.

Quote   Speaker of the House Tip O'Neill sized up the election: "Reagan is the most popular figure in the history of the United States. No candidate we put up would have been able to beat Reagan this year."

MADE famous once by George Orwell, 1984 would be famous again for the way Republicans played the game of modern politics through television. In a sense, they were finally getting back at the Democrats for all the years that Franklin Delano Roosevelt spellbound the electorate at the radio mike. Now, Ronald Reagan, like Roosevelt once, was so reassuring and soothing on camera that he made even "evil empire" sound nice. His Democratic challenger, former Vice President Walter Mondale, in contrast, was "not a TV kinda guy," in *People* magazine lingo. With their camera-ready candidate and campaign, the Republicans also caught and reinforced the public's up-beat mood, while Mondale quickly gained a reputation as "the Great Depressor" for talking taxes and bearing "one another's burdens." It was not surprising that Mondale lost, but a series of bad breaks made it a loss of historic proportions.

From the ashes of his party's 1980 defeat, Mondale built "Fort Fritz," a political apparatus considered so formidable that no primary challenger dare breach its walls. But the media likes, at least, a two-man race and with eight Democrats running for the nomination there was more than enough potential. The early caucus vote in Iowa that had brought Jimmy Carter into focus in 1976 now did the same for Colorado senator Gary Hart, who not only modeled himself on John F. Kennedy but talked a streak of "new ideas" and independence from old, read Mondale's, interest groups. By lengths, Mondale came in first with 45 percent and Hart was behind with 15, but still the spotlight was on the senator as the "new face." It helped bring in funds and votes, for Hart went on to win the next three primaries in New Hampshire, Maine, and Vermont. Suddenly, March 13, the first "super Tuesday," loomed as a make-or-break day for Mondale. He sought an audience with Carter in critical Georgia, after years of distancing himself from his former boss, and reluctantly used a line, urged on him by advisers, from a hamburger-chain commercial he had never seen to answer Hart's call for newness: "Where's the beef?" Mondale took Georgia and Alabama, enough to survive, while Hart won Florida, Massachusetts, and Rhode Island.

Now it was on to Illinois, New York, and Pennsylvania and a more vigorous Fighting Fritz. Of course, the ads helped—one that Mondale put on the air and one that Hart could not get off the air. Mondale's showed a red phone, its red light blinking, ominously, with an announcer warning of an "unsure, unsteady, untested hand" answering it. Hart's pictured Mondale alongside Chicago's Cook County Democratic boss Edward Vrdolyak, with an announcer calling the election a choice between "the past and the future." The ad became too hot and Hart told the press he was pulling it off the air. But it was already locked into a schedule and his words had no effect. At the same time, what the media gave, it was taking away with questions about Hart's change of name, age, and signature. Finally, it was Frontrunner Fritz.

When Mondale declared on June 6, "I've got the votes," Hart retorted, "Welcome to overtime," vowing to continue the race. So did black activist Jesse Jackson, who had polled over three million votes, 22 percent among white voters, but stumbled along the way, by using the terms Hymie and Hymietown for Jews and New York City and having the very vocal support of "Nation of Islam" leader Louis Farrakhan who referred to Judaism as a "gutter religion." But at the convention, Hart and Jackson were only shadow candidates and in the limelight stood Mondale and at his side, a promising running mate, Congresswoman Geraldine Ferraro of New York. The Democratic couple never really had a chance. As Mondale later said, "Except for a day or two after the convention, I never thought I'd win."

In his book *Behind the Front Page*, *Washington Post* political seer David Broder wrote that the 1984 election "was probably sealed well in advance, when Reagan escaped an assassin's bullet in 1981, when he showed his mastery of Congress in that summer's tax and budget fights, when he cut short his mistaken military intervention in Lebanon, and when the economy soared from recession in 1983 without reigniting inflation." Critics claimed that Reagan's was a Teflon-coated presidency, that bad things just did not stick, that the "Reagan Revolution" hurt the needy and that only a "Great Communicator" could have sold such a program in the first place, but, as the campaign began, audiences roared back "Yes!" when he asked: "Are you better off than you were four years ago?" And that's what he would run on.

Reagan's campaign stops came packaged with so much bunting, balloons, and leftover Olympic glow that it was often hard to tell the difference between nightly news spots and presidential campaign ads, which suited his advisers just fine, as they liked the seemingly endless score of patriotism and optimism.

The Democrats did not even have the luxury of an easy beginning. First, Ferraro set herself up for a fall by promising to disclose both her own and her husband's financial returns, when only her own would do, and when she did, the questions came. She answered them well, but doubts remained. Then, Labor Day dawned disaster, when Mondale and Ferraro got started too early and faced a "puny" turnout in New York.

As the campaign went on, it became no easier. Reagan never spelled out a program for his second term, so the Democrats were left to rant about such generalities as the deficits. When Mondale did accuse Reagan of being "the most detached, the most remote, the most uninformed" chief executive, he was cautioned about being too hard on a popular president. Mondale had one high after the first debate in early October, when the president's wan performance raised the age issue. "We have a new race," he beamed. But, two weeks later, Reagan uttered a now famous one-liner: "I am not going to exploit, for political purposes, my opponent's youth and inexperience." "Well, you know," shrugged Reagan at his victory celebration, almost a redo of four years earlier, "good habits are hard to break."

★ THE CAMPAIGN OF 1988 ★

Major Candidates George Herbert Walker Bush, 64, Texas, Republican
Michael S. Dukakis, 55, Massachusetts, Democrat

Credentials Bush served in the Navy during World War II (1942–1945), rising to lieutenant, was a member of the House of Representatives from Texas (1967–1971), United States ambassador to the United Nations (1971–1973), chairman of the Republican National Committee (1973–1974), chief of the United States liaison mission to China (1974–1975), director of the Central Intelligence Agency (1976–1977), and vice president under Ronald Reagan (1981–1989).

Dukakis was elected to the Massachusetts state legislature (1962–1971) and served three terms as governor of Massachusetts (1974–1978, 1982–1990).

Tickets The Republicans convened in New Orleans with much more excitement and tension over the vice presidential than the presidential nominee. Vice President George Bush's nomination was propelled by his comeback in the New Hampshire primary, after his self-proclaimed "humiliation" in the

GEORGE H. BUSH

Iowa caucuses, and a sweep of the Southern primaries on Super Tuesday. He was nominated without opposition on the first ballot. Bush surprised almost everyone by choosing Indiana senator J. Danforth Quayle as his running-mate.

The Democrats met in Atlanta after a long, testy primary fight among seven challengers. Paralleling George Bush, Massachusetts governor Michael Dukakis ended up in third place in Iowa, but won New Hampshire, and on Super Tuesday took seven out of nineteen primaries. By the time of the convention, only the Reverend Jesse Jackson was still vying for the nomination with Dukakis, but Dukakis took the nomination ballot on the first ballot. As his running-mate, Dukakis selected conservative Texas senator Lloyd Bentsen to balance the ticket.

Campaign Notes   Following in the footsteps of his political father, Bush, like Reagan in 1984, made himself scarce to the press once the campaign began. Events were staged to perfection with little chance for spontaneous Q and A with reporters, much less press conferences. Dukakis also tried to limit press access as the campaign continued, but was not as adamant or successful.

In a last hurrah, Dukakis traveled 8,500 miles in fifty-three hours. Meanwhile, the Republicans tried to minimize last-minute mistakes by keeping

Quayle under wraps and almost exclusively before solidly Republican audiences.

Symbols Both candidates played up the theme of patriotism and used the image of the flag.

The negative image of Willie Horton became a symbol of Dukakis' supposed softness on crime.

Slogans Republicans bragged "Let's Keep the Progress Going" and "Let's Keep America Moving, while Bush made famous "Read my lips, no new taxes."

Democrats favored "Good jobs at good pay in the good old U.S.A." and promised "The Best Is Yet to Come."

Songs Bush's favorite was "Don't Worry, Be Happy."

Democrats wore out "Fanfare for Michael Dukakis" written by John Williams. Neil Diamond's "Coming to America" was used in commercials to emphasize the candidate's immigrant background.

Paraphernalia Republicans emphasized patriotism with "Americans for Bush" stickers and red, white, and blue signs promoting "Bush–Quayle."

Not to be beat, Democratic buttons pictured Dukakis with the American flag and the tag line "Michael DUKAKIS for President—1988."

Popular Labels Bush has been called "Poppy" since childhood.

Dukakis was called "Duke." He wanted to be known as "The Great Builder." He campaigned on his economic success as governor or "The Massachusetts Miracle."

Name-calling Bush was "Silver-Spoon George," a "lapdog," a "wimp," a "blank slate," "elitist," and "preppy." His running mate was the "Indiana kid" and a "blond bombshell."

Dukakis was a "Liberal," a "technocrat," "The Ice Man," "the Stealth Guy," "Zorba the Clerk" and was likened to a walking pocket calculator. He and Bensten were the "Brookline Bantam and Texas Tory."

The Democratic primary challengers were named "the Seven Dwarfs" and Hart was specifically "Sleazy."

The Press An unusually large number of newspapers—55 percent, up from 32 in 1984—declined to endorse either candidate.

Spending Estimated as the most expensive presidential campaign in history, Bush spent about $115 million and Dukakis spent $105 million in public and private funds. Forty-six million was the public allotment for the general election.

Firsts Bush was first sitting vice president since Martin Van Buren to be elected president.

Trends Sound-bite campaigns.

Vote Bush carried forty states, receiving 426 electoral votes and 47,946,422 popular votes (54 percent) to ten states and the District of Columbia, 111 electoral votes, and 41,016,429 popular votes (46 percent) for Dukakis. One elector from West Virginia voted for Bentsen for president and Dukakis for vice president.

Benchmarks The Democrats' seventh loss in ten presidential elections.
   One of the most negative campaigns in recent memory.
   The lowest turnout since 1924.
   "Super Tuesday" with nineteen primaries was created, changing fundraising and electioneering strategy.

Quote On election night, Bush reached out: "To those who supported me, I will try to be worthy of your trust, and to those that did not, I will try to earn it . . . I want to be your President too."

"B IFF! Bang! Powie!" was how Bruce Morton of CBS prepared viewers for one of the most ridiculous sights of the campaign: Governor Michael Dukakis, looking for all the world like Snoopy in his army-issue helmet, riding an armored tank right into the living rooms of evening news watchers. In fact, those three little words could have been used to describe the whole campaign, filled with so much silly sound and negative fury that it ended up, for the most part, signifying nothing.

The candidates seemed to play sound bites like issues in this campaign. In San Diego, Bush guaranteed himself more than a voice-over by a snappy statement about Dukakis and defense: "I wouldn't be surprised if he thinks that a naval exercise is something you find in Jane Fonda's workout book." Shortly, Dukakis zapped back that Bush had changed his position on offshore oil: "George Bush is like a coin. They just flip him: Sometimes he lands on his head, sometimes on his tail." On the same day, Bush hit Dukakis with: "He won't win unless he convinces the electorate that everything is bad with America. I am dismayed by the divide-and-conquer strategy." Dukakis even dared to take a dig at President Ronald Reagan when decrying "sleaze" in the administration: "Fish rots from the head first." Ever boyish Dan Quayle, Bush's running mate, also got into the act by quipping that Dukakis "lost his top naval adviser last week. The rubber duck drowned in his bathtub." The most memorable line, though, was uttered by ever senatorial Lloyd Bensten to his opponent during the vice presidential debate: "Senator, you're no Jack Kennedy."

The campaign started out on a low note, produced by the candidates themselves, the press, and other interested parties. Polls showed Democratic senator Gary Hart of Colorado had it made when he announced his candidacy in April 1987, saying, "Ideas have power." But before he could articulate any, he was caught dallying with Donna Rice, and ended up answering questions about adultery rather than big weapons systems and dropping out of the race. In September 1987, Senator Joseph Biden of Delaware, then ranked first in fund-raising among Democrats, was doomed by a so-called attack video, leaked to the press by John Sasso, the genius behind Dukakis' candidacy. The video spliced together a speech by Neil Kinnock, leader of the British Labor party, and one by Biden at the Iowa State Fair. The similarities added up to plagiarism and Biden also left the race. A month later, Bush had a comeuppance of sorts. But instead of killing him off, it seemed to steel him as a candidate. On October 12, 1987, the day that he announced, *Newsweek* magazine showed up on stands with a cover photo of Bush, looking manly at the wheel of his boat. However, the bold-faced cover line read: FIGHTING THE "WIMP FACTOR."

And it went on. In February, Bush, in his après-wimp mode, got into an on-air shouting match with CBS anchorman Dan Rather. Bush had said, in the past, that he reluctantly went along with the sale of arms to Iran in exchange for hostages and never knew that funds were diverted to the Nicaraguan contras, but Rather, along with many others, wanted to know more. Bush fumed that he thought their interview was supposed to be about politics, not Iran. When Rather persisted, Bush protested that he should not be judged "by a rehash of Iran," then threw Rather a curve ball: "How would you like it if I judged your career by those seven minutes you walked off the set in New York?" (It was in Miami that Rather had walked off the set for six minutes to protest a decision to let a U.S. tennis match end before the news began.) Later that month, Senator Robert Dole of Kansas, the Republican winner in Iowa and Bush's fiercest competitor, got hit with a Bush "Straddle Senator" ad that knocked him for a loop in New Hampshire and eventually out of the race. In June Bush started focusing his attention on Dukakis, calling him a "card-carrying member of the ACLU" and using furloughed Massachusetts murderer and rapist Willie Horton's name for the first time in a speech. (Pro-Bush ads with his mug shot and the line: "Horton Received 10 Weekend Passes from Prison" would soon follow.)

Until right before the Republican convention, Dukakis was ahead by as much as 17 percent in the polls. But after his "thousand points of light" speech in which he talked of a "kinder gentler nation," Bush led by seven percentage points and gradually widened the difference to double-digit size. With both candidates, in a way, blank slates—Bush because for so long he stood in Reagan's shadow and Dukakis because he was a national unknown—they could be defined by others. The vice president took the initiative in describing Dukakis to the public in cryptic index-card fashion: against the Pledge of Allegiance, for furloughs for murderers, a card-carrying liberal, and the "Ice Man." The Republicans even used Dukakis' own "Snoopy" scene against him in a "tank ad," claiming he opposed several weapons (in fact, Dukakis supported some, as news organizations pointed out) with the tag "America can't afford the risk."

Dukakis did not help himself by giving technocratic defenses of his veto of the Pledge bill, endorsement of the prison-furlough program, and, from the start, scampering away from the "liberal" label. He did further damage, especially to his "likability," in the second presidential debate, answering a question posed by CNN's Bernard Shaw ("Governor, if Kitty Dukakis were raped and murdered, would you favor an irrevocable death penalty for the killer?") without a breath of emotion: "No, I don't, Bernard. And I think you know that I've opposed the death penalty during all of my life." Finally, Dukakis did find some fire in his belly. With shirt sleeves rolled up, "liberal" on his lips, and a populist passion, Dukakis started reaching the people, and some polls closed to within four points. Bush, who had been making "kinder, gentler" sounds, went back to war words. After winning, Bush seemed to want the campaign to fade from memory. "That's history," he told ABC's Barbara Walters. "That doesn't mean anything anymore."

★ SELECTED BIBLIOGRAPHY ★

Abels, Jules. *Out of the Jaws of Victory*. New York: Holt, 1959.

Abels, Jules. *The Degeneration of Our American Election*. New York: Macmillan, 1968.

Alexander, Herbert. *Financing Politics*. Washington, D.C.: C.O. Press, 1984.

Ambrose, Stephen. *Nixon*. Vol. 2. New York: Simon and Schuster, 1987.

American Enterprise Institute for Public Policy Research. *The Candidates 1980*. Washington, D.C.: American Enterprise Institute, 1980.

Ammon, Harry. *James Monroe: The Quest for National Identity*. Charlottesville, Va.: University Press of Virginia, 1990.

Anthony, Carl S. *First Ladies*. New York: William Morrow and Company, Inc., 1990.

Bagby, Wesley M. *The Road to Normalcy: The Presidential Campaign and Election of 1920*. Baltimore, Md: Johns Hopkins University Press, 1968.

Bailey, Thomas and David M. Kennedy. *The American Pageant*. Vols. 1 and 2, 8th edition. Lexington, Mass.: D.C. Heath and Company, 1987.

Bailey, Thomas. *Presidential Saints and Sinners*. New York: Free Press, 1981.

Bailey, Thomas. *The Pugnacious Presidents*. New York: Free Press, 1980.

Barber, David. *The Pulse of Politics*. New York: Norton, 1980.

Barone, Michael. *Our Country: The Shaping of America from Roosevelt to Reagan*. New York: The Free Press, 1990.

Bendiner, Robert. *White House Fever*. New York: Harcourt, Brace, 1960.

Blaisdell, Thomas C., Jr. *The American Presidency in Political Cartoons: 1776–1976*. Salt Lake City: Peregrine Smith, Inc., 1976.

Blumenthal, Sidney. *Pledging Allegiance: The Last Campaign of the Cold War*. New York: HarperCollins, 1990.

Boller, Paul F. *Presidential Anecdotes*. New York: Oxford University Press, 1981.

Boller, Paul. *Presidential Campaigns*. New York: Oxford University Press, 1985.

Boot, William. "Campaign '88: TV Overdoses on the Inside Dope." *Columbia Journalism Review*, January–February 1989, pp. 23–24.

Broder, David S. *Behind the Front Page*. New York: Simon and Schuster, 1987.

Burner, David et al. *The American People*. New York, 1980.

Chambers, William N. and Burnham, Walter D. *The American Party Systems*. New York: Oxford University Press, 1967.

Congressional Quarterly. *Presidential Elections Since 1789*. Washington, D.C.: Congressional Quarterly, 1983.

Congressional Quarterly. *Historical Review of Presidential Candidates from 1788 to 1968*. Washington, D.C.: Congressional Quarterly, 1969.

DeGregorio, William A. *The Complete Book of U.S. Presidents*. New York: Dembner Books, 1989.

DiClerico, Robert. *The American President*. Englewood Cliffs, N.J.: Prentice-Hall, 1990.

Dinkin, Robert. *Campaigning in America: A History of Election Practices*. New York: Greenwood Press, 1989.

Drew, Elizabeth. *Campaign Journal: The Political Events of 1983–1984*. New York: Macmillan, 1985.

Fischer, Roger. *Tippecanoe and Trinkets Too*. Urbana, Ill.: University of Illinois Press, 1988.

Gammon, Samuel. *The Presidential Campaign of 1932*. Westport, Conn.: Greenwood Press, 1971.

Goldman, Peter, et al. *The Quest for the Presidency, 1984*. New York: Bantam Books, 1985.

Gould, Lewis L. *Reform and Regulation*. New York: Alfred Knopf, 1986.

Gosnell, Harold F. *Champion Campaigner: Franklin D. Roosevelt*. New York: Macmillan, 1952.

Greene, Bob. *Running*. Chicago: Regnery, 1973.

Gunderson, Robert. *The Log-Cabin Campaign*. Westport, Conn.: Greenwood Press, 1977.

Holland, Barbara. *Hail to the Chiefs*. New York: Ballantine Books, 1990.

Jamieson, Kathleen H. *Packaging the Presidency*. New York: Oxford University Press, 1988.

Johnson, Donald. *National Party Platforms*. Urbana, Ill: University of Illinois Press, 1978.

Kane, Joseph N. *Facts About the Presidents*. New York: Wilson, 1989.

Knappman, Edward. *Presidential Election 1968*. New York: Facts on File, 1970.

Lorant, Stefan. *The Glorious Burden*. New York: Macmillan, 1968.

Lorant, Stefan. *The Presidency*. New York: Macmillan, 1951.

Malone, Dumas. *Jefferson and His Time*. Vol. 4. Boston: Little, Brown, and Company, 1970.

McGinniss, Joe. *The Selling of the President, 1968*. New York: Trident Press, 1969.

Melder, Keith. "The Whistlestop: The Birth of Modern Campaigning." *Campaigns & Elections* 6, No. 2 (Summer 1985): pp: 48–53.

Miller, Hope Ridings. *Scandals in the Highest Office*. New York: Random House, 1973.

Miller, Lillian B. *"If Elected . . ." Unsuccessful Candidates for the Presidency, 1796–1968*. Washington, D.C.: Smithsonian Institution Press, 1972.

Minnigerode, Meade. *Presidential Years, 1787–1860*. New York: G.P. Putnam's Sons, 1928.

Minnigerode, Meade. *Some American Ladies*. New York: G.P. Putnam's Sons, 1926.

Mitofsky, Warren J., ed. *Campaign '78*. New York: Arno Press, 1980.

Moore, Edmund. *A Catholic Runs for President.* New York: Ronald Press, 1956.

Nash, Gary et al., eds. *The American People.* New York: Harper & Row, 1986.

New York Times. *The Road to the White House: The Story of the 1964 Election.* New York: McGraw-Hill, 1965.

Ogden, Daniel. *Electing the President: 1964.* San Francisco, Calif.: Chandler Publishing Company, 1964.

Peterson, Merrill D. *Thomas Jefferson and the New Nation.* New York: Oxford University Press, 1970.

Pious, Richard. *The American Presidency.* New York: Basic Books, 1979.

Polsby, Nelson and Wildavsky, Aaron. *Presidential Elections.* New York: The Free Press, 1980.

Remini, Robert V. *The Election of Andrew Jackson.* Philadelphia: Lippincott, 1963.

Rienow, Robert and Leona Train Rienow. *The Lonely Quest.* Chicago: Follett Publishing Company, 1966.

Reinsch, J. Leonard. *Getting Elected.* New York: Hippocrene Books, 1988.

Roseboom, Eugene and Alfred Eckes, Jr. *A History of Presidential Elections: From George Washington to Jimmy Carter.* New York: Macmillan, 1979.

Ross, Irwin. *The Loneliest Campaign: The Truman Victory of 1948.* New York: New American Library, 1968.

Ross, Shelley. *Fall From Grace: Sex, Scandal, and Corruption in American Politics From 1702 to the Present.* Lawrence, Kansas: University Press of Kansas, 1990.

Rutland, Robert Allen. *The Presidency of James Madison.* Lawrence, Kansas: University Press of Kansas, 1990.

Safire, William. *Safire's Political Dictionary.* New York: Random House, 1978.

Schlesinger, Arthur, Jr., ed. *History of American Presidential Elections, 1789–1984.* Vols. 1–4 and supplement. New York: Chelsea House Publishers, 1971–86.

Schlesinger, Arthur, Jr. *The Age of Jackson.* Boston: Little, Brown, and Company, 1953.

Schram, Martin. *Running for President, 1976.* New York: Stein and Day, 1977.

Schram, Martin. *The Great American Video Game.* New York: William Morrow and Company, Inc., 1987.

Sevareid, Eric. *Candidates 1960.* New York: Basic Books, 1959.

Shields-West, Eileen. " 'Give 'em hell' These Days is a Figure of Speech." *Smithsonian* 19, No. 7 (October 1988): 148–160.

Silber, Irwin. *Songs America Voted By.* Harrisburg, Pa.: Stackpole Books, 1971.

Simon, Roger *Road Show.* New York: Farrar, Straus, Giroux, 1990.

Smith, Page. *John Adams.* New York: Doubleday & Company, Inc., 1962.

Smith, Page. *The Shaping of America*. Vol. 3. New York: McGraw-Hill Book Company, 1980.

Southwick, Leslie. *Presidential Also-Rans and Running Mates, 1788–1980*. Jefferson, N.C.: McFarland & Co., 1984.

Stanwood, Edward. *A History of the Presidency*. Boston: Houghton, Mifflin and Company, 1898.

Stanwood, Edward. *A History of Presidential Elections*. Boston: Houghton, Mifflin and Company, 1884.

Stoddard, Henry. *Presidential Sweepstakes*. New York: G.P. Putnam's Sons, 1948.

Stone, Irving. *They Also Ran*. New York: Doubleday & Company, Inc., 1966.

Stroud, Kandy. *How Jimmy Won*. New York: William Morrow and Company, Inc., 1977.

Thompson, Hunter. *Fear and Loathing: On the Campaign Trail '72*. New York: Warner, 1983.

Tugwell, Rexford G. *How They Became President: Thirty-Five Ways to the White House*. New York: Simon and Schuster, 1964.

Warren, Sidney. *The Battle for the Presidency*. Philadelphia and New York: J.B. Lippincott Company, 1968.

Wayne, Stephen J. *The Road to the White House*. New York: St. Martin's Press, 1988.

Weisbord, Marvin. *Campaigning for President*. Washington, D.C.: Public Affairs Press, 1964.

White, Theodore. *America in Search of Itself: The Making of the President, 1956–1980*. New York: Harper & Row, 1982.

White, Theodore. *The Making of the President, 1960*. New York: New American Library, 1967.

White, Theodore. *The Making of the President, 1964*. New York: Atheneum Publishers, 1965.

White, Theodore. *The Making of the President, 1968*. New York: Atheneum Publishers, 1969.

White, Theodore. *The Making of the President, 1972*. New York: Atheneum Publishers, 1973.

Williams, R. Hal. *Years of Decision*. New York: Wiley, 1978.

Young, Michael. *The American Dictionary of Campaigns and Elections*. Lanham, Md.: Hamilton Press, 1987.

★ INDEX ★